Financial Developments in National and International Markets

Financial Developments in National and International Markets

Edited by

Philip Arestis
Jesus Ferreiro
and
Felipe Serrano

palgrave
macmillan

First published 2006 by
PALGRAVE MACMILLAN
Houndmills, Basingstoke, Hampshire RG21 6XS and
175 Fifth Avenue, New York, N.Y. 10010
Companies and representatives throughout the world.

PALGRAVE MACMILLAN is the global academic imprint of the Palgrave Macmillan division of St. Martin's Press, LLC and of Palgrave Macmillan Ltd. Macmillan® is a registered trademark in the United States, United Kingdom and other countries. Palgrave is a registered trademark in the European Union and other countries.

ISBN-13: 978–1–4039–9629–9
ISBN-10: 1–4039–9629–6

This book is printed on paper suitable for recycling and made from fully managed and sustained forest sources.

A catalogue record for this book is available from the British Library.

Library of Congress Cataloging-in-Publication Data
Financial developments in national and international markets / edited by Philip Arestis, Jesus Ferreiro, and Felipe Serrano.
p. cm.
Includes bibliographical references and index.
ISBN 1–4039–9629–6 (cloth)
1. Capital market. 2. Capital market – Developing countries.
I. Arestis, Philip, 1941– II. Ferreiro, Jesus. III. Serrano, Felipe, 1953–
HG4523.F54 2005
332′.0415—dc22 2005048138

10 9 8 7 6 5 4 3 2 1
15 14 13 12 11 10 09 08 07 06

Printed and bound in Great Britain by
Antony Rowe Ltd, Chippenham and Eastbourne

Contents

Notes on the Contributors

Philip Arestis is University Director of Research, Cambridge Centre for Economics and Public Policy, Department of Land Economy, University of Cambridge, and Professor of Economics at the Levy Economics Institute, New York. He is also Visiting Professor, University of Leeds and the School of Oriental and African Studies (SOAS), University of London. His research interests are in the areas of macroeconomics, monetary economics, applied econometrics, political economy and applied political economy. He has published a number of books, contributed invited chapters to books, and has published widely in academic journals.

David Cantarero has a PhD in Economics and is currently Assistant Lecturer at the University of Cantabria. His principal research areas are fiscal federalism and health economics. From 2003 he has participated in projects for National Research (Ministry for Science and Technology) and the Institute for Fiscal Studies. Dr Cantarero has two Young Research Awards and several published papers.

Emmanuel Carré is a PhD student at the University Montesquieu-IFREDE in Bordeaux. He has Master's degrees in Economics and Sociology. His research interests are in the areas of monetary policy strategy, inflation targeting regimes, central banking in general, and deliberation inside monetary policy committees. He is the author of papers on these subjects in foreign edited books in the USA and Mexico.

David Ceballos has a PhD in Economics and is currently an Assistant Lecturer at the University of Barcelona. His principal research areas are financial mathematics and financial time. In 1999 he co-founded IAFI (Investigación en Análisis Financiero y de la Incertidumbre), a finance research group at the University of Barcelona. Dr Ceballos has participated in and organized several congresses and seminars in financial mathematics.

Eugenia Correa is a Professor in Economic Finance at the National University of Mexico. She has a PhD degree from the National University of Mexico and is a member of the Mexican Science Academy. Her research interests are in the areas of macroeconomic finance policy and foreign direct investments. She is the author of several books, a number of papers on her research subjects in refereed Spanish and foreign journals, and of chapters in edited books.

Korkut A. Erturk is Associate Professor of Economics at the University of Utah, where he has been serving as Chair of the Economics Department since 2002, and a Research Associate at the Levy Economics Institute. He gained his BA and PhD at New York University and New School University, respectively. He is the author of numerous articles on heterodox macroeconomics and currency crises.

Jesus Ferreiro is a Reader in Economic Policy at the University of the Basque Country in Bilbao. He has a PhD degree from the University of the Basque Country. His research interests are in the areas of macroeconomic policy, incomes policy, labour markets and foreign direct investment. He is the author of a number of papers on these subjects in refereed Spanish and foreign journals, and of chapters in edited books.

Davide Furceri is a PhD student at the University of Illinois at Chicago. He gained a Laurea Degree in Statistics and Economics from the University of Palermo in 2001, and an MS in Economics from the Coripe, in 2002. His research interests are in the areas of macroeconomics, international economics and European integration. He is the author of a number of papers on these subjects in refereed Italian and foreign journals.

Claude Gnos is Associate Professor of Economics at the University of Burgundy and Director of the Centre for Monetary and Financial Studies in Dijon. He is the author of *L'Euro* and *Les grands auteurs en économie*, and co-editor, with Louis-Philippe Rochon, of *Post Keynesian Principles of Economic Policy* (Edward Elgar, forthcoming), and *The Keynesian Multiplier* (Routledge, forthcoming) also with Louis-Philippe Rochon. He has also published a number of articles in refereed journals on monetary economics, circuit theory and the history of economic thought (*Journal of Post Keynesian Economics, Review of Political Economy, International Journal of Political Economy, Economie Appliquée*).

Carmen Gomez is a Lecturer in Economics at the University of the Basque Country in Bilbao. She has a PhD degree from the University of the Basque Country. Her research interest are in the areas of foreign direct investments and labour markets. She is the author of several papers and chapters of books on those subjects.

Greg Hannsgen holds a PhD in Economics from the University of Notre Dame, Indiana, is a resident research associate at the Levy Economics Institute of Bard College, Annandale-on-Hudson, New York, and the editor of many Levy Institute publications. His primary research interests are endogenous money, the monetary transmission mechanism, and social economics, and publications include 'Minsky's Acceleration Channel and the Role of Money', *Journal of Post Keynesian Economics*, Spring 2005.

Elias Karakitsos is Chairman of Global Economic Research and an Associate Member of the Cambridge Centre for Economic and Public Policy,

University of Cambridge. He was at Imperial College for twenty-five years, where he held the Chair of Economics and was Head of Economics for ten years. He has acted as an adviser to UK, US and EU governments, and as an investment adviser to many financial institutions, including Citibank, Oppenheimer, Allianz, Credit Agricole and Standard Chartered. He is the author of five books/monographs, seventy-six papers in learned journals and 188 reports on financial markets.

Edwin Le Heron is Maître de Conférences in Economics at the Institut d'Études Politiques in Bordeaux and a member of the CRECQSS (Centre de Recherche et d'Études sur le Canada et le Québec en Sciences Sociales). He is also the president of the ADEK (Association for the Development of Keynesian Studies), which gathers French economists interested in post-Keynesian works (adek@free.fr). ADEK was created by Alain Barrère for the organization of the Keynes Today conference in 1983 (published as *Keynesian Economic Policy* by Macmillan, 2 vols, 1990). His research interests are monetary policy, post-Keynesian monetary theory, and history of thought (French monetary thought in the eighteenth century). His latest published works on monetary policy are in *Investigaciòn Econòmica*, Mexico, no. 249 – 2004.

Louis-Philippe Rochon is Assistant Professor of Economics at Laurentian University, Canada. He gained his PhD at the New School for Social Research in New York. He has published extensively in monetary theory and policy, and post-Keynesian economics. He is the author and editor of several books, including *Credit, Money and Production: An Alternative Post-Keynesian Approach* (Edward Elgar, 1999), *Credit, Money and Interest Rates: Essays on Horizontalism* (Edward Elgar, 2001), *Modern Theories of Money* (Edward Elgar, 2003), *Théories monétaires post keynésiennes* (Economica, 2003) and *Monetary and Exchange Rate Systems: A World View over Financial Crises* (Edward Elgar, forthcoming). He is the author of numerous articles in *Review of Political Economy, Journal of Post Keynesian Economics, Journal of Economic Issues, Economie Appliquée, International Journal of Political Economy* and *European Journal of the History of Economic Thought.*

Carlos Rodriguez is a Reader in Economics at the University of the Basque Country. He has worked in the field of foreign direct investment for several years and authored several publications in leading Spanish journals.

Sergio Rossi is Associate Professor of Economics at the University of Fribourg and at the University of Lugano. He has a DPhil degree from the University of Fribourg and a PhD degree from the University of London (University College). His research interests are in the area of monetary macroeconomics. He has authored and edited a number of books on monetary theory and policy. He has recently published articles in the *International Journal of Political Economy, International Review of Applied Economics, Journal of Asian Economics,* and in the *Swiss Review of Economics and Statistics.*

Malcolm Sawyer is Professor of Economics and Pro Dean for Learning and Teaching at Leeds University Business School. He is managing editor of the *International Review of Applied Economics*. His main research interests include macroeconomic policies of the European Union, including the development of alternative institutional frameworks, the analysis of fiscal policy, including the developing the theoretical arguments on fiscal policy and evaluating episodes of fiscal consolidation, and the analysis of the nature of money and the implications for monetary policy.

Felipe Serrano is a Professor in Economics at the University of the Basque Country in Bilbao. He is the Head of the Department of Applied Economics at the University of the Basque Country. His research interests are in the areas of social security, the welfare state, labour markets, innovation and economic policy. He is the author of a number of books, papers (in journals such as *Économies et Sociétés, Informacion Comercial Española, European Planning Studies, Journal of Income Distribution, International Review of Applied Economics, Journal of Post Keynesian Economics and International Papers in Political Economy*, among others) and contributions to edited books on those subjects.

Pablo Toral is Mouat Junior Professor of International Studies at Beloit College and has a PhD in International Relations from Florida International University. He has published articles about Spanish multinational enterprises and their activities in Latin America, regional integration in the Americas, globalization and nationalism, education and identity in Spain. He is the author of *The Reconquest of the New World: Spain's Multinational Enterprises and Direct Investment in Latin America*. He also serves as a consultant. Before becoming an academic, Toral was a journalist in Latin America, the USA and Europe.

Ulvi Vaarja is a Lecturer in Macroeconomics and Money and Banking at the Estonian Business School and a Senior Economist in the Bank of Estonia. She is a graduate of the Tallinn University of Technology in Estonia. Her research interests are mainly in the areas of macroeconomic policy, and monetary and international economics.

Gregorio Vidal is a Professor in Economic Policy at the Metropolitan University of Mexico. He has a PhD degree from the National University of Mexico and is a member of the Mexican Science Academy. His research interests are in the areas of macroeconomic policies, enterprises and entrepreneurs, and foreign direct investments. He is the author of several books and a number of papers on these subjects in refereed Spanish and foreign journals, and of chapters in edited books.

Introduction

Philip Arestis, Jesus Ferreiro and Felipe Serrano

National and international financial markets have faced an unparalleled transformation since the 1970s. This process has been promoted to a very large extent by financial liberalization and deregulation, the creation and spread of new financial assets (options, derivatives and so on.) and the appearance of new agents in the capital markets (hedge funds, pension funds and so on). All these developments have led to a huge growth in international capital flows. It was assumed that the process of financial liberalization–deregulation would lead to a more efficient working of capital markets, create higher profit opportunities and increase the amount of available resources, a crucial factor for developing economies. All in all, the process would lead to an optimal international allocation of financial resources and, consequently, to an increase in economic activity. However, the growth of financial markets has not been problem-free. The operations of international capital markets have proved to be very unstable, with high volatility in capital flows and the permanent threat of systemic risks. These problems are not distributed symmetrically, with the developing countries being affected the most: developed countries are also affected. Perhaps with the exception of the USA, developed countries are restricted in the implementation of autonomous domestic macroeconomic policies – as France, for example, experienced in the early 1980s. Macroeconomic policies, both fiscal and monetary, are permanently restrictive, thus abandoning the traditional objectives of stabilization policies.

The aim of the book is to deal with these problems affecting both developed and developing economies. The different chapters of the book are classified into three broad groups. Chapters 1 to 4, comprise the first group, and are concerned with international capital markets. The focus here is mainly on the problems that have arisen from the current working of these markets and on the reforms needed for their smoother working, thereby avoiding, among other things, the well-known problems of systemic risk, asymmetries, instability in the amount and direction of flows, and the constraints exerted on national strategies of growth and development. The second group of papers, in Chapters 5 to 8, focuses on the effectiveness and consequences of national macroeconomic policies – mainly monetary and fiscal policies. Finally, the third group, comprising Chapters 9 to 13, analyses the behaviour of financial markets from a case-study perspective, focusing on specific kinds of financial flow, and on a specific region or country.

Chapter 1, by Greg Hannsgen, deals with the disutilities of international debt, and evaluates whether the current international financial system preserves the social equality of agent-country participants by achieving the right access of borrowers to necessary credit. For Greg Hannsgen, the international financial system cannot be considered to be economically or socially efficient. As well as discussing some well-known problems suffered by borrower economies (loss of sovereignty, requirements from lenders and international organisms for tax cuts and limits to government spending, changes in the distribution of income and so on), the author analyses the consequences from the loss of autonomy and utility that small nations suffer when they borrow abroad, or fail to provide international investors with a positive return. Foreign borrowing for small economies may result in negative consequences in terms of national welfare. This potential loss of autonomy, sovereignty and welfare implies that some countries have different values and preferences in terms of their participation in international capital markets.

While the first chapter focuses on the socio-political consequences of the participation of developing countries in international financial markets, Chapter 2 by Korkut Erturk pays special attention to one of the main economic features of the current working of financial markets: the common occurrence of currency crises since the 1970s. Those crises are explained by the explosive expansion of secondary asset markets in developing economies, leading to dynamics in the portfolio inflows driven by speculative expectations on variable price assets. The erratic and volatile dynamics of these portfolio flows is explained by changes in expectations, leading to sudden and abrupt changes in the flows received. Currency crises are therefore 'capital account'- driven, related to speculative expectations about asset prices and the speculative behaviour of foreign investors.

The chapter by David Ceballos and David Cantarero about the regulation of financial systems poses the question of whether the current process of globalization can affect the stable working of financial system in a negative way thus leading to financial bubbles and currency crises. Only an efficient financial regulation that prevents financial disturbances but has a neutral impact on market and financial behaviour can limit the risks of financial crises and their contagion to other economies. Using game-theoretic models, the authors show the existence of a Nash equilibrium of long-term stability in international financial markets, justified by the existence of a leader authority interested in defending the stability of the system; the imitation of the behaviour of the agent with the highest information; and by self-fulfilled interests. These three possibilities lie behind the lines of action of the Basel II proposals. Nevertheless, it does not exclude the existence of instability, for a number of reasons involving the need of additional measures to avoid that instability.

In Chapter 4, Sergio Rossi focuses on the current problems suffered by the international financial and monetary system. The author argues that these problems must be analysed and understood in the light of the architecture set up in Bretton Woods in 1944 following the basic recommendations of the White Plan. Sergio Rossi focuses on the importance of reforming the international financial system in a way that follows Keynes' proposals. Only by adopting a post-Keynesian perspective and analysing international money and credit from an endogenous-money perspective can a stable monetary and financial system be designed that is compatible with financial liberalization, autonomous monetary policy and stable exchange rates.

In Chapter 5, Edwin Le Heron and Emmanuel Carré, the authors analyse the different monetary policy strategies of the European Central Bank (ECB) and of the Federal Reserve System (Fed). While the monetary policy of the ECB is based on a 'credibility strategy', the Fed bases monetary policy on a 'confidence strategy'. The reasons behind these different approaches must be found in the social, political and institutional environment in which both central banks operate, what mirrors in the single mandate for the ECB (price stability) and the dual mandate for the Fed (price stability and level of activity or stabilization policy). The latter allows efficiency and legitimacy, independence and accountability in a system where economy and democracy can co-exist in a balanced way.

In Chapter 6, Philip Arestis and Malcolm Sawyer deal with the case for fiscal policy. The chapter reconsiders the case for the use of fiscal policy based on a 'functional finance' approach, which advocates the use of fiscal policy to secure high levels of aggregate demand, which would otherwise be too low. This 'functional finance' view means that any budget deficit should be seen as a response to the perceived excess of private savings over investment at the desired level of economic activity. The chapter outlines the 'functional finance' approach, and its relationship with fiscal policy. It then considers the three lines of argument that have been advanced against fiscal policy on the grounds of 'crowding out'. These lines are based on the response of interest rates, the supply-side equilibrium and Ricardian equivalence. For the authors, these arguments do not apply when a 'functional finance' view of fiscal policy is adopted. A section on the intertemporal budget constraint considers whether this constraint rules out budget deficits, and concludes that in general it does not.

The aim of Chapter 7, by Davide Furceri, is to investigate how the birth of a central fiscal authority or the creation of fiscal federalism could improve the action of fiscal policy in terms of redistribution and stabilization in the EMU. The chapter estimates the increase in the budget amount at the central level, expressed as a fraction of gross domestic product (GDP) of the individual member countries, which would completely absorb symmetric and asymmetric shocks: the central budget of the European Union (EU) should increase by 9 per cent of its GDP. The increased budget would also have redistributive consequences, reducing inequalities among member countries by up to 18 percent of the disposable national income.

Chapter 8, by Elias Karakitsos, analyses the determinants of the dynamics of the exchange rate of the US dollar. For the author, traditional models are not satisfactory because they do not take into account the role played by the dollar as a reserve currency. Any explanation must be based on a structural model in which the economic policies of the countries concerned play a key role, having a direct impact on the currency. Adopting a game theoretic approach to analyse the euro–dollar exchange rate, the author concludes that four elements related directly to the economy of the USA are the main determinants of the dollar exchange of rate: US fiscal policy, US monetary policy, priorities that the FED assigns to the targets of economic policy and Federal debt.

Chapter 9, by Jesus Ferreiro, Carmen Gomez and Carlos Rodriguez, deals with the pattern of inward foreign direct investment (FDI) geographical distribution. Despite the generalized recommendations for developing countries to rely on FDI as an engine for long-term growth and development, the authors conclude that the analysis of the geographical distribution of world FDI inflows since the 1970s does not provide a basis for this argument, for several reasons. First, the increase in absolute FDI inflows has not led to more foreign private capital resources for developing countries because of the fall in private portfolio flows. Second, the weight of those flows in terms of the GDP of the developing economies has remained nearly unchanged since the 1970s. Third, there is a rising concentration of FDI inflows in a small number of developing countries.

Eugenia Correa and Gregorio Vidal deal in Chapter 10 with financial deregulation and capital flows in Latin-American countries and study the transformations in the financial and banking systems in Latin America. The successive bank crises in the region, and the liberalization and deregulation processes in domestic banking systems, have led to a massive penetration by foreign banks, mainly from the USA and Spain. This denationalization of the banking system has not helped to solve the problems from which the region suffers as a consequence of structural inefficiencies of the financial and banking systems. Foreign banks have not made any radical improvements in the efficiency in the allocation of resources. This, the authors argue, could very well produce possible financial and currency crises in the region.

The penetration of foreign banks in Latin America is also studied in the chapter by Claude Gnos and Louis-Philippe Rochon. The direct implication of the penetration of foreign banks is a fall in the profits of domestic banks. In response to this, domestic banks react by curtailing their overall lending in the short run, thereby preventing small borrowers accessing credit, and eventually increasing their lending to riskier projects and borrowers in the medium term. Either way, the multinationalization of the banking system in emerging markets will tend to increase the fragility of the overall system rather than decrease it. Adopting an endogenous money approach, the authors advocate policies that, while recognizing that deregulation and liberalization might be difficult to stop, would none the less address some of the more contentious consequences of multinational banking.

Chapter 12, by Pablo Toral, deals with Spanish FDI in Latin America, between 1989 and 2004, focusing on the reasons behind the huge amount of Spanish FDI in Latin America. Recently, Spain has become the second major foreign investor in the region, behind the USA. Adopting a constructivist approach, Toral explains the conditions that made possible such massive investments. These include the perception by the managers of Spanish firms that their companies had advantages that could profitably be exploited in the region; political and economic support provided by the Spanish authorities to the internationalization of enlarged firms by domestic operations of mergers and acquisitions; and the reforms implemented in Latin-American countries.

Ulvi Vaarja focuses in Chapter 13 on the role of the International Monetary Fund (IMF) in the economic policy-making and growth of the Baltic countries, analysing the co-operation between the Baltic countries and the IMF. This close co-operation has had substantial positive effects for these three countries, not only because of the IMF's financial assistance but also because of the economic policies pursued. The role played by the IMF in the successful transformation of these economies is recognized, not merely in terms of the macroeconomic outcomes but also in terms of the financial integration that has led to greater confidence among international financial investors, and to a substantial growth in FDI inflows.

The chapters in this volume are only a small sample of the proceedings of the Conference on Developments in Economic Theory and Policy, Institutions and European Integration, held in Bilbao on 15–16 July 2004. We would like to thank the participants and contributors to the conference, and the University of the Basque Country that hosted the event. Financial support from the University of the Basque Country, the Basque government and the Spanish Ministry of Education and Science in particular, is gratefully acknowledged. Finally, special thanks must go to Amanda Hamilton, of Palgrave Macmillan, who suggested this volume, and for her encouragement and support throughout.

1
The Disutility of International Debt: Analytical Results and Methodological Implications

Greg Hannsgen

Through most of history, even when interest payments were illegal, the costs of borrowing have been high (Anderson, 2004). Among these costs have been servile relations to the lender, moral opprobrium, and, in the event of default, harsh punishment and destitution. In recent times, these costs have been reduced throughout the industrialized world. The benefits have arguably included more widespread home ownership, a reduction in the barriers of entry to the small business sector, and the non-monetary advantages of a more egalitarian society.

When developing nations borrow, they too face non-pecuniary costs. A number of such costs could be cited, but the strictures imposed by international financial institutions such as the International Monetary Fund (IMF) would be high on any list. Demands by these organizations potentially count as a cost in two ways. First, they impose economic policies that are contrary to the interests of the borrowing nation; and second, in doing so, they inflict the intangible cost of a loss of national autonomy. As an example, borrowing countries can be forced to adopt contractionary policies during recessions, often cutting needed social services in the process. The international financial institutions may compel countries to cut what they regard as distortionary taxes, thus exacerbating fiscal stress. Borrowers may be forced to adopt 'reforms' that result in a more skewed distribution of wealth. One might argue that the intangible costs of a world divided into the wealthy elite of nations and a subjugated borrower class are just as great as an individual nation so divided.

There exists a vast literature on the benefits of the opening of international debt markets, focusing on certain benefits of capital market openness. These include a spreading of risk that purportedly reduces the volatility of consumption in individual nations. Also, financial openness enables countries to take advantage of differences in the rate of discount across economies, in the same way that trade in goods is mutually beneficial to countries with differing relative prices for goods. Accounts of these benefits of capital markets tend to overlook the effects of the exertion of power by lenders over borrowers, a relevant issue, particularly in connection with small developing economies.

This chapter attempts to incorporate the kind of non-pecuniary costs of borrowing discussed here into a model typical of the existing literature. Specifically, the chapter models a small nation that has access to international financial markets. The nation is free to borrow money to smooth its consumption stream and, in the second of the two models, to make an agreement with lenders to repay a reduced amount during hard economic times. However, the representative nation suffers a loss of utility when it borrows or when it repays a relatively small amount of its debt. Several issues will be examined. First, are there any impacts of the revised utility function on the consumption stream of the borrowing nation? Second, how is local investment affected by the disutility of borrowing? Finally, what affect is there on moral hazard?

In tackling a largely non-pecuniary issue (national autonomy) using a standard rational choice model, this work follows up on and challenges the methodological approach pioneered by Lionel Robbins (1935). Robbins insisted that all conceivable values could be fit into the rational choice framework simply by adding them to the utility function. After developing the models, this chapter uses them as test cases for this methodological claim. In particular, Robbins' claim that economists could and should maintain a rigid fact–value distinction, and resist the temptation to assess values, will be examined.

Conceiving international debt as an imperfect substitute for local funds

One tenet common to most neoclassical models is that one 10 per cent return is the same as any other 10 per cent return with the same risk, regardless of how one comes by it. In orthodox theory, countries invest until the return on investment is equal to the return on risk-free bonds, which is in turn equal to the rate at which countries are willing to trade-off current for future dollars. A key feature of the models of this chapter is that countries have two different ways of transferring current into future wealth (investing in capital equipment, and lending or borrowing on international debt securities markets), but these investments are not symmetric in all senses. This behaviour can be quite rational, in the sense of arising from the successful maximization of an appropriate utility function. The result is that different social rates of discount apply to different types of asset. This is simply a recognition of the fact that conventional theory, in equating all rates of discount, abstracts inappropriately from normative distinctions between markets (bonds and capital stock) that arise as a result of the differing international, political and social consequences of operating in those markets. A return on capital of 10 per cent may not compensate for an equal borrowing cost if the IMF appears to be lurking around the corner.

There are some apparent welfare implications of this recognition. Any time that all social and objective interest rates are not equal, an economy suffers from what would be from a conventional standpoint a Pareto-inferior allocation of resources. In the first model, it will be shown that a country that suffers a loss of sovereignty in borrowing allocates insufficient resources to investment in capital equipment. On the other hand, in a model with investment, the issue is not that a utility cost of borrowing exists, but rather that a disutility exists that applies differentially to investment and to lending or borrowing. Once the stigma is also applied to domestic non-financial (dis)investment, the distortion of investment decisions disappears, and the only inefficiency is in consumption choices.

In another model, we shall show that a nation with a similar utility function will not take advantage of opportunities to use international borrowing to reduce economic risk, even if it has access to insurance provided by a perfectly competitive, risk-neutral provider of contingent securities. It may also become more difficult for a borrower to establish creditworthiness on the basis of reputation.

The models raise some important methodological issues. One is their relationship to welfare. Here, since we are arguing that while the utility function is affected by the amount borrowed or by the amount a borrower fails to repay, utility would not be similarly affected if money could be borrowed without international consequences, such as IMF programmes. This fact is relevant for policy-making, but it might be overlooked by an economist who simply observes an apparent aversion to borrowing. This reflects the fact that the source of utility in this case is relationships between nations, rather than the enjoyment they receive from consumption. The paper demonstrates that such concerns can be modelled in the manner of Robbins, but only at a cost of practicality and real understanding.

Such issues range from finding an appropriate utility function for empirical prediction to characterizing the welfare of the agent. Agents motivated by a disutility of operating in international financial markets may defy the predictions of economists who incorrectly interpret a lack of borrowing as a preference for deferred utility, precautionary saving or an economically based lack of credibility. Such economists may find that their inferences cannot be generalized from one area of behaviour (for example, international borrowing) to a second, apparently identical field. They certainly cannot generalize an increasing distaste for foreign capital to a potentially more just system that garners the enthusiastic support of the developing world. With regard to welfare issues, the economist can make many mistakes, including a failure to ascertain the appropriate conditions for the efficient use of financial markets.

Many developing nations find it difficult to attract foreign capital. Since they often badly need funds, it may seem hard to believe that their behaviour could be affected significantly by a disutility of borrowing or a disutility of incomplete repayment. But disenchantment with the conditions attached to borrowing may be growing. Argentina has recently challenged the financial establishment, expressing a refusal to deal with lenders on their own terms. The government has improved its fiscal position, but it has done so by raising taxes, a policy of which the IMF disapproves (Rohter, 2004). Will a rejection of conditionality lead to a restriction in the availability of credit? It may be difficult for Argentina to re-enter world capital markets without the support of the IMF. Will Argentina and other nations that have suffered ill consequences from foreign borrowing find some alternative way of obtaining capital? So far, the Argentine economy seems to be enjoying an increased flow of capital from its own citizens. This almost deliberate substitution of domestic for foreign capital may reflect the kind of disutility of international capital modelled in this chapter. Perhaps a disutility that had previously been felt by citizens is finally finding political expression in number of nations.

Some nations have failed to attract much foreign capital in the first place. This may be because the types of policies that attract foreign lenders are repugnant to the nations involved and are never adopted. Often, a failure to attract foreign capital is interpreted by economists as a symptom of a lack of credibility. But it is one lesson of this chapter that an apparent lack of credibility may be because of the disutilities imposed by the international financial community.

If this fact is recognized, perhaps international institutions might eventually understand the situation and bow to the necessity of easing their demands. This seems unlikely. Alternatively, it may be that self-interest will bring international capital back to the table; the prospect of lending at a profit may overwhelm any desire to punish 'bad behaviour' on the part of recalcitrant nations such as Argentina. Neoclassical economists would interpret this as a lack of credibility on the part of lenders in a threat to cut a nation off from capital markets. The outcome may thus rest on a tougher test of all parties' credibility than they have encountered to date.

Model I: non-pecuniary costs of international debt in a small country model

We offer two models in this chapter, both based on examples in Obstfeld and Rogoff (1996), with slight modifications to functional form and the addition of unconventional arguments to the utility functions. We shall sometimes refer to the latter additions as 'sovereignty-loss disutility'. Both involve infinitely lived representative agents. The purpose is not to suggest that such models are always insightful, but rather to measure various issues against a sort of neoclassical 'baseline', in order to isolate certain concerns. For the most part, we shall leave to one side other objections that have been raised against representative agent models. One claim sometimes made in defence of neoclassical models is that, in spite of various shortcomings, they offer tools to deal with welfare and policy questions that cannot be answered by non-neoclassical methods, such as Sraffian models. One could see this chapter as a response to such an argument – that we must put up with various theoretical weaknesses to obtain the benefits of a useful theory of welfare and policy choice.

The agent, in this case a small state, chooses a consumption stream to maximize the discounted present value of its stream of utility, subject to its available resources. In the first model, agents have two means of transferring wealth over time. They can invest in domestic capital or in foreign bonds denominated in the consumption good. In the second model, which features an uncertain but given endowment, agents trade securities that pay different amounts to different parties depending on the outcome of random events. This market is similar to an insurance market, but it shares many features of a market for securities such as equities that pay off different amounts depending upon the success of the borrower.

To start the first model, we assume the objective function:

$$\sum_{s=t}^{\infty} \beta^{s-t}(aC_s - (b/2)C_s^2 + cB_s)$$

where C_t is consumption in period t, B_s is the stock of outstanding bonds at time s, and β is a fixed discount factor between 0 and 1. B takes on a positive value if the country is a net lender, and a negative value if it is in debt. The utility function is conventional, with the exception of the term involving B. This is a very crude representation of loss of sovereignty through borrowing. Lenders have greater standing in the world the more they lend, and borrowers lose sovereignty as their debt increases. It should be noted here that this term does not reflect a dislike of borrowing *per se*, or a normal preference to defer consumption. It is a distinct motive. If a country could borrow without losing world standing, then it would be more willing to borrow. The term is very similar to an addition to the interest rate, and will have similar effects. But it is inserted into the utility function to emphasize that it represents a non-monetary cost of borrowing.

As mentioned before, the economy is constrained to consume no more than its current income plus its inherited assets. This leads to the budget constraints:

$$C_t = B_t(1 + r) - B_{t+1} + K_t + F(K_t) - K_{t+1}$$

for all t, where r is an exogenously given world rate of interest, K_t is the amount of the capital good, $F()$ is the production function, and the t subscripts indicate a particular time period. (The notation for the models is for the most part borrowed from Obstfeld and Rogoff.) The representative agent's interest rate is constant because it is a small country and borrows too little to affect world financial markets. K is assumed to be the same as the consumption good, so that goods can be converted to capital and back again. Once capital is used it becomes available again for consumption, investment or foreign lending. Capital is the only input into production. Note that investment (the last three terms of the equation) can be negative. Depreciation is neglected for simplicity. The constraint says that the economy inherits foreign debt or bonds, the capital stock, and newly produced goods. All these resources can then be divided into consumption or next period's capital, bonds or debts.

This sort of model is subject to a number of important critiques that are tangential to the ones emphasized here. First, it becomes analytically very difficult to conceptualize an input called 'capital' when there are many goods that are produced by many capital goods. Normally, this problem renders the determination of the interest rate problematic (Garegnani, 1990). Here, we take the interest rate as a given by the world market. Also, the use of only one factor of production prevents some of the problems of this type, though it does not help us to understand the real-world situation in which there are multiple produced inputs and outputs. Another problem with representative agent models is that many phenomena that occur in a world with a large number of heterogeneous agents do not translate into a model with a single representative agent (Kirman, 1992; Hartley, 1997). Fortunately, here we are dealing with a nation as a whole; it is in this setting that concerns about sovereignty make the most sense. Still, none of this rescues neoclassical models from problems related to the capital controversy or critiques of the representative agent. We neglect such concerns here, to concentrate on another critique which, we argue, carries a great deal of force in its own right.

The first-order condition for this problem is obtained by substituting for consumption in the utility function with the period budget constraint and differentiating by B_{t+1}. (We neglect the condition needed to prevent 'Ponzi games'.) For ease of analysis, we assume that $\beta(1 + r) = 1$. We obtain:

$$C_{t+1} = C_t + \beta c/b$$

Clearly, the consumption path is 'tilted' towards the future, in contrast to a similar model without bonds in the utility function, which would lead to equal consumption in each future period.[1] Agents want to defer their consumption because of the sovereignty penalty of borrowing and the benefits of lending. The degree of tilt depends on the subjective rate of discount, β, and the parameters of the utility function. It is clear that consumption drifts upward indefinitely and in fact, $C_t \rightarrow \infty$.

The next first-order condition is obtained by differentiating with respect to K_{t+1}:

$$\beta(a - bC_{t+1})(1 + F'(K_{t+1})) = a - bC_t$$

This equation determines the level of investment. Normally, it would imply that the marginal product of capital should be set equal to the interest rate $(1 + r) = 1 + F'()$. Then, at the margin, the nation can transfer wealth from present to future at the same rate using international bond markets as it can via investment. Here, though, we combine with the first first-order condition to get:

$$c = (a - bC_{t+1})(1 + F'(K_{t+1}) - (1 + r))$$

The first term in parentheses is the marginal utility of consumption and is assumed to be positive. Since c is a positive parameter, the marginal utility of capital, $F'()$ exceeds the interest rate r. In other words, money could be borrowed at the world interest rate and be invested profitably at the margin. So there is an important welfare issue here: investment takes place at less than an efficient rate, because of the disamenities associated with the capital markets. If money could be obtained in some way without the disutility, a Pareto improvement could be made and a free lunch obtained. This contrasts with a situation in which investment is low because the populace heavily discounts its future well-being. It is pointed out below that there may be serious consequences of the failure of economists to understand this distinction.

For the sake of comparison, consider a situation in which borrowing and disinvesting carry the same disutility, meaning that all means of moving consumption forward in time, regardless of their international ramifications, reduce utility. This would not apply in the previous model, because there we assumed that the disutility stemmed from a diminution of stature in the world because of borrower status, rather than immediate consumption as such. Here we drop the critical assumption that present–future commodity trade-offs have different significance depending upon the international context of the trade-off. To fix ideas, consider the following utility function:

$$U = \sum_{s=t}^{\infty} \beta^{s-t}(aC_s - (b/2)C_s^2 + c'(K_s + B_s))$$

The first first-order condition is the same as before. Agents still tilt their consumption into the future because of sovereignty concerns. The second first-order condition is obtained by differentiating with respect to K_{t+1}.

The result is then substituted into the consumption first-order condition, leading to:

$$(1 + r) = (1 + F'())$$

In this case, there is no underinvestment. As in a conventional model without sovereignty-loss disutility, investment is independent of the discount rate and equal to the world discount rate. There is no Pareto improvement to be made on the production side, even if money could be sneaked in some way into the country without compromising sovereignty. It is thus seen that the underinvestment result depends not only on a disutility of borrowing but also on *unequal* disutilities of borrowing and disinvesting. The conclusion rests on the theme of different utilities associated with the diverging international conditions under which future and current consumption are traded-off. Concerns about such international circumstances of economic activity have consequences for the efficiency issues emphasized by economists.

Model II: an onus on international borrowers in recession

Having established some significant effects for borrowing disutility in a setting of certainty with investment, we now abstract from investment and add an element of what neoclassical economists usually call uncertainty. Here, this means that all random variables are drawn from a known distribution. In many settings, this model does not apply, because there are no known moments or distribution (Davidson, 2002, ch. 3). Still, we proceed, because we wish to investigate a different critique that, we believe, deserves separate consideration.

Here we abstract from production and consider a situation in which each country receives a random endowment of the consumption good in each period. The country can also buy securities on the world market that provide payments in certain states of the world (endowment levels), of which there are a discrete number. Formally, a country's endowment is:

$$Y_t = Y^* + \varepsilon_t$$

where epsilon is a mean-zero, independently and identically distributed discrete random variable with a symmetric distribution, and Y^* is a known constant. Countries can enter into contracts on world markets in advance to receive particular amounts of the consumption good in particular states of the world (particular values of ε). The amount *paid* in period t is $P(\varepsilon_i)$. So, the country presumably signs a contract to pay a positive P in good times in return for an insurance benefit $-P$ in bad times, both of which will depend in general on the exact state of the world. Since nations are risk-averse, they presumably wish to take advantage of this opportunity to at least some extent.

The model once again features a disutility associated with certain sorts of financial dealings. In this case, we assume that the country loses standing in the world if it collects on its insurance contract. This insurance can be viewed as the pay-out of a variable-return bond. It may seem odd that a country could suffer a disutility for collecting money as specified in a previously-signed contract. But often, contracts do not state explicitly what happens when a borrower experiences such hard times that it cannot repay for legitimate reasons. Sometimes, both borrower and lender will deny that default is possible, when they know well that it is. Many more risks are knowingly incurred than are publicly acknowledged. When default happens, the borrower is often blamed, even if both parties were clearly gambling. Under current institutional arrangements, borrowers in this situation are often subjected to the kind of loss of autonomy modelled here. This is broadly the same sort of disutility that might arise as a result of the social stigma of welfare receipt, when what is arguably a right is seen as a kind of largesse. To extend the analogy, in this chapter no one loses utility because of a failure to pay taxes.

We now consider the utility function (for each individual period s):

$$U_s = aC_s - bC_s^2 + dP_s(\varepsilon_s) \text{ if } P_s(\varepsilon_s) < 0$$

and

$$U_s = aC_s - bC_s^2 \text{ if } P_s(\varepsilon_s) \geq 0$$

The P term is added to the end of the objective function to indicate the sovereignty 'cost' of recovering insurance benefits. Naturally, this disutility is suffered only if the country must receive a benefit, rather than paying a premium. The problem has two constraints: first, the insurance company or investor is risk-neutral; and insurance is provided by a competitive world industry, so that profits are measured by their expected value, and the industry earns zero profit. The latter condition can be represented by:

$$\sum_i \pi(\varepsilon_i)P_s(\varepsilon_i) = 0$$

The Lagrangean for the problem is the sum of the expected value of total discounted utility plus a Lagrange multiplier, μ, times this constraint:

$$L = E_t\sum_{s=t}^{\infty}\beta^{s-t}(U_s) + \mu\sum_{i=1}^{N}\pi(\varepsilon_i)P_t(\varepsilon_i)$$

The second group of constraints for the problem shows that consumption in each period is equal to the resources households choose to spend:

$$C_s = B_s(1 + r) - B_{s+1} - P_s(\varepsilon_s) + Y^* + \varepsilon_s$$

Each period, the sovereign has the bonds or debt inherited from the previous period, with interest ($B_s(1 + r)$). It also receives its income, which, as we saw earlier, is composed of a deterministic part, Y^*, and a stochastic part, ε. Consumers also pay a premium, P, based upon the realization of ε. P may be negative or positive. A positive P can be interpreted as an insurance premium and a negative P an insurance benefit. Also, P can also be thought of as the return to a security with a variable payout. The country has to pay back more of its borrowings when times are good. All available resources are split between consumption, C, insurance premiums, P, and borrowing or lending, B_{s+1}.

The bond first-order condition is obtained by using the second constraint to substitute in the Lagrangean for C and differentiating with respect to B_{t+1}. We assume that $(1 + r)\beta = 1$. This gives:

$$E_t C_{t+1} = C_t$$

which is the standard result that with a quadratic utility function, consumption does a random walk, which will be modified below.

The other first-order condition is interesting. Suppose we differentiate by $P(\varepsilon_s)$, where we assume $P(\varepsilon_s)$ is negative. This means that the country is receiving insurance benefits, rather than paying a 'premium'. The first version of the condition:

$$(a - bC_s(\varepsilon_s)) - d = \mu$$

The second version of this condition, for a country that is *paying* premiums, is:

$$(a - bC_s(\varepsilon_s)) = \mu$$

Equating the left-hand sides of the previous two equations shows a relationship between consumption in 'good times' and consumption in 'bad times':

$$C_s(\varepsilon) = d/b + C_s(\varepsilon')$$

Here ε represents any state in which P is positive and ε' represents any state in which P is negative. From this we surmise that:

$$P(\varepsilon) = P^* + \varepsilon$$

and

$$P(\varepsilon') = P^{**} + \varepsilon'$$

where the *P*s are constants. From the zero-profit constraint, we know that:

$$\sum_{\varepsilon}\pi_i(P^* + \varepsilon_i) + \sum_{\varepsilon}\pi_i(P^{**} + \varepsilon_i) = 0$$

where the summations are taken over positive or negative ε, respectively, or:

$$-\sum\pi_i\varepsilon_i = \sum_{\varepsilon}\pi_i(P^*) + \sum_{\varepsilon}\pi_i(P^{**})$$

Since the distribution has a mean and median of zero, this becomes:

$$P^* = -P^{**}$$

So the sovereign pays a certain average payment in bad times and receives an equivalent amount in good times. In addition to this payment, the insurer compensates the sovereign completely for the positive or negative ε, so that (after insurance) income is $Y^* - P^*$ or $Y^* - P^{**}$.[2]

Now consider the effect of the disutility of low repayment on the ability of reputation to support the maintenance of capital markets. We suppose that the insurer can credibly commit to cutting off the sovereign from capital markets if the insured country fails to pay a premium. Default would occur, if at all, only if ε were positive. The ability of the sovereign to participate in world insurance markets depends in this case on its ability to commit credibly to paying its premiums. It can do so if the gain to be made by failing to pay a premium is less than the cost of the loss of access to world insurance markets infinitely far into the future.[3] Note here that we are referring to an ability to commit to *pay* $P(\varepsilon)$, which is different from the issue of the country's loss of utility when it *receives* $P(\varepsilon)$. The gain in the period in which the sovereign defaulted (did not pay $P(\varepsilon')$ when due) would be:

$$\begin{aligned} immediategain &= a(Y^* + \varepsilon) - b(Y^* + \varepsilon)^2 - a(Y^* - P^*) + b(Y^* - P^*)^2 \\ &= a(\varepsilon + P^*) - b(2(Y^*\varepsilon + Y^*P^*) + \varepsilon^2 - P^{*2}) \end{aligned}$$

The first two terms in the first equality show the utility that the sovereign enjoys by refusing to make its insurance payment. It simply consumes its total income, including the ε, which would have been partly surrendered if the country had paid its premium. The second two terms show the utility that the country would have received from paying its premium and consuming the remainder of its endowment. This immediate gain (the entire right-hand side of the equation) has to be weighed against the present discounted cost of being isolated from world capital markets in the future. This is a cost, because capital markets provide a utility-enhancing protection from the vicissitudes of income. The loss in the future from being cut off from world capital markets is:

$$loss = E_t \sum_{s=t+1}^{\infty} \beta^{s-t}(a(Y^* + \varepsilon_s) - b(Y^* + \varepsilon_s)^2)$$

$$- \sum_{s=t+1}^{\infty} \beta^{s-t}\big[a(-0.5P^* - 0.5P^{**} + Y^*)$$

$$- b(0.5(Y^* - P^*)^2 + 0.5(Y^* - P^{**})^2) + 0.5\, dE(P(\varepsilon'))\big]$$

Using the fact that $P^{**} = -P^*$ and that ε has a mean of zero:

$$= \beta(1-\beta)^{-1}\big[aY^* - bE_t(Y^{*2} + \varepsilon^2) - aY^* + b(Y^{*2} + P^{*2}) - 0.5\, dE(P(\varepsilon'))\big]$$
$$= -\beta(1-\beta)^{-1}\big[b(\mathrm{var}(\varepsilon) - P^{*2}) + 0.5\, dE(P(\varepsilon'))\big]$$

Here, losses are negative numbers. The first sum on the right-hand side of the 'loss' equation is the discounted value of the utilities obtained in the future when no insurance is available. The terms after the second summation indicate the discounted value of the future income that would have been obtained if the country had retained access to insurance markets. It would then have received Y^* in each period and paid P^* half the time and P^{**} (a negative 'payment') the other half of the time.

We now wish to compare these results with the standard model in which there is no sovereignty-loss disutility. In the absence of the *d* term in the utility function, there is full insurance (Obstfeld and Rogoff, 1996, p. 364). Specializing the model in Obstfeld and Rogoff to the quadratic functional form used here, the gain becomes:

$$immediategain2 = a(Y^* + \varepsilon) - b(Y^* + \varepsilon)^2 - a(Y^*) + b(Y^*)^2$$

$$= a\varepsilon - 2bY^*\varepsilon - b\varepsilon^2$$

The difference between the gains in the two situations is:

$$aP^* - 2bY^*P^* + bP^{*2}$$

The immediate pay-off for non-payment differs between the cases with and without sovereignty utility. If this difference is positive, the net gain from exiting insurance markets is greater with the *d* term than without. Since P^* is positive, the sign of this expression will depend on the parameter values. The loss in the model without disutility from sovereignty loss is:

$$loss2 = \; - b\beta(1 - \beta)^{-1}\text{var}(\varepsilon)$$

which differs from the earlier loss by the amount:

$$\beta(1 - \beta)^{-1}(bP^{*2} - 0.5\, dE(P(\varepsilon'))$$

Thus, since $P(\varepsilon') < 0$, the loss of utility from default is unambiguously lower when the country has a sovereignty term in its utility function. The fact that the loss and gain change when sovereignty-loss disutility is considered indicates that it is more or less difficult to sustain lending on the basis of reputation. Recall that if the cost of defaulting is less than the benefit, then the borrower or insurance buyer will have an incentive to default, destroying its ability to borrow in the first place. First, consider the future loss from losing access to world capital markets. Without considering the unusual feature in the utility function, this loss (*loss*2) is proportional to the variance of the disturbance to income. This is logical, because the main sacrifice from world market withdrawal is in the steadiness of income in the face of the random shock. Two terms reduce the loss, though: (i) the first term in the second pair of parentheses in the preceding equation shows that the loss is reduced because of the variation in income caused by the lack of full insurance. This term is larger, the larger the amount by which insurance payments fail to even out income across realizations of the disturbance, an amount reflecting the lack of full insurance. Recall that the lack of insurance is caused by the unusual term in the utility function; and (ii) the second term shows that the loss is also reduced because the disutility of participating in world markets – that is, the loss of autonomy discussed above. It is interesting to note that the reduction in the comparative disutility of default involves not just the explicit reduction in the benefits of borrowing because of the modification of the utility function, but also a reduction caused by imperfect insurance, a by-product of the modification.

The gain also differs, by the amount shown in the equation below '*immediategain*2'. Intuitively, this is a reduction in the premium one avoids paying by opting out of the capital market. The reward for breaking the contract to pay a premium in a period of high income is reduced because the premium is lower when insurance is incomplete.

The world capital market is inhibited by a lack of credibility on the part of the borrower, which arises from a disutility from *receiving* payments. The failure of credibility derives from the reduced value of insurance market participation to a potential purchaser of insurance. Sovereignty-loss disutility reduces the value of obtaining insurance by lowering the utility benefits of collecting a given insurance benefit and by reducing the amount of insurance a country will optimally choose. Since the benefits of insurance are low when sovereignty appears in the utility function, incentives may be higher for a nation to effectively opt out of the insurance market by refusing to pay a premium. Once again, the efficiency of the capital market is affected by the non-efficiency issues discussed here. Several policy issues are important. For example, do the results above imply that recipients of insurance payments should not be forced to suffer a loss of sovereignty? In the next section, we argue that while conventional economics purports to subsume all types of utility functions, it does not do a good job in handling the policy issues raised by our model.

Does international borrowing disutility or low-return disutility have methodological implications?

As suggested by Robbins, we have incorporated a non-material value into our analysis by putting it into the objective function, as we would with any other good. Does a slightly unusual utility function have any wider implications? Does Robbins' technique deal adequately with the issue at hand? The model leads to non-standard conclusions largely because sovereignty disutility drives a wedge between what might be called experienced utility and action utility (Sen, 1973; Kahneman, 1994). Action utility is the utility function that drives behaviour. Actors behave 'as if' they are maximizing this utility function; hence it is the correct function for modelling market behaviour. In this case, countries act as if they are maximizing a function with a penalty for borrowing (model I) or with a penalty for making a negative payment on a security or collecting on insurance (model II). This is the function Robbins says we ought to be concerned with. On the other hand, this utility function does not reflect actual welfare (experienced utility) in a certain sense: countries do not in fact lose welfare from borrowing *per se*, as an observation of their action utility function might suggest. They judge, in fact, that they would be better off if they were able to borrow; but their desire to borrow is offset by an overriding dislike of submitting to the wishes of the lender. This fact is not apparent to an economist, who judges welfare strictly on the basis of observed market behaviour (the 'revealed' action utility function) and does not take into account that agents are concerned with their relations with other countries, as opposed simply to smoothing their consumption streams. Robbins would not be particularly concerned with such welfare issues because he rejected Pigouvian welfare economics (Robbins, 1927). But we shall argue that it is difficult to avoid such questions, if economics is to provide any meaningful answers to policy problems.

The misunderstanding of observed capital market behaviour induced by these methodological mistakes leads the economist to make several errors regarding appropriate policies, an logical outcome of a failure to consider the appropriate measure of utility.

• When the utility function should properly be perceived as containing a penalty for international capital-market participation, the incorrect conclusion is drawn that this function is arbitrary or irrational

The neoclassical (Robbinist) economist does not attempt to investigate the reasonable basis for a particular utility function (in this case, the concern about sovereignty). We use the term 'reasonable', as against 'rational', to refer to the motivation or justification for a particular preference. In some cases, a preference may have no more justification than the tastes of the individual, as in, for example, a preference for chocolate over vanilla. Neoclassical economics does not distinguish this case from others, where certain reasons lie behind choices. This fact is reflected in the use of the word 'taste' for matters of immorality such as discrimination. Hence, in this case, the disutility of capital market participation appears to be equivalent to an arbitrary or irrational whim. If it is seen only as such, the appropriate policy response would be to educate sovereign governments that there is no reason to have an irrational desire not to borrow. Indeed, nations might come to that conclusion on their own. On the other hand, once the correct theory (in the sense of a justification for the utility function) is obtained, it would be recognized that the correct policy response would be to eliminate the imposition of sovereignty loss when it is clearly counter-productive. What was perceived initially as an irrational superstition on the part of potential borrowers is revealed to be the logical response to the onerous way that repayment is enforced, and the burden of change is shifted from borrower to lender. This policy conclusion hinges on judging appropriately the agent's rationale for a choice, not merely observing the choice and its implied utility function. The methodological implications of this are discussed later.

• The presumption is made that when capital markets are competitive, a Pareto optimum is attained. In fact, resources are misallocated

In the neoclassical model, free capital markets are good from a policy perspective because they allow capital to be used where it is most productive, and because they allow a diversification of risk. No possible Pareto improvement is possible in this model once capital markets are freed. But this policy conclusion is incorrect. This is because countries are participating less in financial markets for a particular reason, and are not discounting future utility to a small degree. If they were, the allocation in the first model would be optimal. Free capital markets respond well to differences in rates of time discount. Instead, there is a disutility to borrowing under current international arrangements that results in several failures of efficiency: (i) underinsurance; (ii) underborrowing; and (iii) underinvestment. The implication is that the world should not be complacent about observed problems in capital markets.

- **'Deep parameters' are miscalibrated**

Many neoclassical macroeconomists insist that empirical models should be functions of deep parameters such as utility function parameters, rather than behavioural relationships such as consumption functions or Phillips curves. This tack is thought to be an answer to the so-called 'Lucas critique', which argues that Keynesian behavioural relationships can vary as the policy regime varies (Lucas, 1991 [1976]). For example, if the monetary authority starts an aggressive programme of seeking high employment, workers will respond only temporarily, for as long as it takes for them to grasp the changes in the statistical process that generates policy. Thus an empirically estimated Phillips curve will break down once a new policy has been in effect for some time. It is far better to estimate the preference and technology parameters that stay constant over time and across policy regimes. A seminal paper, by Hansen and Sargent (1980, p. 7, quoted in Hartley, 1997),

> describes research which aims to provide tractable procedures for combining econometric models with dynamic economic theory for the purpose of modeling and interpreting economic time series. That we are short of such methods was a message of Lucas's (1976) criticism of procedures for econometric policy evaluation ... The implication of Lucas's observation is that instead of estimating the parameters of decision rules, what should be estimated are the parameters of agents' objective functions and of the random processes they faced historically.

Observations of lending behaviour are often used as a means of obtaining measures of such 'deep' parameters. For example, in one of the seminal papers on real business cycle theory, Kydland and Prescott (1982) estimate the risk aversion parameter of their utility function using the equation:

$$r = \rho + (1 - \gamma)(\dot{c}/c)$$

where r is the interest rate, ρ is subjective rate of time discount, γ is the rate of relative risk aversion, and c is consumption, with the overdot representing differentiation by time.

This equation is based on the Euler equation for a consumer's dynamic optimization problem with a constant relative risk aversion utility function. This estimation method will not work if borrowing appears in the utility function. If the equation above is estimated, then in that case the upward 'tilt' in consumption induced by the form of the utility function in the model above will be attributed incorrectly to a low rate of time discount or a high degree of risk aversion. If the estimate is then used to simulate the behaviour of the economy, as called for in certain types of paper, the results could be misleading.

Moreover, estimates such as this are often used for welfare analysis. For example, cost–benefit analysis often uses estimates of behavioural parameters to judge the merits of public investments. If a rate of subjective discount or degree of relative risk aversion is incorrectly estimated, the cost–benefit analysis would be incorrect.

One way of looking at this point is simply as a factor that renders parameter estimates inconsistent across the contexts in which they are apparently observed. A discount factor or risk-aversion parameter estimated using data on borrowing will not be valid in predicting other types of behaviour, such as investment. Nor will these parameters provide correct policy prescriptions when applied to still other intertemporal problems, such as cost–benefit evaluations.

All these problems have a bearing on several general methodological strategies employed by neoclassical economists.

• 'Preferences can be deduced from behavior and are therefore not unobservable'

In modern economics, this view is best represented by Samuelson and his 'revealed preference' theory. While Robbins disapproved of this theory (1953, pp. 101–2), it is consistent with Robbins' notion that preferences should be linked to actual desires, rather than to hedonistic utility (the pleasure of the agent). In the foregoing models, preferences can be observed, but the observations may lead to incorrect conclusions about the underlying reasons for behaviour. This is because welfare preferences are different from action preferences. Because observations of market behaviour cannot discriminate between a disutility of sovereignty loss and a low rate of time preference (two observationally equivalent sets of welfare preferences), they do not provide enough information to make policy judgements through means such as cost–benefit analyses.

The real problem is not that certain aspects of preferences are unobservable, but rather that the types of observation used must be expanded to gather information that would allow economists to distinguish between otherwise observationally equivalent cases. For example, it may help to study how agents justify their own behaviour publicly, and to other agents. An interview with a policy-maker might reveal that he or she is averse to being subjected to an IMF structural adjustment programme. Another appropriate methodological strategy would be to study the history of relations between countries such as the USA, on the one hand, and small, developing economies on the other. Putting the current situation in its proper historical context would illuminate the cultural sensitivities and existing imbalances of power that are exacerbated by lending relationships.

• 'Economists should not concern themselves with justifications for various preferences. Preferences should be used as data, not questioned. There is no arguing about the rationales for preferences (de gustibus non est disputandum)'

This precept was stated well by Lionel Robbins: 'The general absurdity of the belief that the world contemplated by the economist is peopled only by egoists or "pleasure machines" should be sufficiently clear from what has been said already ... We do not regard it as part of our problem to explain why ... particular valuations exist. We take them as data. So far as we are concerned, our economic subjects can be pure egoists, pure altruists, pure sensualists or – what is much more likely – mixed bundles of all these impulses' (Robbins, 1935, p. 95). Robbins goes on to give an example of a consumer who cares about the well-being of the baker from whom he buys bread. As long as we strive to achieve our ends in a consistent manner, according to Robbins, it does not matter from the standpoint of economic theory what those ends are. Economic theory applies regardless of the utility functions, ends or 'valuations' of the economic agent. Here we have used this conception of value to adapt a conventional utility function to an unconventional 'taste' for sovereignty.

But the analysis above shows that rationales for preferences must be discerned and tested. Different rationales lead to different conclusions about the values of various parameters. One rationale would interpret a low level of borrowing as the result of skewed period utility functions (precautionary savings). Another possible rationale is the one in the model above. As we have seen, the different rationales have different policy implications. Further, to deduce proper policy, it is necessary to judge the validity of rationales for preferences. The policy implications of the above model will differ, depending on whether one believes that the aversion of nations to borrowing is a legitimate one. If the strictures imposed by an international financial institution are in fact justifiable or insignificant, then one would *not* draw the policy conclusion from the model above that such strictures should be eliminated.

The preferences-as-data approach also runs the risk of begging the question. Certainly, economics is consistent with many unusual sorts of preferences. One strategy of Robbins' is to argue that knowledge of ends and their validity should be drawn from outside economics:

> [Economics] does not itself deal with the value of ends ... But I have not urged you to *ignore* such considerations. On the contrary, I would suggest that the whole drift of my discussion goes to show that the economist who is to make most use of his materials must be prepared to be more than an economist, to transcend his subject. Unless he is prepared to go beyond the technique of his subject, to live widely and intensely, to steep himself in the intellectual atmosphere of his time he will not be in a position to apply the machinery at his disposal – he will not be alive to the ends which he will be asked to take account of. (lecture notes on 'Economics and Political Theory', 1932, quoted in Howson 2004)

An economist must take into account the proper ends, but such ends must be drawn from outside economics, which consist of 'technique' or 'machinery'.

Those who might accept this methodology must realize that a theory that simply adopts whatever preferences are found empirically or discovered by other disciplines runs the risk of being overly dependent on reasoning from outside the theory. If behaviour can be motivated by any variables suggested by extra-economic work, one might justifiably adopt the explanation offered by that work, rather than simply 'cooking' preferences to mimic or obtain extra-economic results. Where is the value-added in a theory consistent with any desires at all? Should we not be uneasy with using information that is not in someway theoretically justified? Is it rational to have any arbitrary preferences, which may not make sense from the perspective of economic theory alone? If we have an economic theory, why not examine preferences to determine if they are consistent with that theory? What if the preference in question was an aversion to maximizing? Have we truly *explained* an economic outcome if we simply attribute it to desires that make no sense? To truly explain behaviour, is it sufficient to say that the agent prefers to behave that way? It seems that economics is flexible enough to accommodate many types of preferences, but leaves us without a compass to discern their deeper implications. This is reflected in the results above. Certain analytical results have been derived, but few would regard them as a full analysis of what some regard as imperialism.

As one last question, suppose we observe a preference for sovereignty. We can then rationalize the nation's behaviour in rejecting loans. But is this really rational? In the model above, the preference to avoid loans is 'rational' when there is a sovereignty disincentive. But that disincentive would not be present in the absence of an *irrational* economic doctrine, subscribed to by international financial institutions, that says countries benefit by submitting to the demands of lenders. Thus the sort of behaviour described here might be, quite literally, the result not of (rational) microeconomic optimization, but of macroeconomics (an illogical theory of what is the best policy towards debtor nations) (see Anderson, 2002, for another example). The ultimate source of behaviour is irrational, despite the fact that nations are doing the best they can with the resources they have.

• 'Institutional choice is a matter of efficiency. Since institutions are instruments to achieve individual ends, they can be judged solely on the basis of the goods they "deliver" '

In this model, we deal with an institution called the world capital market. The usual analysis of institutions (at least in the 'new institutional economics') sees configurations of institutions as a reflection of their efficiency properties (their ability to reduce transactions costs). By contrast, the subject of this chapter is not the best instrument for delivering capital to its most efficient use. Rather, this issue is disutilities imposed by the capital market itself. An analogy would be a country that disliked central planning on the grounds of its violation of individual autonomy. In such a country, even though a central planner might be able to effect a Pareto-improving reallocation, citizens would reject the planner on the grounds of the undesirability of planning itself. In the same way, according to this chapter and previous work by Elizabeth Anderson (2004), borrowers lose when they are entangled in certain demeaning social relations or institutions. In this sense, the models above invoke extra-economic considerations, even though they are obtained simply by a modification of the utility function. In turn, these extra-economic factors influence the economic properties of the system. Because of a concern about international institutions, certain standard efficiency results do not hold, as we have shown here. The analysis of institutions as strictly neutral means of attaining independent ends fails.

Conclusion

Two models have been developed in this chapter. In both, the concerns of the representative agent, a nation in this case, went beyond consumption streams to the types of external relations involved in international financial market participation. In both models, the implications of the objective function were shown to go beyond intangibles such as standing in the world. In the first model, the nation did not take advantage sufficiently, from an efficiency point of view, of the opportunity to finance investment with foreign capital. It also tilted its consumption stream towards the future specifically because of the presence of a borrowing variable in the utility function. In the second model, the representative nation either bought insufficient insurance or obtained too little financial investment from a welfare point of view. One result was that it was more difficult to maintain international lending markets strictly on the basis of reputation for repayment.

What are the implications of these findings for the line of argument that supporters of open capital markets develop using similar models? With conventional models, the models studied here agree that capital markets can benefit both borrowers and lenders. On the other hand, this chapter shows that, to reap these benefits, capital markets must be adapted in some way to eliminate the disutilities of borrowing or paying a small return. To some extent, the disutilities may be the result of unenlightened policy driven by the Washington consensus. But the disamenities for which the international financial institutions are responsible are to some extent the result of an imbalance of power that enables lenders to dominate borrowers, a problem that has vexed debt markets for some time and is largely invisible to the developers of standard models of international finance or the new open economy macroeconomics. A sure sign that existing disutilities of debt are the symptom of the power that the developed economies exert over the less developed is that the developed countries, including the USA and the members of the European Monetary and Economic Union, have chosen not to enforce fiscal strictures on themselves.

In spite of whatever insights the models above may offer, it was argued that the developed model revealed some potential limitations of an often-adopted strategy for dealing with non-economic issues. The model thus had broader implications. A summing-up of the methodological points demonstrated by the mathematical analysis is in order. All these points addressed neoclassical stratagems that have been deployed to handle arguments that economics cannot deal with certain types of preferences. In the main, such arguments suggest that economics is neutral among various values, preferences or ends, and can be adapted to suit any of them. The first point made above was that when the justifications for the preferences in the model are not investigated, they are treated as equivalent to mere whims or 'likings'; this denigrates unfairly the moral legitimacy of the concerns of potential borrowers. If developing nations lack a proper 'taste' for foreign capital, they cannot reasonably lay the blame for a lack of capital on the lender. Second, the optimality properties of a competitive allocation are different when an unusual form of preference is involved an economist interested in welfare must dirty his or her hands and dig into the matter of motivation. Only once preferences are fully understood will it be realized that the attenuation of capital markets is not merely an optimal response to a nation's desire to defer consumption or its lack of credibility. Third, the failure to understand the reasoning behind behaviour leads the economist to believe s/he is estimating one parameter (perhaps the subjective discount rate) when s/he is in fact measuring a tendency that does not apply outside a particular international context.

A second list of methodological implications followed. First, the chapter noted that economists often defend the empirical legitimacy of preference analysis by arguing that utility functions can be discerned by observing a consumer's choice of behaviour; it was shown that, in order to draw interesting conclusions from the choices of the nations modelled here, one would have to distinguish between apparently indistinguishable motivations for preferences, a requirement that would lead one beyond the narrow sort of fact-gathering associated in economics with empiricism. Second, the chapter pointed out the limitations of the view that values, while important, were outside the purview of economics. In particular, we argued that the policy implications of the models would depend on whether the fear of loss of sovereignty was a legitimate concern; if not, there would be no reason to deviate from the laissez-faire allocation derived in the model. Another challenge to the view that values were distinct from economics and should be drawn from other fields was that this sort of question-avoidance amounted to question-begging: the adoption of non-economic value judgements causes one to question the value-added offered by a theory that is silent on such crucial matters. If justice and power are important in the relations between international lenders and borrowers, neo-classical economics may not be the best vehicle for understanding the issues at stake. Finally, the sorts of preferences modelled here are simply irreconcilable with the standard view of institutions in neoclassical analysis as neutral instruments for achieving individual ends; the institutions in this case are themselves bearers of value.

All these observations suggest that in dealing with such a fundamental issue as the autonomy of a nation, economics cannot pretend to be neutral about the values at stake. An approach that purports to investigate the implications of a certain set of preferences without judging their validity or investigating their rationale fails to answer even the most basic policy questions at issue, is unable to draw empirical lessons that apply to other spheres of action, and is overly optimistic about the optimality of the status quo political economy.

A modeller who simply observes that foreign governments have an increasing distaste for borrowing, as depicted in this chapter, has only gone a small part of the way towards understanding the moral, political and economic issues at stake. Foreign voters, to the economist, may seem to be rationally maximizing an unreasonable value in rejecting governments that accept the demands of foreign and international institutions. A just and efficient solution to frictions between small developing nations and international financial institutions may rest on the development of an understanding on all sides that, on the contrary, a 'taste' for autonomy is both rational and reasonable. That achievement might allow small developing countries to garner the rewards of open financial markets touted by open-economy macroeconomists and finance specialists.

Notes

The author thanks Philip Arestis for extensive and useful comments. Elizabeth S. Anderson also provided many useful comments and clarifications of her views, most of which unfortunately came too late to be incorporated into this chapter. Kenneth Hannsgen also provided some late comments. Of course, neither Arestis, Hannsgen nor Anderson is responsible for any remaining errors.

1 A word about the no-Ponzi constraint is in order. In this case, it is not restrictive. In models of this type, it is (Obstfeld and Rogoff, 1996):

$$\lim_{t\to\infty}((K_{t+1} + B_{t+1})/(1 + r)^t) = 0$$

Now, at some point 0, as consumption grows, the total assets of the representative agent reach zero from above. Its debts will climb faster, the lower its income, Y. Suppose then (without loss of generality) that $Y = 0$ in all periods from time 0 onward. In time 0, $K + B$ will become $-C^*$, where C^* is some constant level of consumption in that period. Subsequently, according to the Euler equation, consumption will rise by $\beta c/b$ in each period, and each period's consumption will be subtracted from $K + B$. Hence, in time 1, $K + B$ will be $-2C^* - \beta c/b$, then in time 2, $-3C^* - 3\beta c/b$, etc. As Gauss realized as a schoolboy, the nth partial sum of this infinite arithmetic series in $K + B$ is $-0.5n(C^* + C^* + n\beta c/b)$ (Weisstein, 2005).

Under our assumption that all consumption is financed by borrowing or capital decumulation, the condition above then becomes

$$\lim_{t\to\infty}(- 0.5(t + 1)(2C^{*} + (t + 1)\beta c/b)/(1 + r)^{t}) = 0$$

One can then apply L'Hopital's rule twice by differentiating both numerator and denominator of the expression after the limit sign twice with respect to *t*, then taking the limit as *t* goes to infinity. The limit is indeed zero, which can be verified numerically.

2 We must rule out anomalous solutions where P^* and P^{**} are greater in absolute value than the lowest epsilon.

3 We do not consider certain outcomes when this conditions is not met: less-than-optimal insurance or the posting of bonds.

References

Anderson, Elizabeth S. (1993) *Value and Ethics in Economics* (Cambridge, MA: Harvard University Press).

Anderson, Elizabeth S. (2002) 'Should Feminists Reject Rational Choice Theory?' in Louise M. Antony and Charlotte E. Witt (eds), *A Mind of One's Own: Feminist Essays on Reason and Objectivity* (Cambridge, MA: Westview Press).

Anderson, Elizabeth S. (2004) 'Ethical Assumptions in Economic Theory: Some Lessons from the History of Credit and Bankruptcy', *Ethical Theory and Moral Practice*, 7, pp. 347–60.

Davidson, Paul (2002) *Financial Markets, Money, and the Real World* (Northampton, MA: Edward Elgar).

Garegnani, Pierangelo (1990) 'Quantity of Capital', in John Eatwell, Murray Milgate and Peter Newman (eds), *The New Palgrave: Capital Theory* (New York: W. W. Norton).

Hansen, Lars Peter and Sargent, Thomas J. (1980) 'Formulating and Estimating Dynamic Linear Rational Expectations Models', *Journal of Economic Dynamics and Control*, 2, pp. 91–125.

Hartley, James E. (1997) *The Representative Agent in Macroeconomics* (London: Routledge).

Howson, Susan (2004) 'The Origins of Lionel Robbins's *Essay on the Nature and Significance of Economic Science*', *History of Political Economy*, 36(3), pp. 413–43.

Kahneman, David (1994) 'New Challenges to the Rationality Assumption', *Journal of Institutional and Theoretical Economics*, 150(1), pp. 18–36.

Kirman, Alan (1992) 'Whom or What Does the Representative Individual Represent?' *Journal of Economic Perspectives*, 6(2), pp. 117–36.

Kydland, Finn E. and Prescott, Edward C. (1982) 'Time to Build and Aggregate Fluctuations', *Econometrica*, 50(6), pp. 1345–69.

Ljungqvist, Lars and Sargent, Thomas (2004) *Recursive Economic Theory*, 2nd edn (Cambridge, MA: MIT Press).

Lucas, Robert E. Jr. (1991 [1976]) 'Econometric Policy Evaluation: A Critique', in Edmund S. Phelps (ed.), *Recent Developments in Macroeconomics: Volume I* (Brookfield, VT: Edward Elgar).

O'Brien, D. P. (1988) *Lionel Robbins* (New York: St Martin's Press).

O'Brien, Timothy and Rohter, Larry (2004) 'The Pinochet Money Trail', *New York Times*, 12 December.

Obstfeld, Maurice and Rogoff, Kenneth (1996) *Foundations of International Macroeconomics* (Cambridge, MA: MIT Press).
Petras, James and Veltmeyer, Henry (2001) *Globalization Unmasked* (London: Zed Books).
Robbins, Lionel (1927) 'Mr. Hawtrey on the Scope of Economics', *Economica*, 20, pp. 172–8.
Robbins, Lionel (1935) *An Essay on the Nature and Significance of Economic Science*, 2nd edn (London: Macmillan).
Robbins, Lionel (1953) 'Robertson on Utility and Scope', *Economica*, 20(78), pp. 99–111.
Rohter, Larry (2004) 'Economic Rally for Argentines Defies Forecasts', *New York Times*, 26 December.
Sen, Amartya (1973) 'Behaviour and the Concept of Preference', *Economica*, 40(1), pp. 241–59.
Weisstein, Eric W. (2005) 'Arithmetic Series', *Mathworld* (*Wolfram.com. ArithmeticSeries.html*).

2
On the Changing Nature of Currency Crises

Korkut A. Erturk

Currency crises have become a common occurrence around the world in the era of capital account liberalization. Following numerous crises in Latin America in the 1980s, speculative attacks on currency wreaked havoc in the Scandinavian countries in the late 1980s, the European Monetary System (EMS) in 1991–2; in Mexico in 1994–5; in East Asia in 1997–8; in Russia in 1998; in Brazil in 1999; and in Argentina and Turkey in 2000–1. And, at the time of writing (April 2005) we may soon face a dollar crisis that will have severe repercussions for the USA and the whole world economy. After each major episode a new *generation* of crisis models emerged, and, arguably, we still lack a clear understanding of what has remained the same and what was novel in the different episodes of crisis.

Despite their many differences, the successive generations of currency crisis models can be thought to revolve around the same set of questions. At one level, they appear as a problem of overborrowing made possible by an excessive expansion in bank credit. Often, capital inflow is stimulated by financial liberalization and leads to a credit expansion in the recipient country that is followed sooner or later by a debt problem. Depending on the country, the debt pile-up could be either private or public, and owed to either domestic or foreign investors, but the destabilizing dynamics it sets off appear similar. At yet another level, these crises have resulted from abrupt capital flow reversals caused by capricious shifts in investor sentiment.

In the 'first-generation' models, the problems of both overborrowing and capital flow reversal were explained by the same mechanism. Monetization of government deficits fuelled an explosive rise in credit supply, giving rise to an unsustainable increase in expenditure and rising prices. With a fixed nominal exchange rate, that led to real currency appreciation and usually went hand in hand with a rising current-account deficit. As a result, the devaluation risk rose steadily, brought to an end the capital inflow and re-imposed the foreign exchange constraint. The beginning of the 'end' came when the depletion in foreign exchange reserves set off a rush among speculators to get out of the domestic currency before the inevitable maxi-devaluation struck.

In the crises of the 1990s, the destabilizing processes that needed explanation remained the same. Explosive increases in bank credit gave rise to overborrowing and at some point capital flow abruptly reversed. The reserve depletion caused by monetized government deficits was no longer an explanation that seemed applicable as excessive credit expansion took place even when there were no government budget deficits. Similarly, the devaluation risk stemming from current-account deficits caused by the spending spree and reserve depletion no longer seemed the decisive factors in explaining capital flow reversals. In much of the 1980s, fixed price assets in the form of bank loans were still the main conduit of financial capital flows into developing economies, whereas variable price assets such as bonds and stocks began to take their place by the end of that decade. The explosive expansion of secondary asset markets in developing countries during this period (Grabel, 1996; Singh, 1997, 2003; Singh and Weisse, 1998) meant that portfolio dynamics driven by speculative expectations on variable price assets, and thus the very dynamics of asset price bubbles, could become the driving force behind erratic capital flows. Once capital inflows into developing countries began to finance speculative asset positions first and foremost, capital account dynamics, rather than those associated with the current account have started to become decisive.

In this chapter, I argue that the growing importance of variable price financial instruments as conduits of capital flows in the 1990s has created the potential for destabilizing trend speculation on the part of international investors. This suggests a state of the world where expectations of asset price capital gains rather than arbitrage opportunities emerge as the predominant motivation behind capital flows. Similarly, once the expectations of asset price increases cease, for whatever reason, capital flow reverses regardless of whether devaluation risk and foreign exchange reserves are high or low. This is the sense in which currency crises have become 'capital account' driven.[1]

This differs from Krugman's (2000) influential typology of different generations of models that are thought to reflect the transformation of currency crises. In his classification, the 'first generation' models refer to reserve depletion caused by monetized government budget deficits, while the second generation models focus on governments' willingness to devalue to avoid reserve depletion, and the third generation models emphasize financial balance sheet problems stemming from currency and maturity mismatch. In what appears to be an alternative classification, Krugman also makes a distinction between *fundamentals*-driven first-generation models and *expectations*-driven second-generation models (Williamson, 2001), which might at best correspond imprecisely to the contrast drawn here between 'current account', driven versus 'capital account'-driven crises. As we shall see, the current-account-driven crises need have little to do with monetized government budget deficits and lax public finance, and the capital-account-driven crises' salient characteristics have little to do with the complications caused by currency (and maturity) mismatch, nor how governments prefer to react when faced with the threat of a speculative attack. In the following sections, current-account-driven and capital-account-driven crises are discussed and contrasted. The chapter ends with a brief summary of the main argument.

Current account driven crises

When currency crises first erupted in the Southern Cone countries in Latin America in the late 1970s, disinflation was being attempted for the first time in the context of a liberalized capital account. Also, the nominal exchange rate functioned as an anchor in all these stabilization programmes, because belt-tightening was not thought to be sufficient in itself to bring down the inertial part of inflation. The main objective was to reduce domestic inflation by decreasing incrementally the rate of devaluation. In later years, similar disinflation programmes with the exchange rate as the nominal anchor were used in many other countries in different parts of the world.

Often, inflation did not fall in tandem with the incremental reduction in the rate of devaluation of currency, causing the exchange rate to appreciate in real terms. Initially, it was thought that this would have a contractionary effect, as it would tend to reduce net exports. But, time after time, the result was invariably the opposite: a private-consumption-led boom in output that eventually collapsed in a few years. For example, in both Chile and Argentina, where these types of programmes were first implemented, private consumption rose by more than 10 per cent within a year of the programme being implemented, and the GDP increase was also close to double digits. With such a rapid expansion of output, it was not long before the current account deficits began to balloon as well, reaching, for example, as high a ratio as 14 per cent of GDP in Chile within two years (Calvo and Vegh, 1999). The same pattern – a private-consumption-led explosive increase in output that disintegrated in a few years, repeated itself in many other countries that implemented disinflation programmes with a nominal exchange rate anchor.

The boom phase of the cycles seemed to be explained by the discrepancy in the speeds with which rates of devaluation and inflation declined.[2] Just as the very credibility of the disinflation programme brought down the expected rate of devaluation, the domestic nominal interest rate also fell, in line with the uncovered interest rate parity condition. The decrease in the real rate of interest was even greater, because the decline in the rate of inflation often lagged behind (Rodriguez, 1982). Moreover, the real wages also often rose, because the decline in inflation, though not as fast as the decrease in the rate of devaluation, was nevertheless faster than the decrease in the rate by which nominal wages continued to increase. Thus, falling real interest rates, coupled possibly with rising real wages, was a part of the explanation of the consumption-led boom in output.[3] But what was perhaps more important was the increased ease of access to credit throughout the economy. As economic liberalization, of which the adoption of a credible disinflation programme has often been a part, set the stage for an increase in capital inflow, a steep increase in borrowing usually ensued. Both the consumers' and firms' willingness, as well as their ability, to borrow increased whether or not their real incomes rose.

Taylor (1998) argues that credit expansion and overborrowing begin with the adoption of a credible economic liberalization programme, as it gives rise to a positive interest rate spread, because the nominal interest rate usually falls by less than the decrease in the expected rate of devaluation. This fuels a steady capital inflow, causing the domestic money supply to increase. If the central bank sterilizes, a further increase in the domestic interest rate leads to an even higher interest-rate spread, stimulating even a greater inflow. The capital inflow in fact induces domestic banks to raise the volume of credit they supply, which in turn raises both the money supply on the one hand, and prices and output on the other. As long as the real exchange rate continues to rise, banks can indeed make easy profits by lending inside the country what they borrow from outside at a much lower rate of interest. But, they thereby ignore the devaluation risk and the possibility that the trend of real appreciation of currency can reverse itself. Is this then prima facie evidence of the moral hazard problem?

Indeed, the large, *open* positions banks took in many of the East Asian countries were blamed for setting the stage for the crisis by the proponents of the moral hazard argument. Thus, in McKinnon and Pill's (1997, 1999) view, the problem in East Asia was too rapid financial liberalization that did not allow the time needed to develop the institutional infrastructure for prudential regulation of banks and the financial system. Corruption, cronyism and lack of transparency were thus thought to be the ultimate causes of the large, open positions banks took and overborrowing throughout the economy. A number of arguments can be made against this moral hazard view.

Even in economies with a well-established tradition of prudential regulation and well-developed financial system, a period of rapid profit growth fuels overconfidence and gives rise to a climate of financial exuberance. This was, in fact, one of Minsky's salient points about business cycle dynamics in an advanced capitalist economy such as the USA, where the most recent episode (Enron) of irrational exuberance in the 1990s is too well-known to recount. As it now turns out, the USA has been rife with corruption to a degree more than was ever thought possible, and thus might not be the best example to raise to question the moral hazard argument. But, even then, the Nordic countries that are not known for their corruption and cronyism also experienced an explosive increase in bank credit on the heels of financial liberalization in the late 1980s that eventually ended in a banking and currency crisis. The speculative fervour that develops in episodes of asset price bubbles stimulates corruption rather than reduces it. Thus it is more plausible that corruption is more an effect than a cause. Second, independently of moral hazard, other compelling reasons exist why one would expect bank credit to be procyclical under conditions of economic liberalization, which can explain bouts of overborrowing. Among those that have already come under extensive scrutiny are the strong pro-cyclical effects of the Basel Accords that set minimum capital requirements for banks (Griffth-Jones and Sprate, 2002; Isenberg and Phillips, 2005; Rude, 2005).

Yet another reason – as yet, not well recognized – is the fact that liquidity preference and currency substitution become entwined under conditions of financial and capital account liberalization. This acts as a built-in macroeconomic destabilizer, as it affects procyclical variations in the liquidity position of banks. Because of various problems – high inflation, credibility, exchange rate risk and so on – currency substitution is, unsurprisingly, quite extensive in many developing countries around the world.[4] Thus, it is not unusual for people in these economies to try to keep a large part of their idle balances in foreign currency. Financial and capital account liberalization, when successful, embed currency substitution within the local banking system and lower transaction costs, thereby channelling these inactive balances into foreign exchange deposits in domestic banks. As a result, under normal conditions changes in the liquidity preference entail currency substitution, causing first and foremost *quantity* rather than *price* changes in the form of shifts in the composition of total bank deposits between active and inactive balances. This, in turn, acts as a built-in macroeconomic destabilizer because domestic banks' reserve requirements are invariably much higher for foreign-exchange-denominated accounts than for those denominated in local currency. When inactive balances swell in the banking system at a time of rising liquidity preference and economic slowdown, the effect is to lower banks' liquidity by redistributing deposits within the system from low-reserve to high-reserve accounts. Similarly, banks' liquidity situation is improved during times of rising economic activity and falling liquidity preference, when the relative size of active balances in domestic currency accounts increase in relation to inactive balances consisting mainly of foreign exchange deposits.

Given all this, policies aimed at eradicating practices that are thought to give rise to moral hazard are likely to be counter-productive not only because there might be other causes that are at least as important, as suggested above, but also stamping out such practices can have adverse unintended consequences if these happen to be 'second-best' solutions to other 'distortions' in the economy. For example, deposit insurance and lender of last resort practices of central banks can create moral hazard problems, but they have also been quite effective in containing systemic risks such as bank panics since the 1930s (Eatwell and Taylor, 2000, p. 47). Thus the cost of erasing such practices can plausibly outweigh the moral hazard problems themselves.

When it comes to the 'bust' phase of the cycle, the argument is more straightforward. The output expansion fuelled by excessive credit creation is unsustainable, mainly because the real exchange rate appreciation and rising output give rise to a ballooning current account deficit, causing a steady increase in the devaluation risk. This means that the domestic nominal interest rate now needs to continually increase in order to maintain a positive interest rate spread, to ensure that the capital inflow continues. As a result, rising interest rates and the current account deficit first slow down, and eventually reverse, economic expansion. Depending on the level of the foreign exchange reserves and the rate of their depletion a run on the currency can occur at any time. In capital-account-driven crises that are discussed next, what is fundamentally different is essentially the modality of the capital inflow and its reversal.

Capital account driven crises

Under conditions of capital account liberalization, the exchange rate becomes just another asset price that can be subject to speculation. This means that, just as in the case of any other forward-looking asset price, rumours, noise and investor sentiment, at least in the short run, are likely to be more important than what is happening in the real economy in determining movements in its price. Yet, ever since Friedman (1953) argued that destabilizing speculation would be unprofitable and thus unsustainable in the long run, most mainstream economists have assumed that speculation as a rule could not be destabilizing. Asset price bubbles were considered to be highly unlikely, if not impossible, in a 'normally' functioning market. The rise of the 'efficient market hypothesis' in the 1960s had bolstered the influence of Friedman's argument, as it gave credence to the idea that actual market prices of assets must be the best estimates of their *true* values at a given point in time.[5] The intuition behind Friedman's (1953) argument rested on a simple view of arbitrage, in which the market comprises smart traders who know the true values, and misinformed noise-traders. If securities are undervalued, as the argument goes, then the smart traders would continue to buy them until their prices bid up to their true value. Similarly, if securities are overvalued, smart traders would sell them, bringing their price down to their true value. Indeed, under these conditions, speculation is always stabilizing and profitable. Misinformed noise traders thus create riskless arbitrage opportunities from which smart traders profit, while themselves making losses.

Undoubtedly, the assumption that smart traders or speculators know with certainty the true value is exceedingly unrealistic. But, even under this strong assumption, it does not follow that the deviation of the current price of an asset from its true value creates a riskless arbitrage opportunity. Because traders in general have a finite time horizon, a speculator who sells overvalued assets short can find that by the time s/he is supposed to close his/her position, the true value has increased, or that the assets in question have become even more overpriced.[6] In both situations, the speculators who have sold securities short would make losses. Even if the true value is known, it does not follow that it would be equal to the expected future price. Thus, because the fear of making losses would cause smart traders to limit the initial positions they take in an over- or undervalued asset, current price might not adjust smoothly to its true value. Needless to say, if we drop the assumption that speculators know what the true value is, the risk of loss they perceive is likely to be higher, and the compensatory shift in demand for the undervalued asset smaller. That is why the modern 'noise trader' or the 'behavioural' approach to finance holds that *riskless* arbitrage is not effective in relation to the prices of shares or bonds as a whole, and severely limited even when it comes to the relative prices of individual assets (Shleifer and Summers, 1990; Shleifer and Vishny, 1997).

In this setting, unlike the situation Friedman (1953) foresaw, successful (read *rational*) speculators are those who engage in 'trend' speculation, where they act like noise-traders themselves in the short run, trying to feed the bubble rather than helping to deflate it (Delong *et al.*, 1990).[7] In other words, they chase asset price trends to jump on the bandwagon of noise-traders and know when to get off, while the rest ride on. In a similar manner, the asset price bubbles that have emerged in the aftermath of economic liberalization appear to have created ample opportunities for trend speculation among international investors. Depending on the special conditions of each country, asset price bubbles have emerged in different asset categories. In some countries, it was the real estate market, in others the equities, corporate bonds or government debt instruments. In the following, the simplest type of a debt instrument, such as a short-term government bond, is assumed.

In order to draw a contrast between capital flows motivated by expectations of capital gain in asset prices from those that are driven by arbitrage opportunities, a useful starting point might be the uncovered interest rate parity condition, which, as written below, simply states that the difference between the domestic nominal interest rate and the international interest rate must be equal to the sum of the devaluation risk (*DR*) and the country (or sovereign) risk (*SR*):[8]

$$i - i^* = DR + SR \qquad (1)$$

where i is the domestic nominal interest rate and i^* the international interest rate. The change in foreign exchange reserves is in turn the sum of the current and capital accounts:

$$\Delta F = T(Y,E) + C(i,i^*) \qquad (2)$$

where T is trade balance, Y is output, and E the real exchange rate (where an increase means a fall in the value of the domestic currency). As it is commonly assumed, $T_Y < 0$, $T_E > 0$ and $C_i > 0$, holding i^*, DR and SR constant.

In Taylor's (1998) argument discussed above, the first equation turns into an inequality once a developing country adopts a credible stabilization programme. The interest rate differential on the left-hand side exceeds the sum of *SR* and *DR*, and the greater the interest rate spread, the higher the magnitude of capital inflow. Over time, output expansion and real exchange rate appreciation cause the trade deficit to rise, which eventually pushes up the *DR*. Under these circumstances, a positive interest rate spread can only be maintained with a higher domestic interest rate. Because the domestic interest rate cannot be increased indefinitely, it becomes harder to check the decrease in the foreign exchange reserves by raising the interest rate past a threshold, causing a further increase in the *DR*. This is the beginning of the end, and once reserves begin to fall steadily the actual mechanism of the speculative attack need not be different from Krugman's (1979) account.

In its present form, Equation (1) implicitly assumes that arbitrage works only through assets that are held to maturity for their interest yield, since expectations of asset price changes are not part of the arbitrage condition. If, instead, the prospect of capital gain is the motivating factor behind capital flows, asset price expectations would need to be introduced into the interest parity condition. One simple way in which this can be done is by defining – for want of a better term – the *total* exchange rate risk (*TER*) as the difference between the devaluation risk (*DR*) and the expected increase in asset prices (ΔAP^e):[9]

$$TER = DR - \Delta AP^e \tag{3}$$

and rewriting Equation (1) as:

$$i - i^* = TER + SR \tag{4}$$

Note that in Equation (1) the *total* exchange rate risk is simply assumed to be equal to the devaluation risk, because the expected change in asset prices is set implicitly equal to zero. Now let us assume a situation where a credible disinflation programme with a nominal exchange rate anchor is about to be implemented in some developing country, and that this gives rise to the expectation that the nominal rate of interest on government bonds will decline in the near future. The adoption of the stabilization programme, again, as assumed before, leads to a decrease in the devaluation rate (crawling peg), giving rise to a positive spread. But, in addition, the expected asset price change also turns positive, as it is now expected that the implementation of the stabilization programme will attract capital, which will push down the nominal interest rate in the near future and thus raise the value of old issue bonds. Thus, in this case, the *total* exchange rate risk falls not only because of the lower expected devaluation risk, but also because of the expected increase in asset prices. Again, capital flows in, the supply of bank credit expands, and spending and output rise. But, now, in contrast to the earlier case, the *TER* begins to rise as soon as the expected increase in asset prices peters out – as the interest rate levels off after its initial rapid decline following the first implementation of the disinflation programme – even when the current account deficit might still be insignificant and reserves are high.

To the extent that foreign hedge fund managers begin to believe that domestic asset prices have peaked, they might simply close their positions and move elsewhere. Provided the *SR* is still low, an increasing number of 'local' speculators, who might also think that asset prices have peaked, would switch to foreign-currency-denominated bank accounts within the country. In either case, whether the foreign hedge funds leave the country, or bank deposits shift to foreign-exchange-denominated accounts in domestic banks, there is an unexpected weakness in the value of the home currency – that is, a slowdown at the rate at which the devaluation rate is decreasing (crawling peg), or a fall in reserves. This can undermine market confidence in the stabilization programme, causing the *DR* to rise unexpectedly as well. At this point, it is possible that the current account deficit, that might until then have been seen as a *normal* corollary of the capital account surplus, might all of a sudden be deemed unsustainable and thus a problem. In other words, it becomes a problem because the capital inflow falters as the expected asset price increases peter out. At the end, the *TER* ultimately rises because of both the initial fall in the expected asset price increases and the eventual rise in the devaluation risk.

Even if the exchange rate survives the initial capital outflow, with the *TER* rising, the nominal interest rate begins to rise steeply. Unlike the situation discussed in the previous section, the higher interest rate is unlikely to succeed in keeping the interest rate spread positive and thus buy much time for the country in question. First, to the extent that rising interest rates signal investors that negative asset price changes are ahead, they are likely to stimulate a net outflow rather than an inflow of capital. In the stylized world of the Mundell–Flemming model, this means that the capital flow is a negative function of the expected rate of change of the interest rate. Within a certain range involving higher time frequencies, this effect is likely to be much stronger than the conventional positive relationship that is postulated in Equation (2) between the level of the interest rate and the capital inflow.

Most, if not all, of the IMF-backed stabilization programmes that were in force at the time a currency crisis erupted in one or other developing country barred the central bank from acting as an intermediary and a lender of last resort.[10] The objective of these stabilization programmes was instead to rely on market forces to maintain liquidity, where two self-correcting mechanisms were often presumed (Ekinci and Erturk, 2004). First, because the private banking sector often held a large portfolio of government debt instruments – mainly because some private banks become the primary dealers in these assets after financial liberalization – they would have a stake in maintaining the value of these assets and be inclined to buy what the speculators wanted to unload. Second, the capital outflow would self-correct by pushing interest rates higher, which would then reverse the outflow.

More often than not, neither mechanism worked, as the two tended to clash with each other. As remarked above, the expectation of further increases in interest rates initially stimulated an outflow as investors tried to avoid capital losses by exiting sooner rather than later. Thus interest rates had to reach exorbitantly high levels before the capital outflow could be stopped at all, let alone reversed. The excessively high interest rates in turn raised the cost of short-term borrowing prohibitively for the primary dealer banks, who were supposed to absorb the portfolios speculators were unloading. The result was often a chain reaction of bank failures, where exorbitantly high interest rates pushed them over the edge even if the banking system was strong enough to weather the shock of the initial bursting of the asset price bubble. Moreover, once banks were forced to default on their foreign debts, they also threatened the solvency of the public sector, causing the *SR* to unravel as well (Corbett and Vines, 1999). The solvency of the public sector was also threatened when the public debt was high to begin with, since, with very high interest rates, it does not take very long before it begins to look out of control. Thus, quite often, government guarantees that were meant to reduce the devaluation risk for foreign investors during the good times, whether explicit – as the dollar indexed bonds (*tesobonos*) in Mexico – or implicit, came back to haunt the solvency of the public sector.[11] Once the *SR* unravelled, which was likely to happen one way or another, no interest rate increase, regardless of how big it was could stem the outflow of capital, and a complete meltdown became inevitable.

Conclusion

The objective of this chapter has been to draw a contrast between current-account-driven and capital-account-driven crises. In the former, excessive credit expansion and overborrowing are the destabilizing processes that play a decisive role. Capital inflow is governed predominantly by arbitrage opportunities, where its reversal is tied to a rising devaluation risk associated with reserve depletion. Starting with the late 1980s, capital-account-driven crises have come to predominate, as fixed price assets in the form bank loans are increasingly dwarfed by variable price assets such as bonds and stocks, giving rise to portfolio dynamics driven by speculative expectations on variable price assets. This, combined with the increased predictability of asset prices, in turn set the stage for destabilizing trend speculation on the part of international investors. Typically, the capital inflow continues as foreign investors chase a rising trend of asset prices, and reverses when they begin to think that asset prices have peaked. Once the asset price bubble deflates, the threshold of sustainable debt is drastically reduced and a chain of bank failures is triggered. After a crisis occurs, the single most effective policy response is whether the provision of lender of last resort is made available or not, which is rarely (commonly) the case in the periphery (centre). But, even in the USA, the effectiveness of lender of last resort intervention is not without limit if financial imbalances that are thereby compounded prevent a return to robust growth. Anxiety about the world reserve of currency is bound to rise if lacklustre growth in the USA is accompanied by a steady rise in its net indebtedness.

Notes

1 This is broadly consistent with the approach other heterodox economists have taken, such as Arestis and Grabel (1995) and Glickman (2002), among others. See also Allen and Gale (1999).

2 Interestingly, in neither the detailed individual country studies nor the literature on disinflation programmes do excessive public spending and monetized government budget deficits get the top billing (Taylor, 1999, 2001).

3 Another view argues that the rapid increase in private consumption is caused by the disinflation programme's lack of credibility in the eyes of the public. Because consumers do not think that the fall in inflation will be permanent, they increase their expenditure, especially on big-ticket consumption items and expensive imports, with the idea of buying what they can before inflation begins to go back up (Kiguel and Liviatan, 1992; Calvo and Vegh, 1999). However, this argument does not explain where the extra income to spend comes from.

4 See, among others, Rodriguez (2003) for Mexico; Bahmani-Oskooee and Techaratanachai (2001) for Thailand; Komarek and Melecky (2003) for Eastern Europe; Prock *et al.* (2003) for Latin America; and Civcir (2003) for Turkey.

5 The 'efficient market hypothesis' has gained currency among economists with Samuelson's (1965) 'proof' that in a market that is *efficient* in appropriating all available information stock prices should exhibit a random walk, and Fama's (1965) 'demonstration' that the stock market in fact almost does that. But, it turns out that neither proposition is valid. Empirically, it is shown that stock prices do not exhibit a random walk, and theoretically it is now known that unforeseeable prices are neither necessary nor sufficient for rationally determined stock prices. See, among others, Summers (1990), Shiller (2000), Shleifer (2000), Bossaerts (2002) and Lo and MacKinlay (1999). In light of these developments in the finance literature, Friedman's contention now appears far from persuasive if it ever was. Among the early criticisms of Friedman (1953), see Baumol (1957) and Kemp (1963).

6 Shleifer and Summers (1990) call these, respectively, the fundamental value and noise-trader risk.

7 In the modern finance literature on asset price bubbles, the emphasis, until recently, was on rational traders' risk aversion, which was thought to prevent them from eliminating noise-driven price movements. However, the focus has been

shifting to 'trend' speculation as the winning strategy for speculators, a fact well known to market participants all along (Soros, 1987; Temin and Voth, 2004).

8 The devaluation risk can in turn be decomposed into two components: a major devaluation risk (*MD*) and exchange rate drift (*ERD*), which entails relatively predictable incremental changes in the peg. In a fixed exchange rate regime *ERD* is insignificant or zero, while *MD* is positive; and in the case of floating regime it is exactly the opposite: *ERD* is significant while *MD* is zero or negligible (McKinnon and Pill, 1999).

9 This is discussed in more rigorous terms in Ekinci and Erturk (2004). The devaluation risk and expected asset price increase can be expressed respectively as: $\Delta AP^e = \Delta \ln P_{t+1}$ and $DR = \Delta \ln e_{t+1}$ (where P_{t+1} is the price of the asset at time $t + 1$, and e is the nominal exchange rate), and the modified interest parity condition where assets are held for the expected increase in their price is given by $\Delta \ln P_{t+1} = i^* + \Delta \ln e_{t+1} + SR$. In the case of a simple discount instrument with a face value of X, the price of the instrument is $P_t = X/(1 + i_t)$ at time t, which gives, $\ln P_t = \ln X - \ln (1 + i_t) = \ln X - i_t$, with the reasonable approximation $\ln (1 + i_t) = i_t$. Similarly, because $P_{t+1} = \ln X - \ln (1 + Ei_{t+1}) = \ln X - Ei_{t+1}$ (where E is the expectations operator), it follows that $\Delta \ln P_{t+1} = i_t - Ei_{t+1} = i^* + \Delta \ln e_{t+1} + SR$, or $i_t = Ei_{t+1} + d_t$, where $d_t = i^* + \Delta \ln e_{t+1} + SR$. This means that, in a Keynesian spirit, asset prices (interest rate) follow a forward-looking unit root process (with respect to the expected rate) with drift (d_t). In other words, with given expectations about the drift, the current interest rate is governed by its expected future value. Thus what speculative investors expect about the future determines what happens in the current period.

10 In general, the failure to provide a lender of last resort appears to have caused the greatest harm in transmitting the financial debacle to the 'real' economy. A stark asymmetry often exists in the policy response to banking cum currency crises as to whether it takes place in an advanced or a developing country. Prompt lender of last resort intervention, which in general is very effective (Allen and Gale, 1999), has been a common reaction only in the former, and has generally been held back in crises involving developing countries. Rude (2005) argues that this is functional in terms of how the world economic system reproduces itself in the current neoliberal era, as contractionary adjustment to periodic crises are the means by which market discipline is instilled where political resistance is weakest.

11 In fact, the link between the initial fall in the *DR* and the eventual increase in the *SR* might be more immediate. A strict anti-inflationary policy stance – as was the case, say, in Cavallo's plan in Argentina – that is designed to reduce effectively the *DR*, at the same time can have the effect of raising the default risk on the stock of outstanding domestic debt (and thus the *SR*) because it thwarts the ability of the country in question to inflate its domestic debt if need be. McKinnnon (1994) explains in a similar vein why the risk premium on Italian and Spanish debt increased after the Maastricht Treaty as the member countries in the European Union (Eu) effectively gave up their ability to inflate their debt. See also Vives (2002).

References

Allen, F. and Gale, D. (1999) 'Bubbles, Crises, and Policy', *Oxford Review of Economic Policy*, 15(3), pp. 9–18.

Arestis, P. and Glickman, M. (2002) 'Financial Crisis in Southeast Asia: Dispelling Illusion the Minskyan Way', *Cambridge Journal of Economics*, 26(2), pp. 237–60.

Bahmani-Oskooee, M. and Techaratanachai, A. (2001) 'Currency Substitution in Thailand', *Journal of Policy Modeling*, 23(2), February, pp. 141–5.
Baumol, W. J. (1957) 'Speculation, Profitability and Stability', *Review of Economics and Statistics*, 39(3), pp. 263–71.
Bossaerts, P. (2002) *The Paradox of Asset Pricing* (Princeton, NJ: Princeton University Press).
Calvo, G. and Vegh, C. (1999) 'Inflation Stabilization and BOP Crises in Developing Countries', NBER Working Paper Series, no. 6925 (Cambridge, MA: NBER).
Chang, R. and Valesco, A. (1999) 'Liquidity Crises in Emerging Markets: Theory and Policy', NBER Working Paper Series, no. 7272 (Cambridge, MA: NBER).
Chen, J. (2004) 'The Basle Accord and Macroeconomic Activity', in J. Chen (ed.), *The Role of International Institutions in Globalisation* (Cheltenham: Edward Elgar).
Civcir, I. (2003) 'Money Demand, Financial Liberalization and Currency Substitution in Turkey', *Journal of Economic Studies*, 30(5–6), pp. 514–34.
Corbett, J. and Vines, D. (1999) 'The Asian Crisis: Lessons from the Collapse of Financial Systems, Exchange Rates and Macroeconomic Policy', in P. Agenor, M. Miller, D. Vines and A. Weber (eds), *The Asian Financial Crisis. Causes, Contagion and Consequences* (Cambridge University Press).
DeLong, J.B., A. Schleifer, L. Summers and R. Waldmann 'Positive feedback investment strategies and destabilizing rational speculation', *Journal of Finance*, 45, pp. 379–95.
Eatwell, J. and L. Taylor (2000) *Global Finance at Risk*, New York: New Press.
Ekinci, N. and Erturk, K. (2004) 'Turkish Currency Crisis of 2000–1, Revisited', CEPA Working Paper Series, no. 2004–01, Center for Economic Policy Analysis, New York.
Fama, E. (1965) 'The Behaviour of Stock Market Prices', *Journal of Business*, 38(1) pp. 34–105.
Friedman, M. (1953) 'The Case for Flexible Exchange Rates', *Essays in Positive Economics* (Chicago University Press).
Furman, J. and Stiglitz, J. (1998) 'Economic Crises: Evidence and Insights from East Asia', *Brookings Papers on Economic Activity*, 2, pp. 1–135.
Grabel, I. (1995) 'Speculation-led Economic Development: A Post Keynesian Interpretation of Financial Liberalization Programmes in the Third World', *International Review of Applied Economics*, 9(1), pp. 127–49.
Grabel, I. (1996) 'Marketing the Third World: The Contradictions of Portfolio Investment in the Global Economy', *World Development*, 24(11), pp. 1761–76.
Griffith-Jones, S. and Spratt, S. (2002) 'Will The proposed new Basel Capital Accord have a net negative effect on developing countries?', accessed on www.ids.ac.uk/ids/global/pdfs/basel.pdf.
Isenberg, D. and Phillips, R.J. (2005) 'Will Basel II Hurt Community Banks in the Macroeconomy?', Paper prepared for the annual meeting of the Association for Evolutionary Economics, Philadelphia, Pennsylvania, 7–9 January 2005.
Kemp, M.C. (1963) 'Speculation, Profitability and Price Stability', *Review of Economics and Statistics*, 45(2), pp. 185–9.
Kigiual, N. and Liviatan, M. (1992) 'The Business Cycle Associated with Exchange Rate Based Stabilization', *The World Bank Economic Review*, 6(2), pp. 279–305.
Komarek, L. and Melecky, M. (2003) 'Currency Substitution in a Transitional Economy with an Application to the Czech Republic', *Eastern European Economics*, 41(4), July–August, pp. 72–99.

Krugman, P. (1979) 'A Model of Balance of Payments Crises', *Journal of Money, Credit and Banking*, 11(3), pp. 311–25.
Krugman, P. (2000) 'Crises: The Price of Globalization?', in Symposium sponsored by the Federal Reserve Bank of Kansas City, *'Opportunities and Challenges: Global Economic Integration'*, Jackson Hole, Wyoming, 24–26 August.
Lo, A.W. and MacKinlay, A. C. (1999) *A Non-Random Walk Down Wall Street* (Princeton, NJ: Princeton University Press).
McKinnon, R. (1994) 'A Common Monetary Standard or a Common Currency for Europe? Fiscal Lessons from the Unites States', *Scottish Journal of Political Economy*, 31(4), pp. 337–57.
McKinnon, R. and Pill, H. (1997) 'Credible Economic Liberalization and Overborrowing', *American Economic Review, Papers and Proceedings*, 87(2), pp. 189–93.
McKinnon, R. and Pill, H. (1998) 'International Overborrowing: A Decomposition of Credit and Currency Risks', *World Development*, 26(7), pp. 1267–82.
McKinnon, R. and Pill, H. (1999) 'Exchange Rate Regimes for Emerging Markets: Moral Hazard and International Overborrowing', *Oxford Review of Economic Policy*, 15(3), pp. 19–38.
Prock, J., Soydemir, G. and Abugri, B. (2003) 'Currency Substitution: Evidence from Latin America', *Journal of Policy Modeling*, 25(4), June, pp. 415–30.
Rodriguez, C.A. (1982) 'The Argentine Stabilization Plan of December 20th', *World Development*, 10(9), pp. 801–11.
Rodriguez, M. and Turner, P. (2003) 'Currency Substitution and the Demand for Money in Mexico', *Applied Economics Letters*, 10(1), January, pp. 59–62.
Rude, C. (2005) 'The Role of Financial Discipline in Imperial Strategy', in L. Panitch and C. Leys (eds), *Socialist Register 2005: The Empire Reloaded* (New York: Monthly Review Press).
Samuelson, P. (1965) 'Proof that Properly Anticipated Prices Fluctuate Randomly', *Industrial Management Review*, 6(2), pp. 41–9.
Shiller, R.J. (2000) *Irrational Exuberance* (Princeton, NJ: Princeton University Press).
Shleifer, A. (2000) *Inefficient Markets. An Introduction to Behavioral Finance* (Oxford University Press).
Shleifer, A. and Summers, L. (1990) 'The Noise Trader Approach to Finance', *Journal of Economic Perspectives*, 4(2), pp. 19–33.
Shleifer, A. and Vishny, R. (1997) 'The Limits of Arbitrage', *Journal of Finance*, 52(1), pp. 35–55.
Singh, A. (1997) 'Financial Liberalization, the Stock Market and Economic Development', *Economic Journal*, 107(442), pp. 772–82.
Singh, A. (2003) 'Capital Account Liberalization, Free Long-term Capital Flows, Financial Crises and Economic Development', *Eastern Economic Journal*, 29(2), pp. 191–216.
Singh, A. and Weisse, B. (1998) 'Emerging Stock Markets, Portfolio Capital Flows and Long Term Economic Growth, Micro and Macroeconomic Perspectives', *World Development*, 26(4), pp. 607–22.
Soros, G. (1987) *The Alchemy of Finance: Reading the Mind of the Market* (New York: Simon & Schuster).
Taylor, L. (1998) 'Capital Market Crises: Liberalization, Fixed Exchange Rates and Market Driven Destabilization', *Cambridge Journal of Economics*, 22(6), pp. 663–76.
Taylor, L. (ed.) (1999) *After Neoliberalism. What Next for Latin America?* (Ann Arbor, MI: Michigan University Press).

Taylor, L. (ed.) (2001) *External Liberalization, Economic Performance, and Social Policy* (New York: Oxford University Press).
Temin, P. and Voth, H. (2004) 'Riding the South Sea Bubble', CEPR Discussion Paper, no. 4221, Centre for Economic Policy Research, London.
Vives, X. (2002) 'External Discipline and Financial Stability', *European Economic Review*, 46, pp. 821–8.
Williamson, J. (2001) '*Currency Crisis*. Book Review', *Journal of Economic Literature* 39(3), pp. 916–7.

3
Financial System Regulation Stability versus Instability: Some Strategic Consideration

David Ceballos and David Cantarero

Since the 1990s, both frequency and magnitude of financial crises have increased, affecting above all the emerging economies (Latin America and South East Asia), but also Europe and the European Monetary System (EMS), the USA, Mexico, Thailand, Korea, Indonesia, Russia, the Long-term capital management (LTCM) hedge fund, Argentina, Brazil, the technological bubble, dot.com companies and many others. These events have had a variety of causes and a range of different consequences, but each crisis supposes a deterioration of (i) a system's credibility; (ii) its credit solvency; and/or (iii) the productive economy. For these reasons, it is clear that financial stability is the desired state.

The financial notion of stability draws on the idea of a financial system that is exposed to neither abrupt nor regular fluctuations, and above all to those that might induce financial losses. In practice, stability supposes controlling financial risk so that when an unfavourable contingency does occur, it does not exceed expected loss levels and has a negative impact on the solvency and credibility of the financial system, and by extension on the real economy. What is required, therefore, are a number of preventive measures that might act to regulate the system or provide prudential supervision so as to maintain a stable macroeconomic environment and thus avoid inefficient agents that serve to undermine the system.

Public regulation means that, in times of crisis, if preventive measures are seen as being insufficient, large and generalized losses could occur as a result of moral hazard, adverse selection, loss of market credibility or speculation and so on. Such losses spread quickly by a process of feedback throughout the financial system because of the globalization of financial products and contracts, the transnationality of economic agents, and the availability of information in real time.

Since the second half of the nineteenth century, financial systems have taken on the characteristics of information markets (Eichengreen, 2003), thanks in the main to developments within the field of telecommunications. The greater levels of security and the velocity that this allows has permitted a boom in capital transfers, and the design of increasingly sophisticated financial operations. All these developments mean that globalization has not arisen simply out of a growth in international trade, but has been linked strongly to the birth and expansion of the international finance system.

Globalization can have detrimental effects on this financial system because of the diffusion of information, which generates contagious or herding behaviour among economic agents (Bikhchandani, 2000). These elements can magnify market fluctuations, resulting in financial bubbles and crises. Financial regulations seek to limit this effect of globalization, while aiming at the dissemination of quality information and preventing fraudulent behaviour. However, such measures of control generate, at the same time, the subsistence of inefficiencies, since arbitrage is neither cheap nor quick. Thus what we see is a trade-off between financial regulations, on the one hand, which seek to reduce the frequency and dimensions of financial crises, and market efficiency on the other, which seeks to exploit these inefficiencies and failures to regulate.

Financial regulation and globalization are therefore key elements in the stability (or instability) of the financial system. If we focus our analysis on these two factors, then stability will be reached when the frequency and magnitude of such crises are minimized (regulation to control financial risks and fluctuations, and to supervise the globalization of information and capital movements by the authorities), while instability will be a consequence of the entire system being affected by a crisis or being undermined by a crisis (failure of regulation on the part of the authorities to defend the financial system).

A financial crisis means suffering losses above the confidence threshold of unexpected losses. Such a crisis becomes global if other sectors and/or other economies are affected by these rational or irrational effects, a phenomenon known as 'systemic risk' (De Bandt, 2000). Underlying the international regulation of the financial system is the need to avoid, as far as possible, 'irrational' contagion, and to reduce the magnitude of 'rational' contagion. Such regulation comprises the implementation of agreements and recommendations by sovereign states, or forums, such as Basel II, or the coordination of fiscal policies that tax capital movement.

This chapter undertakes an analysis of proposed regulations for the financial system in a globalized world, and seeks to take into consideration the recommendations of the international financial institutions and the impact of international taxation on capital movement. We present a study in four parts, beginning by examining financial regulation – its causes and consequences for the stability/instability of the financial system – by calling on the strategic tools provided by game theory. Following this introduction we analyse the corresponding international regulations and then examine the strategic bases of resistance to such regulatory measures. The final section presents the conclusion that can be drawn from our study.

Regulating the financial system

The regulation of the financial system seeks a desired level of system stability within a context of continuous fluctuation. In other words, regulation is a preventive measure, but it seeks to have a neutral impact on market and financial behaviour.

Thus national and international regulations – the result of various decisions, including Basel II, agreements concerning taxation on capital transfers, 'permitted' fluctuation bands, measures to uncover fraudulent practices and so on, seek to prevent, or at least to minimize, the economic and social problems that stem from losses of stability and credibility in the financial system. As the cost of controlling the financial system is high, and because international co-ordination gives rise to many difficulties, we consider the financial aim of such regulation to be a reduction in the frequency and magnitude of financial crises. Through the supervision of information and risk management, and the control over market security, regulation seeks above all to limit the contagious effects produced by globalization and information distortion, such as rumours, accounting reliability and so on, and by destabilizing fluctuations.

In our strategic analysis of financial regulation, we distinguish between the regulation of capital movements, on the one hand, and the regulation that has an impact on the fragile nature of the financial system because of excess risk in the adopting of financial positions and the taking of decisions, on the other.

International taxation

In today's globalized framework, the considerable freedom enjoyed by capital movements, together with the development of new financial products, has meant that various tax reforms affecting capital earnings have been introduced at the international level, aimed at discouraging national capital transfers to foreign economies and the consequent pernicious effect on national economies. According to Bacchetta and Caminal (1991),

> a greater mobility of capital permits investors to choose with more facility the country of the most favourable fiscal processing and, consequently, the political tax decisions of each economy are influenced by the decisions taken by the other economies. This interdependency introduces a strategic element in tax policies of different governments, given the existence of important incentives to compete for capital, cutting off tax levels. Some European economies are conscious of the negative consequences of this competitive behaviour and have tried to prompt a process of negotiations in order to coordinate or to harmonize taxes, although so far without complete success.

In this context, the 'Tobin tax' is an autonomous financial measure that can be adopted by national authorities, which can place a tax on international monetary speculation and the existence of tax havens.

The optimum model of tax policies, in terms of efficiency and equity, in an international context of capital mobility, requires the establishment of (i) basic principles of international tax assignment in direct taxation; (ii) the definition of co-ordination mechanisms that avoid the imposition of double international taxation; and (iii) tax neutrality criteria (efficiency) (Frenkel *et al.*, 1990) in the international allocation of capital as of equity among agents and nations (Álvarez *et al.*, 2003).

By way of summary, Table 3.1 shows the different criteria of efficiency with regard to the international taxation of capital movement, their aims and conditions, and the instruments used in their application. Logically, this scheme should be complemented with the basic principles of equity among individuals (that is, both vertical and horizontal equity) and nations (the equitable distribution among the different countries of the taxable income generated in the international transactions conducted between them, for which a harmonization of fiscal relations is required).

The paralysis of the fiscal process of the harmonization of direct taxes, especially in the case of the European Union (EU), means that a generalized

Table 3.1 Direct taxation and international co-ordination

Efficiency	**Objectives**	**Instruments**
Neutrality of international efficiency on world capital export allocation	Efficiency in investment allocation Equal tax independent of the source of income	Tax system based on residency and exemption-at-source as the general method Full fiscal credit
Neutrality of national efficiency on world capital export allocation	To avoid the exit of capital. Equal national tax: equals full profitability marginal of national investment with marginal profitability of net external investment	Deduction in tax base of international tax
Neutrality of international efficiency on world capital import allocation	Efficient distribution of saving. This equals profitability of investments in the country for residents and non-residents. Equity on distribution of tax base of bilateral transactions. To burden residents' income without discriminations; not to discriminate against income obtained by non-residents	Tax system based on source and exemption-at-residency as the general method Fiscal co-ordination

Sources: Zubirí, 1987 and 1997; Albi *et al.*, 2000; Cordón, 2001; Álvarez *et al.*, 2003.

discount is being recorded in capital taxation, because measures that seek to attract capital from other jurisdictions are being adopted for different economies and as a means of avoiding the outward flow of national capital. Nevertheless, according to Zubirí (2001) and Álvarez *et al.* (2001) there are as many economic (improving the conditions for the creation of employment and promoting economic growth) as political arguments (displacement of the income of the average voter or society's perception that fiscal pressure is excessive, and the preference for tax reduction over an increase in public expenditure) to justify lower taxes.

Financial risk control according to Basel II

Since Bretton Woods, international financial system regulation has undergone a qualitative change with the creation of the International Monetary Fund (IMF) and the World Bank, which, however, was to lose some of its effectiveness following the demise of the gold standard. Subsequently, we have witnessed the early stages of the Basel Committee of Banking Supervision, closely associated with the Bank for International Settlements. Against this backdrop, the first Agreement on Capital Minimums, Basel I, was introduced in 1988. However, this agreement proved ineffective in preventing the financial crises of the 1990s and in the early years of the new millennium: the European Monetary System (EMS) crisis, the Mexican crisis, the bankruptcy of Barings Bank, the Asian crisis, the Russian crisis, the bankruptcy of the LTCM hedge fund, the technological bubble, and the Brazilian and Argentine crises, among many others.

To avoid, as far as possible or to reduce the frequency of these crises, initiatives were taken to draw up a New Basel Capital Agreement, Basel II, in 1998. Basel II focuses its efforts on the financial regulation of market risk, credit risk and operational risk.

Basel I defended risk measurement and control according to a risk typology in the function of the counterpart, but this proved ineffective in the successive financial crises of the 1990s, because, on the one hand, each country and each business was subject to a different risk, even though they belonged to similar groups, and because, on the other, each operation incurred a different risk depending on its characteristics and on the counterpart's experience.

Basel II rectified these shortcomings by means of the internal measurement of risk, adopting a risk typology based on the nature of the operation, the counterparts and the stratification of default rates according to historical statistics.[1] It also introduced procedures of risk management based on ratings and benchmarking, and supervisory procedures that verified the internal systems' quality of financial risk measurement and management systems, requiring a minimum risk exposure of 8 per cent as capital to guarantee company solvency.

In 2005, Basel II will seek to adapt, in a larger measure than in the past, capital requirements by credit and operational risks, thereby reducing the distance between required regulatory capital and necessary economic capital. In this way, banking supervision will be improved in a world marked by globalization, internationalization, increasing sophistication and competence in the financial sector, and thus contribute to the greater stability of the financial system. In seeking to achieve these aims Basel II is constructed around three central pillars. The first pillar has a direct bearing on financial system regulation, since it is concerned with gathering recommendations for minimum capital requirements (credit, market and operational risks), and because it defends a minimum solvency coefficient. The second pillar is concerned with the revision of the supervisory, monitoring and evaluating functions of solvency, and with the quality control of risk measurement and management systems so that they adapt to the regulations derived from the first pillar. The third and last pillar is concerned with market discipline as a financial mechanism of efficiency, because it provides incentives to promote financial system solvency and security through the greater transparency of information. In this way, Basel II seeks to contribute not only to the stability of the financial system, but also to a competitive equality that prevents bad practices and avoids weakening the system, in other words, an equality that impedes large financial fluctuations and crises.

Specifically, Basel II seeks to introduce an internal model to calculate and estimate default probabilities, a sophisticated model that can estimate the degree of recovery of an investment in the case of default, and the value of the risk to which it is exposed.

The formula of regulatory capital calculation proposed by Basel II does not restrict the use of advanced risk measurement techniques through risk exposure estimates, such as VaR methods, conditional VaR (catastrophic loss), extreme values, copulas and so on, using sensitivity analysis, case generation or simulation.

But this apparent flexibility has its constraints, above all with regard to financial stability, and the possibility of contagion risks because of the procyclicality of Basel II regulations (Borio *et al.*, 2001).

Strategic bases of financial regulation

At the macroeconomic level, financial crises are related to the instability of economic nominal fundamentals, such as the exchange rate, inflation or the interest rate. At the microeconomic level, such crises are related to local episodes of bankruptcy affecting banks. In this section, we analyse financial crises at the macro level, because it is at this level that they have a more marked influence on financial system fluctuations, and where we observe greater international co-ordination to overcome their effects, in terms of capital movement control as well as risk management and measurement supervision. This does not mean, however, that the regulation of banks is not affected by general financial regulation, since microeconomic financial crises can have international effects if transferred to the whole economy, and from there are able to affect the rest of the financial system. In this study of banking crises we should take into consideration the so-called herding behaviour that can weaken the national credit sector and cause a loss of confidence in neighbouring countries or economies within the same block. Such contagion effects can be classified as being either 'rational' or 'irrational'. The former arise when the contagion effects are a response to factors within the real economy, and are a consequence of the variation in the nominal fundamentals brought about by a fall in international commerce because of the financial crisis, business losses transferred to headquarters or devalued position liquidation. Herding situations in the financial liquidation of positions motivated by an unexpected increase in risk perception are considered 'irrational' – for example, those arising from asymmetric information, feedback of financial fluctuations (panic) or the generalization of financial management standards (De Bandt, 2000). A number of models are discussed in Barberis and Thaler (2002).

In this section we present models that might be considered useful, didactically or strategically, in any discussion concerning the effects of instability prevention and regulation in the global financial system. These financial crisis models are of the second generation, since they permit a better synthesis of the effects of fluctuation because they do not affect the real economy. Three types of financial crisis, in function of their specific nature, can be distinguished: first generation or macroeconomic crises (which were typical of the period up to the 1980s, and which affected exchange rates and the balance of payments), generally caused by an inadequate combination of fiscal and monetary policies or preceding a chronic public deficit (Krugman, 1979); second generation crises, typical of the 1980s and 1990s, which had net effects on the financial economy because of the importance of free capital transfers and financial globalization (Obstfeld, 1994); and third generation or twin crises, which combine currency and banking crises (Kaminsky, 1998). Here, we focus specifically on the second type of crisis, which has essentially financial effects.

We shall undertake a strategic analysis to justify regulation in a globalized financial system, presenting this analysis in the form of a payoff matrix, using game theory to account, on the one hand, for the actions of national and international authorities (regulation), and on the other, for the actions of the various economic agents of the market (efficiency). In order to do this, we divide the next section into two parts: in the first we describe a model for the control of capital movements, and, in the second, a model to control financial stability.

Modelling the effects of international capital movements

The forecasts of processes of fiscal competence among national states can be analysed by applying simple game theory models – in fact, the same as those used in fiscal decentralization (Álvarez *et al.*, 2003; Zubirí, 1987). Let us

Table 3.2 Pay-off matrix

		Country B	
		COMPETITION	CO-OPERATION
Country A	COMPETITION	(4, 4) case *a*	(7, 3) case *b*
	CO-OPERATION	(3, 7) case *c*	(5, 5) case *d*

suppose that two countries, A and B, submit the earnings obtained in their territory by residents from another fiscal jurisdiction to taxation, and that in designing their own tax system they can adopt two types of strategy: on the one hand, a competitive strategy (aimed at attracting foreign capital by increasing the net profit value of taxes by means of fiscal discount) or a co-operative strategy (that is, non-competitive, designing a fiscal system without taking into consideration the possibility of attracting foreign capital). The results of such a situation can be shown in a pay-off matrix (see Table 3.2). If both jurisdictions are symmetrical in all their relevant characteristics and because a country is affected by fiscal competence, one country will have to adopt a competitive strategy if the other adopts this strategy so as not to lose resources. Then, case (a) (in which both countries compete because each seeks optimum conditions for themself, given the behaviour adopted by their opponent) is the only Nash equilibrium in this competitive game, in which the doubt remains as to what constitutes the actual incentive, so that either of the two countries will initiate this process of competition, which is also known as *competitive harmonization*.

Logically, the origin of this competitive process might be attributed to a break in the symmetry of conditions between countries (that is, some countries have more incentives than others to collaborate, and it is not easy to determine and to distribute the benefits of co-operation, which complicates agreements), the possible breaking of pacts (given that although these were entered into, it would be difficult to sustain them over time, for a variety of reasons – for example, the outbreak of a crisis in a country might well force it to compete) and the fact that governments can base their actions on considerations of short–medium time limit (as is often the case in practice).

In short, there are several incentives that will ensure co-operation between countries does not occur (Zubirí, 1987). Finally, competition between countries to attract foreign capital cannot necessarily be generated for reasons of tax but rather for other motives such as the protection of a country's banking system or its financial markets, as is the case with various countries in the European Union. In practice, problems such as double international imposition lead to the establishment of mechanisms of co-ordination (methods of tax-exemption and of accusation) for the sake of the unilateral character or, in the framework of international agreements, with the purpose of eliminating, or at least partly correcting, this problem.

Modelling the effects of financial stability

In order to analyse stability in the global financial system, the possibility of systemic risk needs to be considered. Furfine (1999) distinguishes two types of crisis: (i) a simultaneous crisis that affects the whole market; and (ii) a successive crisis in which bankruptcy or the difficulties of one or several institutions, businesses or economies affects the whole system. Here, we analyse both possibilities, but focus our study on just the financial effects, and taking into consideration that systemic crises can be avoided by the regulation or defence of the financial system by the competent authorities. We adopt a second generation model similar to the Krugman model (Krugman, 1998) and drawing on ideas in Obstfeld (1996) for a financial system with competitive agents.

In Tables 3.3 and 3.4 we show the co-ordination effects and their absence in the case of the actions of supervision and regulation authorities with market agents. The co-ordination effects on financial stability can be both short-term and long-term. Both tables show strategic aspects of the defensive stability of the financial system, which differ in the short and long-term.

In the short term, what is observed is the 'prisoner's dilemma', where the only Nash equilibrium is to move towards a crisis in a difficult situation, without the regulator or supervisor wasting resources in defending the system against attacks of financial weakness by market (efficient) agents. The justification for this result in the short term is that the speculation and forecast benefits of financial instability are higher than those in a stable financial system. Financial adjustments in search of greater efficiency do not generate enough profits over such a short period, and so all agents incur losses. Nevertheless, speculation or financial instability produces a zero sum game, where those who forecast correctly the system direction earn unjustly the resources used by others.

In the long term, because there is sufficient time for recovery or for the significant generation of profits thanks to stability, two Nash equilibria exist. The first is the same as that of the short-term non-defence of the system in a difficult situation, allowing an adjustment towards a more efficient system. The second constitutes the efficient defence of the system with greater profits as a result of the continuity in stability.

This strategic analysis reveals the best supervisory and regulatory actions to prevent financial fluctuations or to defend the system's stability: namely, to encourage a long-term strategy for risk control and the management of financial participants with a credible, healthy and efficient system. The Nash

Table 3.3 Pay-off matrix (short-term)

		Market	
		DEFENCE	NO DEFENCE
Authority	DEFENCE	(0, 0) stability	(−1, 1) speculation
	NO DEFENCE	(1, −1) fluctuation	(−1/2, −1/2) crisis

Table 3.4 Pay-off matrix (long-term)

		Market	
		DEFENCE	NO DEFENCE
Authority	DEFENCE	(1, 1) stability	(−1, 1/2) speculation
	NO DEFENCE	(1/2, −1) fluctuation	(1/2, 3/2) crisis recovery

equilibrium of long-term stability can be justified in three ways:

(i) By non-simultaneity of decision between the authority and the market with a leader that the other imitates. When the authority is the leader, it is interested in defending the stability of the financial system because solvency and 'good' economic growth imply larger and more sustained public income. Then the equilibrium is (defend, defend) or long-term stability. Nevertheless we can suppose that the market is not interested in defending the stability of the financial system and it tries either to accumulate profits from system instability or to force efficient reforms. In this case, if the market is the leader, in a difficult situation, it would begin by not defending the system and causing the crisis.

(ii) By the existence of asymmetric information that causes the player with the least information to imitate the strategy adopted by the other. In other words, we have a situation that is similar to that of the previous case of leader–follower. Here the results are determined by the player with the most information and by the degree of confidence in the system's stability.[2]

(iii) By self-fulfilled expectations. In this case, market and authority are considered as acting simultaneously in the choice of long-term equilibrium. This equilibrium will be conditioned to existing expectations about the future stability of the system. Expectations will be self-fulfilled because the financial agents will believe in their occurrence, and they will act accordingly. This is the typical situation of 'second generation' models. In our model, the reason why the authority and the market defend the system is associated with the profits assured from not using their resources, and the long-term stable growth of public and private income. The third element of circular logic in this 'second generation' model is that the authority's defence of costs is greater when the market thinks its defence will be fruitless (financial weakness), because of a lack of resources (damaged economy) or because of a lack of confidence (system inefficiency).

These three possibilities incorporate the lines of action of the Basel II proposals. In the first place, it is the authority (system regulator and supervisor) that takes the initiative in the control of the stability and health of the financial system. Basel II aims to supervise private risk management, to provide incentives for more sophisticated, as well as internal, models for risk measurement and management, and to regulate the major risks: market, credit and operational risk. Second Basel II defends greater transparency of information because, by so doing, both the financial market as well as the authority are aware of the solvency of the system, and so market efficiency is enhanced. Excessively risky and fraudulent operations do not survive market arbitrage and supervisory controls. Third, and last Basel II allows the financial authorities the possibility of creating a confident environment for system stability, because of international co-ordination in fluctuation and solvency control.

Nevertheless, self-fulfilled expectations create certain difficulties for Basel II or weaknesses in its ability to guarantee the stability of the financial system. There are certain financial phenomena that undermine investor confidence in the long-term stability of the system. This problem is a direct consequence of the procyclicality of risk measures, management and control, and of the crisis feedback that arises from the fact that most financial agents follow similar risk standards.

Procyclicality means that during periods of economic growth, or an expansive stock market cycle, provision demands are reduced (smaller risk), because risk measurement is based, when it is estimated internally, on the most probable event (point in time – PIT), which differs with cycle evolution.

External agencies of risk measurement are used in adopting an approach classified as the most unfavourable possibility (through the cycle – TTC), with an unchanged probability throughout the cycle. But this last case can lead to an infravaluation of real risk in terms of its stress testing, because when negative aspects are higher than a threshold, the whole system fails. Borio *et al.* (2001) carried out an extensive study of the procyclicality effects of control measures, which can result in a financial crisis because of the greater demands for provisions and cascades of liquidations because of a rise in risk.

On the other hand, similar risk monitoring and risk management standards foment herding behaviour in financial trading, which in its turn generates financial bubbles and panic. Moreover, contagion effects appear among investors with different standards of risk measurement, with different horizons, different profit and loss distributions, different portfolio diversifications, and so on, because of the generation of a downward or upward trend in all financial products.

The symptoms (causes) of financial instability and the possibilities of preventing it (recommendations and Basel II) are summarized in Table 3.5.

Conclusions

In this chapter we have considered the strategic action undertaken by the three parties making up the financial system: the authority or international institutions, the market, and national states. Financial stability, in the context of the dependence and availability of information that characterize globalization, is subordinated to the actions of the former. There exist strategic incentives to defend or attack financial stability, according to the solvency, credibility and/or inefficiencies of the financial system.

The optimum design of taxation policies in terms of efficiency and equity in an international context of mobility of capital requires the establishment of (i) basic principles of international tax assignment in direct taxation; (ii) the definition of co-ordination mechanisms that avoid double international imposition; and (iii) the establishment of tax neutrality criteria (efficiency) in the international allocation of capital as equity among individuals and countries. The paralysis of the fiscal process of harmonization in direct taxes, especially in the case of the European Union, has caused a generalized discount of capital taxation in order to avoid national capital leaving the country.

The forecasts of processes of fiscal competence among national states can be analysed by applying simple game theory models – in fact, the same as those used in fiscal decentralization. Thus the results obtained from the payoff matrix, as long as it is supposed that both jurisdictions are symmetrical in all relevant aspects, mean that the case in which both countries compete

Table 3.5 Symptoms and prevention of financial instability

Causes	Recommendations	Basel II
Free capital movement	International co-ordination Tax harmonization	–
Economic cycle and expansive credit	Anticyclicality provisions Sophistication of risk measures and control Improved credit risk methods	PIT methodology Stress testing Benchmarking
Financial market deregulation	Regulation to produce positive externalities with international co-ordination and control	Risk measurement and management supervision Market discipline
Financial liberalization[3]	Government intervention to guide liberalization and to ensure fiscal and monetary discipline	–
Procyclicality of risk measures/standards[4]	Anticyclicality provisions Flexibility of risk measures Fiscal measures for intertemporal adaptation of capital requirements Averaging measures over the cycle Contracyclical adjustments over the cycle of the prudential parameter Improve credit risk methods	Sophistication and diversity of risk standards (measures and management)
Contagion effects Systemic risk	Diversification and non-standard portfolio selection Improve credit risk methods	Internal risk management
Investment herding behaviour	Portfolio diversification	Flexibility in horizons and risk correlations Internal risk control Market discipline
Macroeconomic expectations error Risk evaluation error	Sophistication in risk measures and control Information transparency	Internal risk control Higher information transparency Market discipline

Sources: Mayer, 1999; Borio *et al.*, 2001; Goodhart *et al.*, 2004.

is the only Nash equilibrium. Nevertheless, the competition to attract foreign capital cannot necessarily be produced for motives related to taxation and it implies the establishment of agreements to avoid the double international imposition.

In relation to the stability of the financial system, the public authorities and market actions are constrained by recommendations of the New Basel Capital Accord of Basel II, and by its wide acceptance by international institutions and national states, so that it constitutes virtually a common international regulation of the financial system. Basel II grew out of the absence of financial risk measures and techniques for the management of fluctuation and crisis prevention. To overcome these shortcomings, a greater degree of sophistication in quantitative risk estimation is proposed in management models, in supervision and the provision of public information.

The effectiveness of these measures and recommendations can be analysed strategically by simplifying the actors in authority (international institutions) and in the market (economic agents), where it is deduced that long-term stability and efficiency depend on the financial system's credibility and solvency. It has been observed that the fluctuation in financial variables depends on rumours, opinions, legislation and so on, which while they do not affect the real economy, do form the basis of economic agents' expectations and their financial undertakings.

Thus we can conclude that today's effectiveness in the defence of the solvency and efficiency of the financial system is the consequence of 'second generation' crises and of the strategic considerations of the participants. System instability can have an impact on other investors, sectors or economies because of the contagion effects derived from the international relations of globalization, from the correlations among investment or hedging macro-portfolios, from herding behaviour, and from the generalization of similar risk management standards.

Notes

1 Three forms of credit and operational risk measurement are proposed: from traditional external qualifications, basic internal qualifications (only estimation of loss probability), and advanced internal qualifications (estimation of all risk factors related to expected loss). The last two possibilities belong to the Internal Rating Based (IRB) methodology proposed by Basel II.

2 This would change the associated pay-off to case (no-defence, no-defence) from (1/2, 3/2) of little confidence in stability to (1/2, 1/2) of confidence.

3 Mayer (1999) and Arestis (2004) highlight the problems of financial liberalization, guided by Washington Consensus commands, and IMF and other economic recommendations, which are at the root of many recent cases of financial fragility and crises.

4 Borio *et al.* (2001) and Goodhart *et al.* (2004) defend the thesis that the normative in order to measure and supervise bank solvency is procyclical, magnifying periods of recession. They analyse the financial and macroeconomic effects of this procyclicality empirically with special reference to the Basel Agreements (I and II), and comment on various alternatives for non-procyclical regulation.

References

Albi, E., González Páramo, J. M. and Zubirí, I. (2000) *Economía Pública II*, [Public Economics III] (Barcelona: Ariel Economía).

Álvarez, S., Fernández, M. L. and González, A. I. (2003) 'La fiscalidad del ahorro en la Unión Europea: Entre la armonización fiscal y la competencia de los sistemas tributarios nacionales', [Taxes on savings in European Union: Between tax harmonization and tax system competition], *Documento Trabajo Instituto de Estudios Fiscales*, 15/03 (Madrid: Instituto de Estudios Fiscales).

Álvarez, X.C., Alonso, J., Gago, A. and González, X.M. (2001) 'Tendencias recientes de la fiscalidad internacional', [Current trends in international tax], *Papeles de Economía Española*, 87, pp. 10–32.

Arestis, P. (2004) 'Washington Consensus and Financial Liberalization', *Journal of Post Keynesian Economics*, 27(2), pp. 251–72.
Bacchetta, P. and Caminal, R. (1991) '¿Es deseable la coordinación internacional de la imposición sobre el capital?', [Is it international co-ordination about capital tax desirable?], *Moneda y Crédito*, 192, pp. 247–78.
Bank for International Settlements (2001) 'Continued progress toward Basel II', Press announcements, 15/01 (Basel: Bank for International Settlements) (www.bis.org/press/p040115.htm).
Barberis, N., Thaler, R. (2002) 'A Survey of Behavioral Finance', *NBER Working Paper no. 9222* (Cambridge: NBER) (www.nber.org/papers/w9222).
Basel Committee on Banking Supervision (1999) 'Credit Risk Modelling: Current Practices and Applications', *Consulative paper*, June (Basel: Bank for International Settlements) (www.bis.org/publ/bcbs92pdf).
Basel Committee on Banking Supervision (2003) 'Overview of the New Basel Capital Accord', *Consulative paper*, April (Basel: Bank for International Settlements) (www.bis.org/bcbs/cp3ov.pdf).
Bikhchandani, S. and Sharma, S. (2000) 'Herd Behavior in Financial Market: A Review', IMF Working Paper No. WP/00/48 (Washington: International Monetary Fund) (www.imf.org/external/pubs/ft/wp/2000/wp0048.pdf).
Borio, C., Furfine, C. and Lowe, P. (2001) 'Procyclicality of the Financial System and Financial Stability: Issues and Policy Options', BIS papers, 1 (Basel: Bank for International Settlements) (www.bis.org/pu/bispapola.pdf).
Cordón Ezquerro, T. (Director) (2001) *Manual de Fiscalidad Internacional* [Handbook of International Tax] (Madrid: Instituto Estudios Fiscales).
De Bandt, O. and Hartmann, P. (2000) 'Systemic Risk: A Survey', *Working Paper of the European Central Bank*, 35 (Frankfurt: European Central Bank) (www.ecb.int/pub/pdf/scpwps/ecbwp35.pdf).
Eichengreen, B., and Bordo, M. D. (2003) 'Crises Now and Then: What Lessons from the Last Era of Financial Globalization?', in P. Mizen (ed.), *Monetary History, Exchange Rates and Financial Markets* (Cheltenham: Edward Elgar).
Frenkel, J., Razin, A. and Sadka, E. (1990) 'Basic Concepts of International Taxation', NBER Working Paper No. 3540 (Cambridge: NBER) (www.nber.org/papers/w3540).
Furfine, C. H. (1999) 'Interbank Exposures: Quantifying the Risk of Contagion', BIS Working Paper No. 70 (Basel: Bank for International Settlements) (www.bis.org/publ/work70.pdf).
Goodhart, C., Hofmann, B. and Segoviano, M. (2004) 'Bank Regulation and Macroeconomic Fluctuations', *Oxford Review of Economy Policy*, 20(4), pp. 591–615.
Kaminsky, G. L. and Reinhart, C. M. (1998) 'The Twin Crisis: The Causes of Banking and Balance-of-Payments Problems', *American Economic Review*, 89(3), pp. 473–500.
Krugman, P. (1979) 'A Model of Balance-of-Payments Crisis', *Journal of Money, Credit and Banking*, 11, pp. 311–25.
Krugman, P. (1998) 'Current Crises' (web.mit.edu/krugman/www/crises.html).
Lowe, P. (2002) 'Credit Risk Measurement and Procyclicality', BIS Working Papers no. 116 (Basel: Bank for International Settlements) (www.bis.org/publ/work116.pdf).
Mayer, C. (1999) 'The Assessment: Financial Instability', *Oxford Review of Economic Policy*, 15(3), pp. 1–8.
Obstfeld, M. (1994) 'The Logic of Currency Crises', NBER Working Paper no. 4640 (Cambridge: NBER) (www.nber.org/papers/w4640).
Obstfeld, M. (1996) 'Models of Currency Crises with Self-fulfilling Features', *European Economic Review*, 40, pp. 1037–147.

OECD (1991) *Taxing Profits in a Global Economy. Domestic and International Issues* (Paris: OECD).
OECD (1994) *Taxation of Household Savings* (Paris: OECD).
Zubirí, I. (1987) 'Sobre la distribución de recursos en un sistema federal', [On resource distribution in a federal system], *Papeles de Economía Española*, pp. 426–36.
Zubirí, I. (1997) 'La fiscalidad de los rendimientos del ahorro con movilidad del capital', [Taxation of saving returns with capital movement], *Hacienda Pública Española* (Monograph) (Madrid: Instituto de Estudios Fiscales), pp. 109–23.
Zubirí, I. (2001) 'Las reformas fiscales en los países de la Unión Europea: causas y efectos', [Tax reforms in European Union economies: causes and effects], *Hacienda Pública Española* (Monograph) (Madrid: Instituto de Estudios Fiscales), pp. 13–52.

4

The Bretton Woods Institutions Sixty Years Later: A 'Glocal' Reform Proposal

*Sergio Rossi**

The current international monetary architecture was set up in Bretton Woods in 1944 as a result of debate between Harry Dexter White (heading the US delegation) and John Maynard Keynes (for the UK). Both White and Keynes presented a series of plans and proposals for the creation of an international monetary and financial system with the aim of avoiding the troubles they were observing as a result of the Second World War. Because of the different economic situation in the USA with respect to that in the UK at the end of the Second World War, it should come as no surprise that White's and Keynes' plans were quite different from each other. The US economy was indeed in a strong position, as its production system had not been destroyed by the war and its current account recorded huge surpluses as a result of the need to rebuild the economies of those European countries devastated by the war. Further, the USA had an enormous stock of gold in its reserves, and could thereby guarantee convertibility of US currency into the precious metal. The UK, by contrast, experienced current account deficits as a result of the need to import a number of commodities from the USA without the possibility of paying for them by means of an equivalent flow of commercial exports. Views on the international payment system were therefore very different when seen from Europe or the USA.

White was asked by the then US Treasury Secretary Morgenthau to elaborate a plan for a new international monetary order, which he did in March 1942 as a 'Preliminary draft outline of proposal for a united and associated Nations Stabilization Fund'. In his plan, White suggested modifying the gold standard system to create an international monetary institution to which

---

* The first draft of this chapter was presented at the conference on 'Developments in Economic Theory and Policy, Institutions and European Integration' held at the University of the Basque Country, Bilbao, Spain, 15–16 July 2004. The author would like to thank Philip Arestis, Eugenia Correa, Paul Davidson, Korkut Erturk, Malcolm Sawyer and Domenica Tropeano for their helpful comments. Research assistance by Dante Caprara is also gratefully acknowledged. The usual disclaimer applies.

countries could apply for financial assistance. In particular, White's plan proposed the setting up of an international monetary fund with the task of stabilizing exchange rates, and to create a world bank whose task would be to help in financing post-war reconstruction and development in the countries most in need of them. For his part, Keynes was persuaded that the UK had to put forward an alternative proposal to limit US domination worldwide – and in particular with respect to his own country. On 8 September 1941, Keynes published two memoranda in which he called for a new monetary order, and from which he started to develop his own ideas about the new monetary architecture to be set up internationally. He put forward the idea of creating a world central bank – for the creation of a truly international money (which he was to call 'bancor') – which, in his own words, 'might become the pivot of the future economic government in the world' (Keynes, 1980, p. 189).

The debate between White and Keynes was tough, as was the confrontation between the Stabilization Fund plan advocated by the US delegation and the Clearing Union plan put forward by UK delegates at the Bretton Woods conference. Criticizing the White plan, Keynes (1980, p. 370) stated that '[t]his is intolerable. It is yet another Talmud. We had better simply break off negotiations'. To this, White replied provocatively that the US delegation 'will try to produce something which Your Highness *can* understand' (Keynes, 1980, pp. 370–1). According to Skidelsky (2000, p. 245), the divergences between White and Keynes can be traced to different views of capitalism as seen from either side of the Atlantic:

> The White and Keynes Plans were based on different concepts. The Stabilisation Fund made loans out of subscribed capital; the Clearing Union created overdrafts out of nothing. In the Fund a member's maximum liability was fixed by its subscription; in the Clearing Union a member might be required to accept 'bancor' (in payment for its exports) up to the total of all the other members' overdraft facilities.

In fact, a number of crucial questions that Keynes addressed in his plan, or that the latter plan raised, have still to be answered at the time of writing. To cite only the most important of them: can a local currency such as the US dollar play the role of international money, and thereby guarantee world monetary order? If the answer is negative what are the principles for creating an orderly international monetary system? Which institution should issue international money to guarantee exchange rate stability? What are the links between money, credit and finance at the international level? How should the Bretton Woods institutions work, or be reformed today, to solve the world's main financial problems, as was hoped at the 1944 conference and as is still being promised to governments as well as to the general public some sixty years later?

This chapter focuses on the importance of a structural monetary reform of the present international payment system in the spirit of Keynes. It analyses international money and credit from an endogenous-money perspective, showing that these questions need to be addressed, and solved, together in order to set up an institutional system that can avoid world monetary disorder as well as financial turmoil. It also shows that the so-called incompatible triad of international financial liberalization, monetary policy autonomy, and stable exchange rates can be disposed of, if Keynes' message for a world monetary reform is elaborated, considering the financial issues *pari passu* as the monetary ones.

The remainder of this chapter is structured as follows. The next section expands on Keynes' proposals for world monetary reform, considering the scant academic debate that has occurred since the 1940s. The third section elaborates on a post-Keynesian approach, making sure that international transactions occur in a stable monetary environment, avoiding exchange rate volatility and currency crises. The fourth section applies this approach to regional monetary integration, and provides a case study in addressing the adoption of a common currency by the so-called Barcelona partner countries of the European Union (EU). A final section draws conclusions.

Keynes' proposal for a new international monetary order

Keynes was one of the first proponents of an international payment system using bank money instead of a commodity, such as gold, to settle international imbalances. In the early 1940s, a few economists in Germany were also arguing along similar lines, to propose a German 'new order' as a result of the Second World War (see Keynes, 1980, ch. 1). In particular, Schumacher (1943a, 1943b) had been calling for an international clearing system similar to Keynes' (see also Kalecki and Schumacher, 1943, Schumacher and Balogh, 1944). As is documented by Hession (1986, p. 4):

> [In the 1940s, Schumacher] was very much absorbed in ways to prevent future wars and finally concluded that in international economics, it was the countries with surpluses in their balance of trade which were the greatest threat to peace ... As a possible solution to this problem he devised a new system whereby surplus countries had to spend what they earned in the long term while financing the debts of the economically weaker countries with their surpluses in the short term.

In fact, Keynes' aim was to create an international monetary system in order (i) to make sure that international imbalances are finally settled; and (ii) to provide deficit countries with the means to finance their imbalances with respect to surplus countries. In Keynes' own words:

> We need a method by which the surplus credit balances arising from international trade, which the recipient does not wish to employ for the time being, can be set to work in the interests of international planning and relief and economic health, without detriment to the liquidity of these balances and to their holder's faculty to employ them himself when he desires to do so. (Keynes, 1980, p. 169)

To this end, Keynes (1980) proposed the creation of an international bank money, which he dubbed 'bancor', and further underlined that '[w]e need a central institution, of a purely technical and non-political character, to aid and support other international institutions concerned with the planning and regulation of the world's economic life' (p. 169). In fact, Keynes linked bancor balances to gold, because in his plan the international bank money 'would be defined in terms of a weight of gold' (p. 85).

The starting point of Keynes' analysis relies on the merits of the gold standard for the orderly working of the international payment system that existed before the First World War. As he cogently argued, '[y]ears ago, money was an international thing: if you had the money of one country you could change it into the money of another at a fixed rate, and you never had to think which currency you held' (p. 3). As a matter of fact, under the gold standard system there was an international standard – namely, gold – that rendered the various national currencies homogeneous because of the convertibility principle. Hence Keynes' proposal was to revert to the *structure* of the international gold standard system, which is 'a means for trading goods against goods' (p. 12). To be sure, Keynes did not ever propose a system of barter trade. On the contrary, he insisted on the importance of money as the means of payment at both national and international levels. His argument, however, was that any 'trading transaction must necessarily find its counterpart in another trading transaction sooner or later' (p. 18).

To reform the international payment machinery, Keynes (1980, p. 33) suggested that '[w]ithin any member-country or currency unit the provision of foreign exchange [is] to be concentrated in the hands of its central bank which would deal with the public through the usual banks'. To obtain foreign exchange, non-bank agents have therefore to turn to banks, which in turn ask the central bank for it. Further, '[i]nternationally all transactions [have] to be cleared between central banks, operating on their accounts with an International Clearing Bank' (p. 34). The characteristics of the international monetary order proposed by Keynes are therefore that the bank to set up must act as a *settlement* institution – that is, it must imitate national central banks in their capacity for finally settling interbank debts (see Rossi, 2005a); and it must be an *international* bank – that is, the settlement agent for national central banks:

> Keynes observed that the logic of bank money implied the hierarchical structure of banking systems. Within countries inter-bank settlements are daily proceeded in central bank money after multilateral clearing of net bank exposure. Keynes thought that the same logic could be forwarded to international settlements, if a third stage was built in linking national banking systems together. (Aglietta, 2004, p. 52)

In short, the aim of Keynes' plan was to reproduce at the international level the monetary order that exists in any country, as a result of the workings of domestic settlement systems headed by a central bank. In order to reproduce at the international level the principles governing national monetary systems, Keynes went so far as to maintain that the proposed International Clearing Bank (ICB) create its own payment unit, the bancor, for any transaction it settles:

> If no credits can be removed outside the banking system but only transferred within it, the Bank *itself* can never be in difficulties. It can with safety make what advances it wishes to any of its customers with the assurance that the proceeds can only be transferred to the bank account of another customer. (Keynes, 1980, p. 44)

This is the loans-to-deposits causality on which the modern endogenous-money paradigm is based (see Gnos, 1998).

There is no doubt that Keynes' plan was ingenious; since participating countries would have been entitled to obtain a credit in terms of bancor by paying in gold to the ICB for the credit of their clearing account (Keynes, 1980, p. 175), this plan would have turned 'a stone into bread' (p. 177) and hence led to an expansion of foreign trade, with ensuing positive effects on the world economy in terms of growth, employment and effective demand. Because of political factors and imbalances of power between the US and UK delegations gathered in Bretton Woods, however, Keynes' plan was put aside, the White plan closely inspired the Bretton Woods agreements, and the US dollar thereby became the leading currency at the international level. To date, despite some efforts to provide the international economy with international bank money (the Special Drawing Rights, and the European Currency Unit), foreign trade and all sorts of cross-border transactions are still settled using national currencies, in the form of US dollars and a small number of other local currencies, among which the euro has a prominent place. In particular, at the European level, the creation of a single currency for EU countries has led to the formation of a wide currency area within which local currencies have been abolished. Is this enough to provide a solution to the problems that Keynes pointed out in the 1940s, particularly with regard to 'the substitution of an expansionist, in place of a contractionist, pressure on world trade' (Keynes, 1980, p. 176)? Some post-Keynesian economists, following Arestis and Sawyer (1996, 1997), answer in the negative. In fact, the 1999 changeover to the European single currency may have reinforced the economic slowdown that continental Europe has been experiencing since the beginning of the new millennium (see Arestis *et al.*, 2001, 2002; Hein and Truger, 2005). Let us therefore elaborate on Keynes' plan in order to put forward an alternative solution for integrating different countries monetarily, without abolishing their currencies and the ensuing monetary sovereignty, which is instrumental for domestic policy-making conducive to economic growth and a high level of employment.

The principles for a proper international settlement system

In his speech to the House of Lords on 18 May 1943, Keynes (1980, p. 270) pointed out that the principal object of his plan was 'to provide that money earned by selling goods to one country can be spent on purchasing the products of any other country. In jargon, a system of multilateral clearing. In English, a universal currency valid for trade transactions in all the world. Everything else in the plan is ancillary to that'. Now, as Schumacher (1943a) explained in his *Economica* article on 'Multilateral Clearing', the settlement of international transactions on real goods and services by way of clearing means that:

> The importer in country *A* pays for the goods he buys from country *B* by handing over to the Clearing Authority in his own country a sum of *A*-money which is deemed to discharge his debt. The exporter in country *B* receives from the Clearing Authority in his country an equivalent sum of *B*-money which is deemed to satisfy his claim. (Schumacher, 1943a, p. 150)

Hence multilateral clearing implies that every single international transaction has to be finally settled, in local currency within the countries concerned and in an international monetary unit, say bancor, between them. In this system, '[b]eing linked to equivalent payments by and to individuals in their respective currencies, [every international settlement in bancor] only transfers existing purchasing power from one country to another' (Guttmann, 1994, p. 433).

Suppose, for instance, that country *A* has a trade deficit worth *x* units of money *A*, *MA*, or, equivalently, *z* bancor. For expositional ease, let us assume that country *A*'s deficit is country *B*'s surplus, as if the multilateral clearing system were composed of two countries only. To make sure that the monetary circuits of local monies are clearly separated from the bancor circuit, let us introduce a two-department bookkeeping system in each national central bank involved (see Schmitt, 1973, for an analogous proposal at the international level). If so, then each transaction across borders – be it for commercial or financial reasons – will be recorded by the relevant central bank in two separate monies: the Domestic Department enters the payment in local currency, while the International Department enters it in international money (bancor). Table 4.1 shows the result of the payment of the trade imbalance between countries *A* and *B*.

Following Keynes' plan, a 'supranational' tier to the two-tiered banking structure existing at present in each country has to be created, to allow for the ultimate settlement of international transactions using international bank money (bancor). An international institution in charge of the final

Table 4.1 The result of an international payment in bancor: step I (goods market)

Central bank of country A			
Domestic department		**International department**	
Assets	**Liabilities**	**Assets**	**Liabilities**
Bank *B1* (importer) +*x MA*	International department +*x MA*	Domestic department +*z* bancor	International Clearing Bank +*z* bancor

International Clearing Bank	
Assets	**Liabilities**
Central bank of country A (International Department) +*z* bancor	Central bank of country B (International department) +*z* bancor

Central bank of country B			
Domestic department		**International department**	
Assets	**Liabilities**	**Assets**	**Liabilities**
International department +*y MB*	Bank *B2* (exporter) +*y MB*	International Clearing Bank +*z* bancor	Domestic department +*z* bancor

Note: *x MA* = *z* bancor = *y MB*.

settlement of international transactions must head this 'supranational' tier of the payment system. This calls for a truly international money, which will be provided by the very international institution heading the international settlement system, every time a final payment takes place between two participating countries or currency areas. In particular, the system that we propose here will be based on the principles listed below, which expand on the Davidson (2002, ch. 14) design of an international system that does not require the surrender of national monetary sovereignties in order to create a homogeneous monetary area at the international level (see Schmitt, 1985):

1 Analogously to what would happen under an international gold standard, the exchange rate between each currency and the international bank money (to be created) will be set by the country concerned.
2 Settlements between non-bank agents will continue to be made in any currency as permitted by their country's legislation and agreed upon by the contracting parties.
3 The international monetary unit to be issued is an electronic, interbank money at the supranational level, and is not available to the public, who therefore cannot speculate on it.
4 The Clearing Union being a closed system by nature, the deposits at the ICB of a country are necessarily equal to the debts to the ICB of another country, so that there are no settlement risks for either the participating central banks or the ICB itself.
5 The ICB will also act as a financial intermediary in so far as it lends to deficit countries the amounts of bancor saved by surplus countries.

Let us elaborate on the last point, which to the best of our knowledge has not yet been fully developed in the post-Keynesian literature (see, however, Arestis and Sawyer (1996, 1997) for an outstanding exception), before considering the workings of the proposed international settlement system through a stylized example in the framework of the Barcelona partner countries of the EU. This shows that our reform proposal applies to regional as well as global monetary order (hence it is 'glocal' and has many possible applications in the modern world).

In the stylized example of Table 4.1, when the central bank of country *B* is informed that it is entitled to a deposit in international money at the ICB, it should decide whether to lend this amount directly to a deficit country (such as country *A*) or to spend it in buying interest-bearing securities in the international financial market. (To accelerate the latter decision, deposits at the ICB should bear no interest at all.) In our stylized example, if country *B* spends its deposit at the ICB on purchasing financial assets, this means that these assets are sold by country *A* – there are indeed no other countries in our example. If so, the bookkeeping situation after this financial transaction has taken place, and has finally been settled thanks to the ICB, is depicted in Table 4.2 (previous entries are shown in italics).

As a result of the international payment in bancor through the ICB, no country has a *monetary* deficit, because trade imbalances are finally settled by a transfer of eligible assets in a multilateral framework. To be sure, country *A* ultimately has a net *financial* outflow, as it sells an amount of securities to fund its final payment to country *B* (via the ICB). In other words, country *B* spends on the international financial market the deposit in bancor it gets as a result of its trade surplus for a sum total of *z* bancor. Country *A* thus finds on the international financial market the funds it needs to reimburse the

Table 4.2 The result of an international payment in bancor: step II (assets market)

Central bank of country A			
Domestic department		**International department**	
Assets	**Liabilities**	**Assets**	**Liabilities**
Bank B1 (importer) +x MA	*International department +x MA*	*Domestic department +z bancor*	*International Clearing Bank +z bancor*
International department +*x MA*		International Clearing Bank +*z* bancor	Domestic department +*z* bancor
Financial assets (sold to country *B*) −*x MA*			
Bank *B1* (*importer*) +*x MA*			
Financial assets (sold to country *B*) −*x MA*			

International Clearing Bank	
Assets	**Liabilities**
Central bank of country A (International department) +z bancor	*Central bank of country B (International department) +z bancor*
Central bank of country B (International department) +*z* bancor	Central bank of country A (International department) +*z* bancor

Central bank of country B			
Domestic department		**International department**	
Assets	**Liabilities**	**Assets**	**Liabilities**
International department *+y MB*	*Bank B2 (exporter)* *+y MB*	*International Clearing Bank* *+z bancor*	*Domestic department* *+z bancor*
Financial assets (bought from country A) *+y MB*	International department *+y MB*	Domestic department +*z* bancor	International Clearing Bank +*z* bancor
Financial assets (bought from country A) *+y MB*	Bank *B2* (exporter) *+y MB*		

Note: $x\,MA = z$ bancor $= y\,MB$.

overdraft it obtained at the ICB. In the end, international money disappears as the reflux principle indicates (and as the ICB balance sheet in Table 4.2 shows unequivocally).

Now, the question that pops up at this juncture asks what happens if country *B* does not spend its bancor deposit at the ICB to buy those securities sold by country *A*, which seeks to finance its trade imbalance.[1] It is at this juncture that the ICB can intervene and operate as a financial intermediary. In fact, instead of selling its securities to country *B*, country *A* may sell them to the ICB, which, in buying these securities, would advance a payment that country *A* will benefit from when exporting real goods and/or services. If so, there may be two distinct kinds of securities behind the entries in Table 4.2: country *A*'s securities sold to the ICB, and the ICB's securities sold to country *B*. Needless to say, in order to avoid a 'buffer-stock' problem in the long run – namely, to make sure that the ICB does not end up with a stock of poor-quality (risky) securities – some form of quality control has to be devised: for example, adopting international best practices and Basle-II-like standards. These regulations and institutional arrangements, however, will impose no conditionality on the loans that the ICB will be able to grant on a long-term basis. Therefore, they will differ from the present policies of both the International Monetary Fund (IMF) and the World Bank, but will also differ from the Meltzer (2000) proposal to transform the IMF into an international lender of last resort dealing with short-term loans only. This is so much so that the ICB may collect private as well as public capital, and invest it in those areas where capital does not flow spontaneously. Let us expand on the last point with respect to the Barcelona partner countries of the EU, to show how the proposed international structural–monetary reform might lead to implementing a new world monetary order on regional grounds, without abolishing national currencies and the monetary room for manoeuvre that they offer (see Rossi, 2004, for an application to the new EU countries' case).

The case of the Barcelona partner countries

Recently, the European Central Bank has established bilateral contacts with the central banks of the partner countries of the 'Barcelona Process' (which seeks to set up a free-trade area between the EU and a number of Mediterranean countries by 2010), in order to discuss common economic policy issues arising from geographical proximity and a long historical record of extensive commercial and financial flows between the countries around the Mediterranean Sea.[2] In particular, the financial ties result from euro-area bank lending to the Barcelona partner countries, foreign direct investment, and workers' remittances. For most Barcelona partner countries, commercial ties with the euro area are also very important: on average, the Barcelona partner countries' trade with the euro area accounts for some 40 per cent of their total trade in recent years. As the European Central Bank (2004, p. 72) notes, 'the euro area has constantly registered a trade surplus with the Barcelona partner countries'. The formation of a free-trade area by 2010 between the EU and these partner countries is likely to increase the number as well as the amount of both trade and financial flows across the Mediterranean Sea. International capital flows may therefore become a serious threat to financial stability if the exchange rate regime is not appropriate to control this situation with a view to making the Barcelona partner countries' economy grow and develop along a stable monetary–financial path.

As a matter of fact, most of the Barcelona partner countries suffer from insufficient economic growth and from a number of structural difficulties, which are particularly worrisome in the light of their high rates of unemployment, both overall and for the young. In these countries, monetary policy is orientated towards stabilizing the local currency's exchange rate *vis-à-vis* the euro or the US dollar, or against a basket of currencies. The corresponding exchange rate regimes are most of the time intermediate arrangements, as only the shekel and the Turkish lira float independently and no country has a hard peg (Table 4.3).

Intermediate exchange rate regimes, such as a crawling peg or a managed float, may provoke financial instability in countries where capital movements *vis-à-vis* the rest of the world are set free as a result of financial liberalization. Additionally, since a number of Barcelona partner countries are experiencing significant political instability, foreign investors may be reluctant to direct capital flows into the region, so that exchange rates are likely to be under capital volatility pressure, bearing the risk of speculative attacks.

Table 4.3 Exchange rate strategies of the Barcelona partner countries, 2004*

Country	Currency	Exchange rate regime as of 31 December 2004
Algeria	Dinar	Managed float
Cyprus	Pound	Peg to the euro with a ±15% fluctuation band
Egypt	Pound	Managed float
Israel	Shekel	Free float
Jordan	Dinar	Peg to a single currency**
Lebanon	Pound	Peg to the US dollar
Malta	Lira	Peg to a basket of currencies***
Morocco	Dirham	Peg to a basket of currencies
Syria	Pound	Peg to the US dollar
Tunisia	Dinar	Crawling peg
Turkey	Lira	Free float

Notes: * Although West Bank and Gaza (Palestinian territories) belong to the so-called Barcelona partner countries of the EU, they are not sovereign countries and thus have no currency of their own, but use the Israeli shekel. Cyprus and Malta are members of the EU as from 1 May 2004, but have not as yet adopted the euro.

** The Jordanian dinar is pegged *de jure* to the Special Drawing Right, but *de facto* to the US dollar.

*** 70% euro, 30% US dollar and pound sterling.

Source: International Monetary Fund (http://www.imf.org/external/np/mfd/er/index.asp).

Floating exchange rates, however, do not represent a solution, since they tend towards volatility, which raises the exchange-rate risk premium and thereby decreases potential capital inflows (mainly in the form of foreign direct investment) to the detriment of the economic development of the countries adopting this exchange rate strategy. Hence the question of what kind of exchange rate strategy the EU's Barcelona partner countries should implement to enable them to boost their economic development and growth, hence job creation, without creating (the risk of) financial instability and breakdown, with a view to speed up the catching-up process of at least part of the so-called 'euro time zone' with respect to the EU (see Mazzaferro *et al.*, 2002).

The answer this chapter provides to the above question combines the macroeconomic benefits of exchange rate stability with the flexibility offered by an exchange rate that can be adjusted over time by the country concerned. Certainly, for all the Barcelona partner countries a certain degree of exchange rate flexibility will remain necessary in the near future: 'sufficiently flexible exchange rates would facilitate the catching-up process, in conformity with stability. They safeguard the requisite monetary room for manoeuvre' (Deutsche Bundesbank, 2001, p. 24). In fact, even a small open economy will be able to implement monetary and fiscal policies orientated to its domestic needs, and this even in case of an extremely high degree of capital mobility, as long as the country controls its own currency and hence refrains from entering a single currency area such as Euroland or from dollarizing/euroizing its economy (see Rochon and Rossi, 2003).

In light of the risk of speculative attacks on the foreign exchange market pointed out above, the Barcelona partner countries need in particular an exchange rate arrangement by which they can prevent the destabilizing effects on their economies elicited by trade integration and international financial liberalization. This reform requires an agreement between the Barcelona partner countries, and preferably also between them and the euro area (to enhance foreign direct investment from this area), to enable them to set up an international settlement structure based on a double-entry bookkeeping agent to record any payments between participating nations or currency areas. Let us call the proposed international payment institution 'European settlement agent' (ESA), and dub the 'euror' the monetary unit in which this institution will record the settlement of a participating country's transactions with the rest of the world.

Three stylized cases may be singled out. Let us consider them very briefly in turn.

Payments between two Barcelona partner countries

Suppose that a Barcelona partner country – say, Turkey – imports from another such country – say, Lebanon – goods worth 2 billion Lebanese pounds (LBP) or, equivalently, 2,000 billion Turkish lira (TRL) (assuming an exchange rate of 1 LBP to 1,000 TRL). The Turkish importer is invoiced in Lebanese pounds by the exporter. Today, s/he may pay for his/her imports by writing a cheque on a bank account in Lebanese pounds, or by buying the necessary amount of Lebanese pounds on the foreign exchange market. Any other payment arrangement may be conceived, of course, but in any case there is an exchange rate risk, since the LBP/TRL exchange rate floats. If the ESA system were implemented along the lines we propose in this chapter, then the Turkish importer would pay for his/her imports in local currency, while the Lebanese exporter would be paid in his/her own local currency, at an exchange rate that is kept stable by the workings of the system. Table 4.4 shows the relevant entries under the proposed settlement system in euror.

In this system, the Turkish importer asks his/her bank (Bank *B1*) to pay 2,000 billion TRL to his/her correspondent in Lebanon. In order to do this, Bank *B1* gets in touch with the central bank of Turkey, whose international department asks the ESA to provide the amount of international money necessary for the ultimate settlement to take place between the two countries involved (let us suppose an exchange rate of 2,000 Turkish lira for 1 euror). As a result, Turkey is debited with an amount of 1 billion euror, a sum credited to Lebanon, whose central bank is entitled to the corresponding euror deposit at the ESA.

Table 4.4 The result of an international payment via the ESA (Case I)

Central bank of Turkey			
Domestic department		**International department**	
Assets	**Liabilities**	**Assets**	**Liabilities**
Bank *B1* (importer) +2,000 TRL	International department +2,000 TRL	Domestic department +1 euror	ESA +1 euror

European Settlement Agent	
Assets	**Liabilities**
Central bank of Turkey (International department) +1 euror	Central bank of Lebanon (International department) +1 euror

Central bank of Lebanon			
Domestic department		**International department**	
Assets	**Liabilities**	**Assets**	**Liabilities**
International department +2 LBP	Bank *B2* (exporter) +2 LBP	ESA +1 euror	Domestic department +1 euror

Note: Entries in billions.

Payments between a Barcelona partner country and a country of Euroland

Suppose now that Lebanon imports from the euro area (say from Germany) goods worth 2 billion euros or, equivalently, 4 billion Lebanese pounds (assuming an exchange rate of 1 euro for 2 LBP). In Lebanon, the importer asks his/her bank (Bank *B3*) to pay 4 billion LBP to the German exporter, who holds an account in the German banking system (say at Bank *B4*) and is thereby paid in local currency – namely, in euros. In this respect, Bank *B3* has to get in touch with its central bank to enable the international transaction to finally be settled. When Bank *B3* asks the central bank of Lebanon to pay an amount of 2 billion euros to Bank *B4*, this payment order gives rise to an entry in both departments of the central bank of Lebanon: its domestic department enters the transaction in local currency (4 billion LBP), carrying it over to the international department of the same central bank, which enters this payment in euror (let us assume that 2 LBP = 1 euror). The result of this double-entry bookkeeping is shown in Table 4.5.

Table 4.5 The result of an international payment via the ESA (Case II)

Central bank of Lebanon			
Domestic department		**International department**	
Assets	**Liabilities**	**Assets**	**Liabilities**
International department +2 LBP	*Bank B2 (exporter) +2 LBP*	*ESA +1 euror*	*Domestic department +1 euror*
Bank *B3* (importer) +4 LBP	International department +4 LBP	Domestic department +2 euror	ESA +2 euror

European Settlement Agent	
Assets	**Liabilities**
Central bank of Turkey (International department) +1 euror	*Central bank of Lebanon (International department) +1 euror*
Central bank of Lebanon (International department) +2 euror	Bundesbank (International department) +2 euror

Bundesbank			
Domestic department		**International department**	
Assets	**Liabilities**	**Assets**	**Liabilities**
International department +2 €	Bank *B4* (exporter) +2 €	ESA +2 euror	Domestic department +2 euror

Note: Entries in billions. Balances carried over from the previous case are in italics.

As Table 4.5 shows, the corresponding partner of a central bank's international department is not another central bank – as is the case under a correspondent central banking model, which can only represent an interim solution to the problem of finally settling cross-border transactions (as European Central Bank (1999) notes) – but the international settlement institution that we labelled ESA. In practice, the international department of the central bank of Lebanon asks the ESA to pay an amount of 2 billion euror to the benefit of Germany, which at the international level is represented by (the international department of) the Bundesbank. As a result, the international department of the Bundesbank is credited by the ESA with an amount of 2 billion euror, carrying this flow over to its domestic department, to the benefit of the local exporter, who is paid via Bank *B4* in local currency (2 billion euros) at the prevailing exchange rate.

Payments between a Barcelona partner country and a third country

Suppose now that Turkey exports goods worth 2,000 billion TRL to Switzerland, a non-EU and non-Barcelona partner country. Again, the relevant bookkeeping entries under the proposed new system follow the same logic as above, and are recorded in Table 4.6 with no need of further explanation (let us assume that 2,000 TRL = 1 euror = 2 Swiss francs (CHF)).

If we draw the balance once all these stylized international payments have taken place, we notice that the deposit at the ESA owned by the Bundesbank for 2 billion euror may finance the current account deficits of both Lebanon and Switzerland, which each owe 1 billion euror to the ESA. To this end, the proposed international settlement system may be complemented by a multilateral agreement between all the participating countries, according to which creditor countries spend the positive balances they hold with the ESA in order to provide the necessary finance to deficit countries (that is, Lebanon and Switzerland in our example).

In fact, the newly formed deposits in euror can be spent in three ways by the country entitled to them – namely, for:

(i) purchasing goods and services from any other member of the ESA system;
(ii) purchasing financial assets directly from deficit members of the ESA; and/or
(iii) purchasing financial assets issued and sold by the ESA itself, which accepts to lend to deficit countries on a long-term basis (see above for the case of the ICB).

The first kind of expenditure is likely to induce a trade balance adjustment in so far as surplus countries import goods and services from deficit countries. The second kind of expenditure may imply that creditor countries enter into new foreign direct investment projects with deficit countries. The

Table 4.6 The result of an international payment via the ESA (Case III)

Central bank of Turkey			
Domestic department		**International department**	
Assets	**Liabilities**	**Assets**	**Liabilities**
Bank B1 (importer) +2,000 TRL	*International department +2,000 TRL*	*Domestic department +1 euror*	*ESA +1 euror*
International department +2,000 TRL	Bank *B5* (exporter) +2,000 TRL	ESA +1 euror	Domestic department +1 euror

European Settlement Agent	
Assets	**Liabilities**
Central bank of Turkey (International department) +1 euror	*Central bank of Lebanon (International department) +1 euror*
Central bank of Lebanon (International department) +2 euror	*Bundesbank (International department) +2 euror*
Swiss National Bank (International department) +1 euror	Central bank of Turkey (International department) +1 euror
Central bank of Lebanon (International department) 1 euror	Bundesbank (International department) 2 euror
Swiss National Bank (International department) 1 euror	

Swiss National Bank			
Domestic department		**International department**	
Assets	**Liabilities**	**Assets**	**Liabilities**
Bank *B6* (importer) +2 CHF	International department +2 CHF	Domestic department +1 euror	ESA +1 euror

Note: Entries in billions. Balances carried over from previous cases are in italics.

third kind of expenditure makes sure that deficit countries can borrow multilaterally the credit balances owned by surplus countries, via the ESA financial intermediation as shown in the previous section with respect to the ICB. All these expenditures help to accelerate economic development and growth of the Barcelona partner countries, to the benefit of these countries as well as the rest of the world.

Conclusion

The creation of an International Clearing Bank as proposed by Keynes is an important step towards solving the problem of funding, and finally settling economic transactions between trading countries. This chapter has shown that a structural monetary reform of the international payment system is needed to put the Keynes plan into practice. In this chapter we analyse international money and credit with the endogenous-money paradigm. Our conclusion is that these issues need to be addressed, and solved, together, to set up an institutional system that can avoid world monetary disorder and foreign exchange crises. The structural reform of the international payment system we propose in this chapter combines the benefits of exchange rate stability with the flexibility offered by an exchange rate that can be adjusted over time by a unilateral decision of the country concerned – analogously to the gold standard system.

This structural reform is particularly needed in today's world of free international capital flows and multi-currency international banking. Certainly, these are essential characteristics of modern open economies, and their importance has been growing in line with the emergence of globalized financial markets. In spite of highly integrated financial markets, however, the international infrastructure for the settlement of cross-border transactions is still fragmented today, because it lacks a truly international bank money through which countries themselves can finally settle their position. This represents a limitation of cross-border transactions, because in the current international monetary architecture these transactions can generate destabilizing effects on exchange rates, current and capital accounts, and nominal and real interest rates, and therefore affect economic performance negatively (see Rossi, 2005b).

The reform of the international settlement system we propose in this chapter will guarantee that each monetary transaction between any two countries gives rise to both a fund transfer at the ICB and a securities transfer between the countries involved, in line with the delivery-versus-payment protocol that an ever-increasing number of countries around the world are implementing for their domestic settlement systems, to avoid systemic risks as well as financial instability (see Committee on Payment and Settlement Systems, 2003). Further, when international settlements are carried out via the monetary and financial intermediation of the ICB, each national money will be exchanged instantaneously against itself via international money (say, bancor or euror). For example, *x* units of *MA* will be supplied (against *z* bancor) in the payment of country *A*'s trade deficit, at the same time as *x* units of *MA* will be demanded (against *z* bancor) in payment of the financial assets sold by country *A*. Similarly, *y* units of *MB* will be demanded (against *z* bancor) in the payment of country *B*'s trade surplus, at the same time as *y* units of *MB* will be supplied (against *z* bancor) in payment of those securities bought by country *B*. Each local money being supplied and demanded simultaneously against an identical amount of international money, its exchange rate will never be affected by international transactions – be they on products or financial markets. As a result, speculation can never alter exchange rates in such a system.

The first benefit of our system would indeed consist in introducing a mechanism by means of which any creditor country spends its positive balances in bancor as soon as it earns them, so that at the end of each settlement day no credit balances will be held idle at the ICB. International hoarding would thereby be mechanically impossible. Further, and more importantly, in the system we propose any participating currency will have an exchange rate that is stable in terms of international money, hence also in terms of any other participating currency, in a framework of fully liberalized international capital flows[3] – without this being incompatible with a higher degree of flexibility in domestic policy-making. In fact, our plan grants another important benefit to the nations adopting it, because it increases their room for manoeuvre when gearing their economic policies (particularly an autonomous and independent monetary policy) to the real needs of their domestic economy, including output growth and hence employment. Indeed, the reform of the international settlement system we propose in this chapter will make sure that all international payments take place in an orderly manner – that is, with no disturbances on the foreign exchange market that might jeopardize the goal of exchange rate stability and its ensuing benefits. The age-old conflict between the internal and external goals of a country's monetary policy would thus be resolved definitively, to the benefit of growth, employment and effective demand all around the world.

Notes

1 To be true, a country recording a financial deficit, especially one elicited by a capital outflow, is hardly in a position to issue new debt instruments on favourable terms. If so, it must accept either the onus of paying higher rates of interest on new debt, or of slowing down the national economy by a hike in domestic interest rates in the hope of attracting foreign capital (both short- and long-term). Alternatively, or additionally, such a country might devaluate, hoping thereby to boost exports and improve its trade balance in the not too distant future. Indeed, the bancor standard is not a system of irrevocably fixed exchange rates. Generally speaking, '[c]hanges in parities can take place when money wages and profit margins relative

to productivity are permanently out of line, or when countries experience chronic difficulties in their balance of payments for other reasons' (Arestis and Sawyer, 1997, p. 363).

2 The Barcelona partner countries of the EU are Algeria, Egypt, Israel, Jordan, Lebanon, Morocco, Syria, Tunisia, Turkey, and West Bank and Gaza (both represented by the Palestinian National Authority). Cyprus and Malta were among the Barcelona partner countries before joining the EU on 1 May 2004.

3 Two-way convertibility between any participating currency and the bancor through the proposed two-department bookkeeping system in the national central banks (see Tables 4.1 and 4.2) amounts, in fact, to free international capital flows. This contrasts with the one-way convertibility mechanism called for in the Davidson proposal (2002, p. 232), which permits each nation to control and regulate international capital flows, but which seems unrealistic these days, characterized by '[t]he dominance of purely financial motives over the needs of trade in foreign exchange markets' (Arestis and Sawyer, 1997, p. 361).

References

Aglietta, M. (2004) 'The International Monetary Fund: Past and Future', in M. Desai and Y. Said (eds), *Global Governance and Financial Crises* (London/New York: Routledge), pp. 43–69.

Arestis, P. and Sawyer, M. (1996) 'European Monetary Integration: A Post Keynesian Critique and Some Proposals', in P. Arestis (ed.), *Keynes, Money and the Open Economy: Essays in Honour of Paul Davidson,* Vol. I (Aldershot/Brookfield: Edward Elgar), pp. 144–64.

Arestis, P. and Sawyer, M. (1997) 'Unemployment and the Independent European System of Central Banks: Prospects and Some Alternative Arrangements', *American Journal of Economics and Sociology*, 56(3), pp. 353–67.

Arestis, P., Brown, A. and Sawyer, M. (2001) *The Euro: Evolution and Prospects* (Cheltenham/Northampton: Edward Elgar).

Arestis, P., Brown, A., Mouratidis, K. and Sawyer, M. (2002) 'The Euro: Reflections on the First Three Years', *International Review of Applied Economics*, 16(1), pp. 1–17.

Committee on Payment and Settlement Systems (2003) *Payment and Settlement Systems in Selected Countries* (Basel: Bank for International Settlements).

Davidson, P. (2002) *Financial Markets, Money and the Real World* (Cheltenham/Northampton: Edward Elgar).

Deutsche Bundesbank (2001) 'Monetary Aspects of the Enlargement of the EU', *Deutsche Bundesbank Monthly Report*, 53(10), pp. 15–30.

European Central Bank (1999) *Correspondent Central Banking Model (CCBM)* (Frankfurt: European Central Bank).

European Central Bank (2004) 'The Barcelona Partner Countries and Their Relations with the Euro Area', *European Central Bank Monthly Bulletin*, 6(4), pp. 67–75.

Gnos, C. (1998) 'La théorie monétaire de Keynes: les enseignements du plan d'une Union de Compensation', *Économie Appliquée*, 51(2), pp. 79–94.

Guttmann, R. (1994) *How Credit-Money Shapes the Economy: The United States in a Global System* (New York: M. E. Sharpe).

Hein, E. and Truger, A. (2005) 'European Monetary Union: Nominal Convergence, Real Divergence and Slow Growth?', *Structural Change and Economic Dynamics*, 16(1), pp. 7–33.

Hession, C. H. (1986) 'E. F. Schumacher as Heir to Keynes' Mantle', *Review of Social Economy*, 44(1), pp. 1–12.

Kalecki, M. and Schumacher, E. F. (1943) 'International Clearing and Long-Term Lending', *Bulletin of the Oxford University Institute of Statistics*, 5, Supplement, pp. 29–33.

Keynes, J. M. (1980) *The Collected Writings of John Maynard Keynes, Vol. xxv: Activities 1940–1944. Shaping the Post-War World: The Clearing Union* (London/New York: Macmillan/Cambridge University Press).

Mazzaferro, F., Mehl, A., Sturm, M., Thimann, C. and Winkler, A. (2002) 'Economic Relations with Regions Neighbouring the Euro Area in the "Euro Time Zone" ', *European Central Bank Occasional Paper*, 7 (Frankfurt: European Central Bank).

Meltzer, A. H. (2000) *The Meltzer Report* (Washington: United States House of Representatives) (http://www.house.gov/jec/imf/meltzer.pdf).

Rochon, L.-P. and Rossi, S. (2003) 'Dollarization Out, Euroization In', *International Journal of Political Economy*, 33(1), pp. 21–41.

Rossi, S. (2004) 'Monetary Integration Strategies and Perspectives of New EU Countries', *International Review of Applied Economics*, 18(4), pp. 443–69.

Rossi, S. (2005a) 'Central Banking in a Monetary Theory of Production: The Economics of Payment Finality from a Circular-Flow Perspective', in G. Fontana and R. Realfonzo (eds), *The Monetary Theory of Production: Tradition and Perspectives* (Basingstoke: Palgrave Macmillan), pp. 139–51.

Rossi, S. (2005b) 'Cross-Border Transactions and Exchange Rate Stability', in L.-P. Rochon and S. Rossi (eds), *Monetary and Exchange Rate Systems: A World View of Financial Crises* (Cheltenham/Northampton: Edward Elgar).

Schmitt, B. (1973) *New Proposals for World Monetary Reform* (Albeuve: Castella).

Schmitt, B. (1985) 'Un nouvel ordre monétaire international: le plan Keynes', in F. Poulon (ed.), *Les écrits de Keynes* (Paris: Dunod), pp. 195–209.

Schumacher, E. F. (1943a) 'Multilateral Clearing', *Economica*, 10(38), pp. 150–65.

Schumacher, E. F. (1943b) 'The New Currency Plans', *Bulletin of the Oxford University Institute of Statistics*, 5, Supplement, pp. 8–28.

Schumacher, E. F. and Balogh, T. (1944) 'An International Monetary Fund', *Bulletin of the Oxford University Institute of Statistics*, 6(6), pp. 81–93.

Skidelsky, R. (2000) *John Maynard Keynes, Vol. 3: Fighting for Britain 1937–1946* (Oxford University Press).

5

The Monetary Policy of the ECB and the Fed: Credibility versus Confidence, a Comparative Approach

*Edwin Le Heron and Emmanuel Carré**

The *rule versus discretion* debate is used frequently to shed light on monetary policy, in particular to contrast the strategies of the ECB and the Fed: the ECB is rule-based, while the Fed is discretionary. This approach is irrelevant, because both central banks reject opposition as a misperception of their strategy. We also believe that this debate is no longer relevant. *Credibility versus confidence* appears to be much more useful for understanding the changes in monetary policy and the differences between the ECB and the Fed. By a strategy of 'credibility', we mean that a central bank that adopts a model of behaviour and then follows it. It says what it does, and does what it says. The simplified chain of the credibility strategy is Rule – Commitment – Enforcement – Transparency – Credibility. Credibility has evolved from new Classical Economics to propound an alternative to the rule issuing from the quantity theory of money.

There is 'confidence' when there is a mutual understanding between the central bank and the economic agents. This 'common understanding', which implies a high level of communication, can be understood on two levels: in the first place one takes into account the opinions of the other party and, second, the expectations of the economic agents are similar to the strategy and conventions of the central bank. Therefore, it is possible to have credibility without confidence. The central bank should not only account for, but also take into account the economic model that the agents hold. The simplified chain of the confidence strategy is Communication – Common understanding – Governance – Accountability – Confidence. A single or predetermined equilibrium does not exist, and strong uncertainty makes the management of expectations necessary, so good co-ordination between the central bank and economic agents is therefore essential. This implies a high

* Our grateful thanks to Michael Hughes, who helped us with the translation.

level of communication and a definition of the objectives of monetary policy accepted by all. The ECB has agreed to define its strategy as a 'credibility strategy', and its view conforms to the credibility literature. The latter starts with Kydland and Prescott (1977) and their time-inconsistency and inflation bias, continues with Barro and Gordon (1983) – that is, reputation as a solution to time inconsistency, and ends with Rogoff (1985) – strategic delegation to a conservative banker, Walsh (1995), Svensson (1997) or Woodford (2003). For the ECB: 'Ultimately, however, credibility will have to be built over time by establishing a reputation' (Issing *et al.*, 2001, p. 38); 'Credibility is won through systematic, coherent action... A good track record' (Issing, 2005, p. 71).

The ECB exhibits a 'cross checking' strategy. Nevertheless, this transparency does not lead to a clear understanding of the ECB strategy by the markets.[1] More generally, 'reputation' is an outdated conception of 'credibility'. Transparency about its strategy could be seen as a commitment technology to price stability, and not a democratic explanatory device: 'The public announcement of a strategy effectively works as a form commitment' (Issing *et al.*, 2001, p. 38). The ECB's transparency is a 'new Lady in old clothes' (the credibility literature). The ECB acts and communicates as a conservative central bank with a unique mandate. It explains the lack of regulation in the economy and the lack of policy mix. More generally, it generates both a prosperity deficit and democratic deficit. The Fed argues that the time-inconsistency problem and, generally speaking, the credibility literature, are second order issues. Its strategy of 'balance of risks' can be defined as a 'confidence strategy'. It is now a commonplace that the Fed is no longer 'cryptic' or leading an informal ' "just do it" strategy' (McCallum, 1995). It has changed since 1994. The Fed's efficiency stems from explanations (deliberative process) that allow building of a common understanding between itself and market participants. In contrast to the ECB, the Fed does not pursue a reputation of providing a culture of stability – that is, credibility for low inflation. People have confidence that the Fed will be aggressive in response to shocks – that is, to lead stabilization policies that maintain prosperity. Hence, the Fed has a social role to play, 'regulating public conflict over inflation's redistributive powers' (Faust, 1996, p. 267).

If inflation targeting stands out as the dominant regime in monetary policy today, the ECB and the Fed prefer to follow their own ways. We shall compare them from the position of credibility (ECB) versus confidence (Fed). The objective is not to judge the efficiency of their monetary policy, but to clarify its foundations and innovations. We shall develop successively five conflicts between a credibility strategy and a confidence strategy: (1) independence versus governance; (2) responsibility versus accountability; (3) common knowledge versus common understanding; (4) transparency versus openness; and (5) credibility versus confidence.

Independence versus governance

Governance is the delegation of power, not the separation of power as with full independence. Governance aims to balance the independence of instrument and the independence of goal. It means that independence is always limited in a representative democracy because it remains subservient to the elected representatives who define the mandate.

ECB: an extraordinarily full independence

The ECB claims that 'maximum' or 'full independence' is a condition for implementing and maintaining price stability. 'When exercising their powers and carrying out their tasks and duties, neither ECB nor any NCB (National Central Bank)nor any member of their decision-making bodies shall seek or take instructions from Community institutions or bodies, from any government of a member state or from any other body' (Article 108 of the Treaty).

A creature of central bankers

Unlike the Bundesbank (Buba), the ECB was not founded on civic society. But the ECB is based on the same theory of an economic order independent from the political order (Scheller, 2004, pp. 121–5). Full independence of the ECB is the institutionalization of a monetary sovereignty. The specific German ordoliberalism cannot be directly applied to a supranational central bank such as the ECB. The Buba rests upon a constitution while the ECB is the result of a simple treaty.

A simple majority in Parliament could change the Bundesbank law. ECB's mandate cannot be changed by the European Parliament. The novelty is that the economic order is radically independent from the political order. Moreover, ECB's statutes are difficult to shift because the modification of the treaty requires a unanimous vote of Euroland members.

The Buba had a social role to play: to safeguard a common good – namely, money. The ECB has two economic or technical tasks: first, to ensure price stability; and second, to support the general economic policies in the European Community. While the Buba was the inheritance of the German hyperinflation crisis of the 1920s, the ECB is a consequence of the theoretical dogma of independence that emerged in the 1980s. The Buba's case illustrates that central banking is a political question. The Buba could anchor inflation expectations because it had a democratic role derived from the doctrine of ordoliberalism. In the ECB literature, full independence is a requisite for ensuring price stability, which is presented as a public good:[2] 'The ECB's independence is a corollary of its primary objective of maintaining price stability' (Scheller, 2004, p. 121). With price stability, the ECB tries to preserve the inheritance of the disinflationary credibility earned during the 'fight' against high inflation. Price stability is presented as the wisdom of central banking inherited from 'the great experience of the 1960–1970s'.

Today, the ECB is a special kind of central bank, since it follows the credibility literature of the 1980s. It is not a creature of elected representatives, but rather a creature of the folk wisdom theory of central bankers. From a theoretical point of view, the full independence of the ECB results from time inconsistency, institutional design (Persson and Tabellini, 1993) and the 'free lunch' literature. 'This evidence points to a potential free lunch: delegating monetary policy to an independent central bank with a clear price stability mandate leads to lower and less variable inflation without increasing the volatility of output' (Issing *et al.*, 2001, p. 130).

Full independence is a maximum interpretation of Rogoff's solution (1985): delegation and the conservative central banker. Delegation becomes insulation from political oversight. The ECB's full independence aims to serve its own interests: namely its reputation and its credibility. The ECB scheme does not organize the delegation, but rather the separation of monetary policy from the democratic order. To avoid short-term political pressures (time inconsistency and inflation bias), monetary policy (a political issue) moves to central banking (a technical issue). Full independence leads to a strict separation of power, but not in order to achieve a balance of power. There is a democratic deficit.

In the institutional design approach, the ECB's credibility is established as soon as a credible commitment to price stability is achieved. But in the credibility literature, commitment technology such as a rule (for example, quantitative theory for monetary targeting) is insufficient to ensure credibility. In order to impose the optimal incentive structure, enforcement is required. Full independence is a constitutional law, which is extremely costly to change. So it derives from the credibility scheme: Rule – Commitment – Enforcement.

The discrepancy between full independence and accountability

The ECB (Trichet, 2004, p.1) states that 'In a democracy, transparency and accountability are the quid pro quo for that independence', but full independence is inconsistent with accountability. Yet, in the responsibility approach of the ECB, effective accountability by elected representatives is impossible because it would entail its independence:

> If any political body – such as parliament or government – were able to intervene or influence directly the policy-making of the central bank, they would actually be taking part in the decision-making process itself and hence would share the responsibility for the policy outcomes. This would not only contradict the independent status of the central bank, but it would also render the concept of accountability meaningless. (Scheller, 2004, p. 126)

Not only is the ECB fully independent, but the Stability and Growth Pact makes it possible to avoid the free rider and chicken game (budgetary expansion with monetary restriction) by enforcing budgetary rules. The European policy mix is dominated by monetary policy without any flexibility. For the ECB, accountability is only judged by the general public on the announced objective of price stability.

The Fed: the challenge of central banking in a democratic society

The Fed is embedded in a larger representative democracy. It benefits from an instrumental independence, but not independence for the objectives, remaining subservient to elected representatives. It is typically a governance arrangement. Kohn (2005, p. 4)[3] talks about 'the governance of central banks in democratic societies'. 'A central bank in a democratic society is a magnet for many of the tensions that such a society confronts. Any institution that can affect the purchasing power of the currency is perceived as potentially affecting the level and distribution of wealth among the participants of that society, hardly an inconsequential issue' (Greenspan, 1996, p. 1).

The Fed rejects both time inconsistency and free lunch theories: 'I have never found the literature on time inconsistency particularly relevant to central banks ... There is no consistent evidence of a relationship between central bank independence and real economic activity nor consistent evidence that central bank independence lowers the cost of reducing inflation or increases the effectiveness of stabilisation policy' (Meyer, 2000, pp. 3–4). Delegation of monetary policy by democratic authorities does not mean insulation from politics. The Fed's independence is the production of elected representatives, not of economic theory. It has a limited delegated power: 'the Fed independence is a product of congressional legislation and can therefore be diminished at the will of the Congress' (Meyer, 2000, p. 16). The Fed represents a political revival in central banking. It is a break with the consensus on independence in the 1980s that led to the full independence of the ECB.

Regarding democracy, the difference between the ECB and the Fed is important: the 'central bank exists to serve the society' (Blinder, 1996, p. 8). The Fed is a 'creature of the Congress' (Meyer, 2000, p. 6), because it remains subservient to elected representatives. So it benefits from political legitimacy. This legitimacy process is strengthened by democratic accountability procedures. It explains why accountability is a key element of central banking: central bankers 'are accountable both to the Congress from which we derive our monetary policy mission and, beyond, to the American people' (Greenspan, 2001, p. 1). For the Fed, independence should be limited by a checks and balances scheme. In this government arrangement, balancing independence and accountability restricts independence. To sum up, full independence of the ECB leads to a political separation of the monetary order in the name of a technical legitimacy. The central banking of the ECB is driven by economics, and this explains the absence of political actors. Full independence is a requisite for disinflationary credibility. The consequence is a democratic deficit. It differs from the governance of the Fed that rests on a delegation of power. Legitimacy is primarily political. Governance insists on the politics of monetary policy and on the democratic founding of the Fed that explains its democratic device for prosperity.

Responsibility versus accountability

Responsibility means that the central bank, and not elected representatives, has the ultimate responsibility for monetary policy in society. On the other hand, accountability reveals a mutual dependency between agents and central banks. This link of confidence rests notably on the possibility of sanctioning the central bank (override procedure).

The democratic deficit of the ECB: an ineffective democratic accountability

'Accountability' appears only twice in the title of a speech of an ECB board member – once each in 1999 and 2001. Accountability is not a leading concern for the ECB, while 'transparency' is used intensively.

An ineffective parliamentary accountability

The ECB is accountable to the European Parliament in the procedure of 'quarterly monetary dialogue', but it is only a formal accountability. The Parliament can change neither the ECB's law nor its objectives or targets. It can neither remove the central bankers nor put a sanction on the ECB. There is no override procedure. It is an effective dialogue, but not an effective democratic accountability. 'Formal sanction mechanisms would be too blunt and would have potentially negative implications for the efficient fulfilment of the central bank's mandate' (ECB, 2002, p. 47).

The European Parliament has limited power, which consists in the ability to call the president and other members of the ECB board to discuss on EMU monetary policy (Art. 109b). The candidates for the ECB board must appear before the European Parliament prior to their appointment. The Parliament has the right to give an opinion on their appointment (Art. 11, ECB Charter), with the exception of the president. Consequently, only Executive Board members can be accountable to the Parliament. Yet since the Parliament has only a consultative role, it is accountability without power. As Buiter (1999, p. 23) puts it, what is required is 'a European Parliament with teeth'.

Ecofin with extended prerogatives could be an appropriate arrangement to reduce the democratic shortages of the ECB. It represents a fiscal government that could take part in a dialogue with ECB in order to elaborate a policy-mix and to avoid the restrictive bias of the Stability and Growth Pact.

A fascinating archetype of responsibility

The ECB has developed a peculiar way of building its legitimacy. It rests on two pillars: the belief in the neutrality of money in the long run; and technocracy. First of all, money does not really matter. Inflation is a monetary phenomenon, justifying the mandate on price stability. The best gift from monetary policy to the general public is price stability. With neutral money in the long run, full independence does not imply a democratic shortage, while monetary policy becomes only a technical problem: inflation. Second, central bankers are experts. They are wise people who have to be insulated from the short-sightedness of politicians. This explains its full independence and the rejection of democratic accountability. The ECB claims to be directly responsible to the general public at large, and not indirectly via elected representatives. This direct responsibility is justified by indirectly effective democratic accountability, which is counter-productive in its reduction of independence and its credibility. Direct responsibility to the public is an elegant way earning legitimacy without passing through the traditional legitimacy by democratic oversight or subservience to elected representatives. Parliamentary sanctions are replaced by a simple public scrutiny as a way earning legitimacy.

This is not a fair argument, for two reasons. First, it contradicts our representative democracies (a political body is generally indirectly responsible to the public, via its elected representatives). Second, the public does not have any direct legal or constitutional power over the ECB. The public cannot change the monetary policy orientation, even if it disagrees with it. The ECB is responsible for price stability and not accountable for its economic policy.

The ECB asserts that democratic accountability is unfeasible: the ECB is an unconventional supranational central bank; there is no government in the EU; and the European Parliament has not written the Treaty on the ECB. So the Parliament does not have the power to modify its Statute. From their own viewpoint, the ECB is only responsible to those who have voted for the Treaty – that is European citizens. For the ECB, accountability is nothing other than a duty of communication: 'Accountability is the legal and political obligation of the ECB to explain and justify its decisions to the citizens of Europe and their electoral representatives. Accountability is enhanced by a high degree of transparency' (ECB, 2002, p. 45).

Using credibility literature, the ECB justifies its doctrine of full independence cum responsibility through the principal–agent theory. In this delegation approach, the principal is the democratic authority (government or Parliament). However, the ECB's approach is based on political authority rejection, the public is the principal in the contract: 'A clearly defined mandate lies at the very heart of the aforementioned "contract" between the people and the independent central bank' (ECB, 2002, p. 50). The problem arises because the people did not write the Statute and did not give the mandate to the ECB. It explains why the ECB has a commitment to transparency and price stability, and not a commitment to a mandate as has the Fed. The people monitor the ECB's performance through the definition of price stability: 'It created a benchmark against which its performance can be assessed' (ECB, 2002, p. 50). But without any public sanction in case of non-fulfilment, the transparency on price stability does not confer a public legitimacy, it only 'imposes self discipline' (ECB, 2002, p. 61) on the ECB.

The Fed: effective democratic accountability

The Humphrey–Hawkins procedure produces an effective accountability with a double meaning. First, there is the subservience to potential sanctions for the central bank. Presentation of the Fed's president in Congress is an effective testimony for the Congress can abolish or remodel the Fed by a simple majority. Second, accountability has an economic effect: it has an impact on market participants' expectations. This communication reduces significantly uncertainty among financial markets (Kohn and Sack, 2003). The Humphrey–Hawkins procedure reveals that political pressure on monetary policy is oriented towards more accountability from the central bank, and not towards more over-expansionary policy (time inconsistency).

In the case of the Fed, accountability is the way that democratic authorities exercise their control over the independent body to which they delegated their power: 'Accountability is the critical mechanism for ensuring both that the central bank is operated in a way consistent with democratic ideals and that the central bank operates under incentives to meet its legislative mandate for monetary policy' (Meyer, 2000, p. 10).

The Fed has a democratic and institutional commitment to its mandate. Monetary policy is not rule-based on economic laws but is founded on democratic principles. However, the people do not elect central bankers directly. Legitimacy is not obtained by the ballot box, but by procedures of accountability: 'Such democratic accountability is even more important for central bankers, because the voting populace does not directly elect them' (Ferguson, 2002, p. 2). Realized by elected representatives, accountability acts as a transfer of democratic legitimacy. The Humphrey–Hawkins testimonies appear to be a procedural institutionalization of the Fed's legitimacy.

The ECB exercises its direct responsibility towards the public by monitoring its performance on the definition of price stability. It is radically different from the Fed, which is democratically accountable to Congress – which verifies the accordance with its mandate with no quantification or prioritization of the objectives.

The ECB's responsibility is to explain, enforce and justify the measures laid down to achieve its chosen targets. As for accountability, the Fed asks how the central bank remains subservient to elected representatives by respecting its mandate? Contrary to the ECB's assertions, accountability does not exist only to justify its action. In a representative democracy, accountability exists primarily to ensure the subservience of the central bank to the elected representatives.

The ECB favours responsibility – that is, a purely consultative political accountability. It has an economic mandate derived from the neutrality of money that allows for a direct responsibility to the public: the ECB is a creature of central bankers. In contrast, the Fed practices an effective democratic accountability to the public indirectly, via the elected representatives: the Fed is a creature of the Congress.

Common knowledge versus common understanding

Both the ECB and the Fed have had their revolutions, which underline the importance of uncertainty. Because central banks evolve in an environment of uncertainty, strict rules are irrelevant and monetary policy acknowledges 'the role of judgmental inputs' (Issing *et al.*, 2001, p. 32). Furthermore, both alleged that the 'true' model underlying the rule has also disappeared: 'a straightforward selection of the "best" if not the "true", reference model becomes a matter of faith' (Issing *et al.*, 2001, p. 40). Common knowledge becomes undefined, even with rational expectations.

This turning point of uncertainty and discretion could be the reason for the movement from secrecy to communication and transparency: 'the need for transparency is also linked to the large degree of uncertainty that characterises monetary policy' (Issing *et al.*, 2001, p. 128). Hence, central bank communication is a consequence of Keynes' radical uncertainty. The more uncertainty there is, the more the rule is unfeasible because it is undiscoverable. There is a certain scope of discretion (choice of the best model) in monetary policy; and discretion makes communication indispensable to the central bank:

> Strict adherence to rules solves the problem of communication and transparency to the extent that it does not allow for any discretion or personal influence to be brought to bear in the decision and its communication. Conversely, the public's need for information increases with the level of discretion exercised in the monetary policy decision. (Issing, 2005, p. 69)

Nevertheless, the Fed and the ECB do not put an emphasis on the same kind of uncertainty. The ECB speaks of an uncertainty regarding the appropriate model of the economy, favouring transparency, but the Fed is more concerned about unpredictable shocks that require flexibility and communication.

ECB: paradoxes of common knowledge

Although everyone knows the ECB has a strategy of transparency, nobody understands it. The paradox is that a transparent focal point does not automatically lead to the agent's co-ordination. It reveals the limits of the transposition from the Buba's model of co-ordination. The Buba's strategy of co-ordination with financial market participants seems to be outdated.

Monetary policy is no longer regarded as a non-cooperative game with agents, where common knowledge intends to implement a complete environment of perfect information in order to co-ordinate agents. Furthermore, the ECB pretends to make monetary policy a benchmark or a salient point for financial market participants in uncertainty by making policy transparent. It tries to create an environment of rational expectations.

This co-ordination of the common knowledge process does not work, for two main reasons:

(i) The salient strategy does not automatically serve as a benchmark, as it is not always understood: transparency is not a sufficient condition; and
(ii) It neglects the expectations formation process: the latter is not a question of induction from information, or anchorage from a focal point – rather, it is an interpretation and conviction process resulting from explanation.

Since the ECB focuses on monetary transmission channels and not expectations channels, communication is not an important side of monetary policy. Communication is only the need for transparency: you are supposed to 'say what you do and do what you say'.

A rule-like monetary policy strategy

It is difficult to make the ECB's two ideas compatible: uncertainty on the model of the economy; and transparency – that is, disclosure of the ECB's model, which defines the systematic character of the policy. Despite its cautions, the solution is that the ECB follows the Friedman–Lucas model of the economy that justifies price stability as a unique goal:

> price stability is unambiguously assigned overriding importance. This provision reflects a broad consensus existing in the economic discipline that the maintenance of price stability is the appropriate objective of monetary policy. The consensus is rooted in the belief that monetary policy makes its best contribution to overall economic welfare by maintaining price stability. (Issing, 2001, p. 7)

We shed light on the lack of robustness of such a 'divine coincidence' between inflation stabilization and output stabilization promoted by the price stability strategy.

There is one type of uncertainty that central bankers should reduce with communication: the uncertainty they create themselves. The ECB's communication does not explain strategy and tactics in a convincing manner. It sends conflicting signals (noise) rather than co-ordinating signals (a focal point). This lack of understanding can be seen through an indicator such as the volatility of the short-term interest rate. Gros *et al.* (2000) find that both actual and implied volatility is higher in the eurozone than in the USA. There are many possible reasons for this misunderstanding: a problem of institutional design, of policy framework, or a lack of clarity in the communication strategy.

This poor perception of the ECB's communication is well documented. In a survey by Goldman Sachs in 2000 and Reuters in 2001 on the understanding of central bank rationale for policy action, the ECB came out badly. The conclusion seems straightforward: 'the ECB is widely perceived as non-transparent' (De Haan and Amtenbrink, 2002).

The ECB itself admits the weakness of its communication (Hämäläinen, 2001). Issing (2000) also recognizes that there is a 'communication gap': 'the overall perception of the ECB by the public, academics, financial analysts, market participants, and not least, journalists continues to remain – at best – rather mixed'.

Communication: information versus explanation

Issing defines communication as 'a specific language used to explain to the public, on the basis of the strategy, the bank's assessment of current and expected developments and the reasoning behind policy decisions' (Issing *et al.*, 2001, p. 45). More generally, he presents communication as the 'hidden pillar' of ECB strategy. It is not in accordance with the current fashion of putting emphasis on clarity and 'communications strategy'. This third pillar should be structured, and open to discussion, not hidden.

Fully independent, the ECB can benefit from communication restricted to transparency. Nevertheless, the ECB (Issing *et al.*, 2001, p. 39) makes a critical appraisal of the Fed's communication. It considers that the Fed has a secret strategy that is counter-productive (and even perilous) for central bank credibility, since it depends on the president's personality. The Fed does not have an explicit nominal anchor, but a personal anchor: the Chairman – Greenspan.

The Fed: monetary policy as a deliberative process

For the Fed, monetary policy is a 'deliberative process' (Ferguson, 2002, p. 4) between the central bank and agents. The Fed's influence on expectations is defined as a 'discussion' (Kohn, 2005, p. 3) or a 'conversation' (Goodfriend, 2004, p. 16). The Fed's communications strategy intends to 'improve the public's understanding' (Kohn, 2005, p. 1). The Fed demonstrates that the expectations channel and communications strategy are intimately related. But the Fed puts priority on action. Communication is not a goal per se, it is aimed at enhancing action: 'Actions speak louder than words', but 'actions and words likely speak louder than actions alone' (Thornton, 2002, pp. 11–12).

The 'quiet revolution' of the Fed in the 1990s: the dual mandate

The Fed underwent a 'quiet revolution' in the 1990s. The turning point was around 1994. First, the Fed began to reveal its action in real-time. Second, it started to implement a fully explicit interest policy (Goodfriend, 2004, p. 16). Third, there was the 'Jackson Hole incident', when Blinder broke the 'Secret of the Temple'. Blinder simply announced publicly that Greenspan was following the dual mandate, and that he was a hawk not only on inflation, but also on employment. It was necessary to return to the democratic mandate of the Fed: Congress had imposed multiple goals without a hierarchy or quantitative numerical definitions. Abolishing the primacy of price stability, the Fed promoted this dual mandate. Common understanding is a critical issue, since the central bank does not perfectly control inflation. Communication is regarded as a framework and an instrument of monetary policy, as it intervenes in the expectations formation process. Numerous papers from the Fed demonstrate the efficiency of the combination between action and communication, open market and 'open mouth' operations. The latter are complementary tools in monetary policy (Gurkaynak *et al.*, 2004). The central bank cannot achieve its objectives without public support – that is, without convincing inflation expectations: 'We confirm a potentially important role for central bank communications to shape public expectations of future policy actions' (Bernanke *et al.*, 2004, p. 4).

Fed communication evolved in the 1990s, and in 1994, the policy decision was immediately announced to the public. In 1999/2000, the announcement of the policy decision was accompanied by the publication of a statement giving an explanation of the current decision, and an explanation of the forward-looking decision through the economic outlook, an assessment of the balance of risks and economic conditions in the 'foreseeable' future. It demonstrates that the timing, number, organization and content of meetings are key components of communication strategy. The Fed communication strategy permits markets to concentrate their attention on eight pre-set dates per year on which it announces its key policy rate. This system is often referred to as the Bank's fixed announcement dates, or simply fixed dates.

The 1999/2000 turning point also modified the process of forming market expectations. Before 1999, agents had to guess at future official rates during the inter-meeting periods, via speeches, testimonies, interviews or macroeconomic data. After 1999, agents were advised of future monetary policy at the time of the meeting through the Fed's communications strategy: immediate release, statement, economic outlook, balance of risks, and so on. This new communication framework also enhances the common understanding between the central bank and agents: 'not only do they have a larger effect on the level of interest rates if they are accompanied by an asymmetric assessment, but also the volatility induced by the FOMC [Federal Open Market Committee] meetings has been significantly lower since 1999. Third, market participants anticipate the next monetary policy decision earlier' (Ehrmann and Fratzscher, 2005, pp. 26–7).

Extensive and forward-looking explanations strengthen the transmission of monetary policy, reduce market participants' uncertainty and reduce transmission lags. The reason is that forward-looking information favours the common understanding of the path of future interest rates. With the expectations theory of the term structure, the Fed shapes the yield curve, thus enhancing and accelerating the linkage between short and long rates: the Fed has a stronger and earlier impact on the economy.

In contrast to the ECB, the Fed uses the expectations channel by giving no explicit nominal anchor, since there is no explicit inflation target. Inflation expectations amplify and accelerate the impact of the nominal interest rate on inflation via the real interest rate. Regarding the expectations channel, we can make the following comparison:

- The ECB tries to neutralize the inflation expectations channel. Compared with the Fed, the impact of the nominal interest decision is more certain, but lower and slower. The time frame of transmission is medium to long-term. It employs an *indirect* channel of transmission to inflation, passing through on output with a two-year lag.
- The Fed uses the expectations channel. The impact of the nominal interest rate decision is more uncertain but faster and stronger. The time-frame of transmission is short to medium-term. It employs a *direct* channel of transmission to inflation with a one-year lag.

Communications should contain relevant explanations – that is, the ability to make the central bank comprehensible to the general public. Comprehensive explanations presuppose three characteristics: explanations should be extensive, clear, and convey forward-looking information.

We need extensive explanations (justification, and motivation of central bank decisions) (Kohn and Sack, 2003, p. 29): 'Before I served on the Federal Reserve Board, I believed the Fed could and should offer much more by way of explanation. Now, having been there, I feel absolutely certain' (Blinder, 1999, p. 75). We move from 'Never explain, never excuse' to 'explaining more it is understanding better' (Ricoeur, 1985, p. 37).

Clear explanations could be defined as follows: 'The aspect of clarity suggests that information needs to be simplified, structured, and interpreted in order to be understood' (Winkler, 2002, p. 422). The public should be able to understand the short-term tactical change in the central bank's long-term strategy (Ferguson, 2002, p. 1). Explanations should be oriented towards the future, because financial markets are uncertain about the future of the economy.[4] Forward-looking explanations ('Policy inclination', 'Economic outlook') participate in the formation of expectations for the market.

Communications strategy: enhancing both efficiency and flexibility

Communication improves monetary policy efficiency and the public understanding of monetary policy, enabling the public to anticipate or react in line with the central bank. It tries to convince agents that the Fed is pursuing the right policy, and it ensures a common understanding. The Fed and agents share a similar representation of the future path of the economy. This common understanding simplifies the link between the Federal funds rate and the market-based long-run interest rate that has a strong effect on the economy. Central bank talk enhances monetary policy transmission. By increasing the speed of transmission, communication reduces one of the major problems of monetary policy – lags: 'Given that one of the limits on the effectiveness of monetary policy are the long lags between policy actions and their effect on aggregate demand, this anticipatory effect on long-term rates potentially speeds the effect of monetary policy and, in principle, can make it more effective' (Meyer, 2003, p. 21).

Uncertainty induces flexibility – that is, tactical deviations from the strategy. This means severe shifts in the direction or in the amplitude of interest rates (from 25 to 50 base points). Flexibility is feasible as soon as market participants understand and validate tactics by following the Fed. Otherwise, agents play a non-cooperative game with the central bank, which inhibits monetary policy efficiency: 'failing to communicate with the public does not create genuine policy flexibility but only reduces the potency and predictability of the effects of given policy actions' (Bernanke, 2004b, p. 8). By ensuring public understanding, communication allows for more flexibility. Open market and 'open mouth' operations are complementary. If the Fed uses flexible policy and communication, the ECB considers that expectations are anchored by rule-like systematic policy.

The opposition between the ECB and the Fed is connected to the leading transmission channel. The ECB defends prominent monetary transmission mechanisms. Common knowledge produces a commitment channel. The Fed, however, chooses the expectations channel. It needs a common understanding to achieve the inflation expectations management required to link the short-term official interest rate and the long-term market interest rate. The common understanding is that the Fed is a 'statue with feet of clay' that needs public support.

Transparency versus openness

ECB: the pitfalls of 'maximum transparency'

The ECB defines transparency as

> an environment in which the central bank provides in an open, clear and timely manner all relevant information on its mandate, strategy, assessments

> and policy decisions as well as its procedures to the general public and the markets. Transparency is ultimately about the genuine understanding by the public of the entire process of monetary policy-making. (ECB, 2002, p. 59)

The ECB associates transparency with efficiency, accountability, predictability and effectiveness. More generally, it is related to 'effective communication' (ECB, 2002, p. 59).

Transparency as 'real time' information

The ECB claims it is transparent because it gives its analysis and the reasoning for its decision in 'real time' – that is, immediately after its decision. It judges itself to be 'one of the most transparent central banks in the world' (Trichet, 2004, p. 9). The ECB states frankly: 'We mean what we say ... even if we have perhaps not always been entirely successful in saying what we mean' (Issing, 1999, p. 505). Transparency is honesty. It clarifies the underlying policy framework of its interest rate setting.

The refusal to be mysterious is connected to the quest of credibility. By showing a pragmatic monetarist model of the economy, the ECB attempts to improve both its reputation and its credibility. With transparency, the ECB wants to avoid time inconsistency – that is, surprise inflation. Previously, with monetarism, secrecy was aimed at reinforcing monetary policy efficiency with independence and surprise, but today, transparency aims at anchoring expectations by displaying a credible rule-like monetary policy.

It is generally agreed that old fashioned secrecy was a way for non-independent central bankers to free themselves from the government (Mishkin, 2004, p. 1). Transparency is the new means used by the ECB to increase its independence from elected representatives. Transparency is of the first importance for the ECB's legitimacy, and practically synonymous with accountability. Fully independent, the ECB (2002) does not benefit from democratic accountability: 'A high degree of transparency helps to ensure accountability to the public.' Direct responsibility to the public, through transparency, can be a substitute for democratic accountability to elected representatives.

Transparency does not mean understanding

In the literature, we find three kinds of criticisms about the ECB's communications. First, its explanations, through the two-pillars strategy, are unclear. Second, the ECB only communicates inflation while at the same time focusing on other objectives, such as growth. It is not transparent. Third, the ECB does not communicate enough with financial markets.

The first problem with the ECB is that transparency does not necessarily mean understanding its reasoning and the strategy behind its action: 'The Federal Reserve and the (old) Deutsche Bundesbank are clearly perceived as more transparent than the ECB' (De Haan *et al.*, 2004, p. 124). The significant efforts made towards communication and transparency provide some knowledge of the ECB but not really a better understanding. One explanation certainly rests on different models of thought. While the ECB maintains, generally speaking, a Friedman–Lucas synthesis, the agents are more worried about a better policy mix.

The second explanation is that the ECB communicates about a strategy built only on inflation, to ensure credibility. But its decisions also focus on growth and other objectives such as the exchange rate. On that score, the ECB is not transparent. Even Issing recognizes that full transparency is impossible, and prefers to talk about maximum transparency, which could be viewed as the folk wisdom of central banking: 'do what you do, but talk only about inflation' (Faust and Henderson, 2004). Communication is supposed to clarify, not to obscure the mandate and the strategy.

The ECB's transparency about its strategy could be seen as a technique of commitment to price stability only, and not a democratic device of explanation: 'The public announcement of a strategy effectively works as a formal commitment' (Issing *et al.*, 2001, p. 38). It appears that transparency is the new solution to credibility: the search for a credible commitment, enforcement or anchor.

The ECB defines predictability as 'the ability of the public to correctly anticipate the monetary policy decisions' (ECB, 2002, p. 65). The ECB pretends to anchor expectations through the predictability of its policy, both short- and long-term: 'Transparency is needed both in the longer run to create overall credibility and in the shorter run to ensure the smooth and efficient transmission of monetary policy' (Hämäläinen, 2001, p. 1). Predictability is a new version of rational expectations.

Generally, predictability exists when market participants can anticipate precisely the ECB's decision. At the time of decision, market rates or forecasts are close to the actions of the central bank. The ECB's predictability is found by internal research (Gaspar *et al.*, 2001), but external research is less conclusive about this evidence: 'In the case of the ECB, the market has had difficulty anticipating, at least in our calculations, – large changes and cuts in policy interest rates' (Ross, 2002, p. 24).

The ECB itself seems to recognize the pitfalls of its transparent communication. Real-time transparency generates a problem of communication frequency. During a press conference, Duisenberg (2001) indicated that:

> We have the impression that the bi-monthly meetings of the Governing Council also lead, every two weeks, to speculation in the markets and higher volatility in exchange rates and market interest rates than would be the case if we had a calmer rhythm of meetings ... We thought that it might inspire some calm in the markets if we made it known that a discussion in the media and the markets on the monetary policy stance will only take place once a month.

In November 2001 the ECB adopted a system of twelve pre-set dates per year on which to announce its key policy rate.

There is effective communication, but neither effective understanding nor effective conviction among agents. However, the ECB is a new and supranational central bank. Common understanding certainly requires a longer history. As a supranational institution, the ECB can easily become the scapegoat of national politicians and its insulation strengthens this propensity.

Fedspeak's revolution: from cryptic statements to openness

Reviewing the Fed literature, we note that communication or 'Fedspeak' (Bernanke, 2004a) is considered to be the key aspect of its policy framework. It is linked with effectiveness and democratic considerations:

> Openness is more than just useful in shaping better economic performance. Openness is an obligation of a central bank in a free and democratic society. U.S. elected leaders chose to vest the responsibility for setting monetary policy in an independent entity, the Federal Reserve. Transparency of our activities is the means by which we make accountable to our fellows citizens to aid them in judging whether we are worthy of our task. (Greenspan, 2001, p. 3)

Traditional central banking: 'Secrets of the Temple'

Previously, 'Fedspeak' corresponded to the enigmatic and esoteric art of the Fed. Greenspan is famous for his declaration in Congress in 1987: 'Since I have become a central banker, I have learned to mumble with great incoherence. If I seem unduly clear to you, you must have misunderstood what I said.' Nowadays, the Fed has changed: 'Fedspeak' means clear and extensive communication.[5]

In the 1990s the novelty of Greenspan's communication is less its accountability or transparency than what he explains: the dual mandate – that is, the respect of its democratic mandate. The appropriate term for the 'risk management paradigm' of Greenspan is 'openness'. This openness about the dual mandate is the cornerstone of Greenspan's Fed. This improvement in monetary policy is evident for Meyer (2003, p. 7):

> What is unique about the Greenspan vision is the synergy presumed between the two objectives: price stability and damping fluctuations around full employment. What is also unique is that the Chairman, based on this vision, is generally viewed as being a hawk when it comes to containing inflation and a dove when it comes to quickly providing support for a weakening economy. This is remarkable combination, politically as well as economically.

Transparency, openness, uncertainty and gradualism

Bernanke (2004a, p. 8) exposes the counter-productivity of full transparency:

> Other possibilities for improved transparency may exist. Importantly as we think about these, we should not simply take the view that more information is always better. Indeed, irrelevant or badly communicated information may create more noise than signal; and some types of information provision – an extreme example would be televising FOMC meetings – risk compromising the integrity and quality of the policy-making process itself.

Moreover, the Fed argues for limited transparency towards financial markets: 'This, of course, is not to say that a central bank will never surprise the market. As I mentioned earlier, the most important task of a central bank is to get monetary policy right. At times, getting policy right will involve taking action unexpected by the market – for example, in its timing and magnitude' (Ferguson, 2001, p. 5). Limited transparency points out the importance of independence towards financial markets, and not only on political authority, as in the case of ECB independence.

The Fed considers uncertainty as a fundamental element of monetary policy: 'Uncertainty is not just an important feature of the monetary policy landscape, it is the defining characteristic of that landscape' (Greenspan, 2003, p. 1).

Openness also concerns inflation targets. With the New Keynesians, the explanation of inflation moves from money to expectations. Money is no longer neutral. There is no natural rate of inflation. In accordance with Greenspan (2001, p. 2), the confidence paradigm considers inflation to be a phenomenon of expectation: price stability is 'when economic agents no longer take account of the prospective change in the general level price level in their economic decision-making ... By price stability, however, I do not refer to a single number as measured by a particular price index'. Greenspan prefers an implicit inflation target that gives flexibility to the policy mix. The implicit inflation target can be 2 per cent, 3 per cent or 4 per cent depending on circumstances.

The explicit reference value of the ECB (2 per cent inflation) is rule-like and generates a restrictive bias. Fixed targets generate rigidity in expectations that reduces the working margin of the monetary policy under unpredictable shocks. If there is a deviation from the target, volatility of inflation expectations will be very high, and the expectations anchorage will be broken. With unpredictable shocks, monetary policy is required and cannot be rule-based. But the Fed can be forecast-based, or forward-looking. The Fed assumes that this forecast-based approach leads to a pre-emptive policy making: 'pre-emption refers to the idea that policy-makers achieve better results when they act in advance to forestall developing problems' (Bernanke, 2004b, p. 6).

Theoretically, it is difficult simultaneously to sustain radical uncertainty and pre-emptive action. In the light of the 1995–2000 episode of the New Economy, it appears that pre-emptive action is very difficult. The Fed could not prevent the boom and bust of the New Economy, but its achievement of a soft landing was brilliant. Because the Fed uses the expectations channel intensively, the appropriate name for its strategy is 'pro-active'. Monetary policy is protracted by the expectations of agents.

The relationship between flexibility and activism is more complex than simply permanent shift of monetary policy orientation. Rough flexibility could lead to misinterpretation, and this misunderstanding could generate an excessive volatility in financial markets by adding uncertainty. Pro-active action requires a smoothing of the federal funds rate. This gradualism of the Fed is a commonplace in the literature. It moves its rate gradually in both amplitude (25 points generally; 50 points in special cases) and direction. Flexibility is slowly and intensively prepared and explained to markets. In the absence of shocks, there are only eight meetings a year, when Federal Open Market Committee (FOMC) can change the rate. Gradualism could have several explanations: the Taylor inflation–output variability trade-off; carefulness, with uncertainty about future developments of the economy; uncertainty about the channel of monetary policy; and to maintain the common understanding between the Fed and agents. Like pro-active action, activism is subservient to agent expectations. That is why gradualism is a more appropriate term to define the Fed strategy and tactics.

The Fed intends to foster the term 'structure of interest rates' via markets expectations. Shaping the yield curve means influencing the link between the Funds rate and long-run market rates. This formation process is not a matter of predicting Fed action, but rather of understanding it. Thornton (2002, p. 8) indicates that the transmission from the official to the market rates is determined solely by how long the policy rate is expected to stay at its new level, and not whether the policy action per se is anticipated.

The Fed's communications indicate future funds rate movements to market participants. The Fed rhetoric regarding a 'considerable period of time' or 'sufficient period of time' indicates that the Funds rate will stay at this level, or/and in this direction; it is not inertia. It allows market participants to understand the future amplitude and direction of the funds rate. This common understanding, through the expectations channel, has a quiet impact on the yield curve.

But the Fed can also lead its interest policy 'loudly'. A spectacular increase of the Funds rate of 50 base points is not a way to 'surprise' financial markets, but rather a signal: 'it wishes to get more attention for its actions' (Goodfriend, 2004, p. 17). It is part of the dialogue with financial markets, and the way that the Fed indicates to markets some stress on the economy.

Table 5.1 Credibility (ECB) versus confidence (Fed)

Institutional Design	**CREDIBILITY STRATEGY** **European Central Bank:** **a conservative central bank**	**CONFIDENCE STRATEGY** **The Fed:** **a democratic central bank**
Monetary policy strategy	• Cross-checking • Stability-orientated strategy • Medium-term orientated strategy	• Risk management paradigm • Balance of risks strategy (since 2000) • Interest rate policy (since 1994)
Credibility versus Confidence	• Quasi-unique mandate, primacy to price stability • Full independence • Transparency and commitment on price stability • Monetary order linked to an independent monetary Power	• Dual Mandate: 'goals of maximum employment, stable prices, and moderate long-term interest rates'. • Neither prioritization nor quantification of the objectives • Balancing independence, delegated power and now governance • Openness, accountability on its mandate • Monetary policy as a deliberative process
Independence versus Governance	• Creature of central bankers • Supranational bank • Goal (2%) and instrument independence	• Creature of Congress (Congress oversight) • Congress sets the goals. Federal Reserve Act (1977), the 'full employment and balanced growth act' (Humphrey~Hawkins Act) • Instrument independence
Responsibility versus Accountability	Responsible directly to the public • Judicial review (Art. 230–233) • Dismissal of members of the executive Board, 'compulsorily retired' by the Court of Justice of the European Community (Art. 11.4) • Annual report to the European Parliament (Art. 113(3)). Monetary dialogue with the European	Accountable to elected representatives • Congress has the power to overrule any interest rate decision made by the FOMC by passing a statute that the President will sign. • Congress can threaten to: – Change the structure of the Fed – Remove a governor

	Parliament. Quarterly hearings to the Committee on Economic and Monetary Affairs (Art. 113(3)) • Quarterly reports on the activities of the euro system • Rule 40a: 'Written questions to the ECB' by all members of European Parliament. • Definition of price stability is a yardstick against which the public can hold the ECB accountable • No effective accountability since the European Parliament cannot change central bank law or Mandate	– Specify particular qualifications for Board members – Alter the composition of the FOMC • Bi-annual hearings at Congress (Humphrey~Hawkins testimony) • Congressional report • The congress can demand accounting of policy by summoning the chairman, board members and reserve presidents to congressional hearings • Effective accountability since the Congress can change central bank law or mandate
Transparency versus Openness	• Monthly press conference (12/year) since 11/2001 (previously press releases every 2 weeks) • Annual Report, Monthly Bulletin, real-time information • No publication of the proceedings of the meetings (Art. 10.4) • The Governing Council may decide to make the outcome of its deliberation public (Art. 10.4) • No publication of voting records or verbatim records • No publication of internal inflation forecasts, but publication of staff macroeconomic projections 2/year (since December 2000)	• Immediate statement after each (8/year) scheduled meetings of the FOMC • Bi-annual report and monthly reports • Immediate public announcement of FOMC decision (since 1994) • Minutes of the FOMC published 3 weeks after the meeting since 2004 with votes and naming names (previously a little over 6 weeks) • Publication of detailed verbatim transcripts after 5 years • Regular speeches by the members to outside audiences • Publication of inflation and output forecasts (2/year)
Monetary policy committee	• The Governing Council has 18 members: – 6 from the Executive Board – 12 national central banks' governors and maximum 15 vote after the enlargement	• FOMC has 19 members but only 12 vote: – 7 from the board of Governors – 5 from regional central banks' presidents. Always New York's Fed that has responsibility for implementing decisions

Openness and democracy: a communicational central bank

A central bank practising openness in a democratic society could be defined as 'communicational';[6] that is to say, a central bank that tries to build a common understanding with the general public of its monetary policy decisions and actions. The central bank should try to convince agents:

> To the extent that it can explain its general approach, clarify its plan and objectives, and provide its assessment of the likely evolution of the economy, the central bank should be able to reduce uncertainty, focus and stabilise private sector expectations, and with intelligence, luck, and persistence develop support for its approach in policy-making. (Bernanke, 2004a, p. 4)

This debate refers to the strategy. The ECB has a communication gap because of a double inconsistency: first, between the mandate and the strategy, since agents consider that there is no possibility to reaching the legal hierarchical mandate with a unique mandate strategy; and second, between strategy and tactics, the ECB does not match explanations of the action (words, strategy) to observable action (deeds, tactics).

By contrast, the Fed is communicational. The openness displayed inside its 'balance of risks' strategy is regarded as being consistent with its dual mandate; and the openness produced by its clear explanations of its tactical movements are understood by agents to be part of the necessary flexibility of the strategy. Communications strategy is the keystone anchoring the agents' inflation expectations.

Conclusion

The confidence strategy of the Fed indicates a revival of politics in central banking. It is simply a reminder that the central bank is a creature of the democratic authorities that serve the public. Because central bankers are not elected by the public, they must be accountable to and under the control of elected representatives. The confidence strategy proposes to combine democracy and economy, principles and performances, communication and action (see Figure 5.1).

From a political perspective, the ECB is the result of the fascination with independence typical of the credibility literature in the 1980s (see Figure 5.2). Full independence from democratic authority is now an outdated way to build legitimacy. The solution of the ECB's democratic deficit does not pass through instrument or targeting rules such as the inflation targeting regime. The ECB should abandon the old tradition of avoiding accountability as has been pointed out by Milton Friedman: 'From revealed preference, I suspect that by far and away the two most important variables

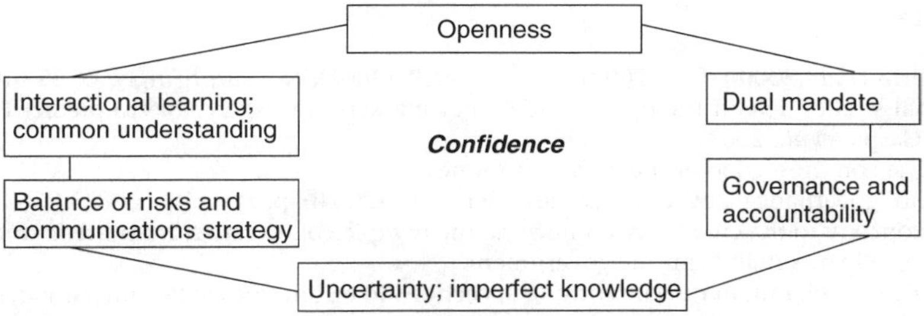

Figure 5.1 Confidence

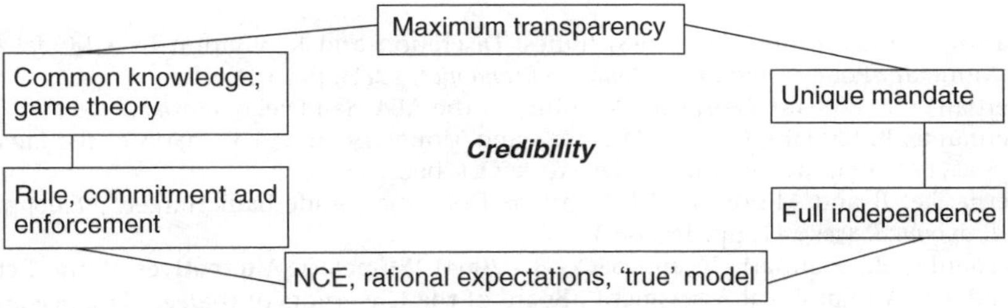

Figure 5.2 Credibility

in their loss function are avoiding accountability on the one hand and [to] achieve public prestige on the other.'

Credibility versus confidence appears to be useful for understanding the changes in monetary policy and the differences between the ECB and the Fed. Inflation targeting stands out as the dominant regime in monetary policy today, but only the middle-sized powers (New Zealand, Canada, Great Britain, for example) develop this policy, while the ECB and the Fed prefer to go their own way. The new ECB is a creature of central bankers and follows an out-of-date 'credibility strategy'. The ECB is a 'new Lady in old clothes' (the credibility literature of the 1980s). On the other hand, the Fed is a creature of Congress and has changed dramatically since 1994. The Fed's strategy of 'balance of risks' can be defined as an up-to-date 'confidence strategy'. These oppositions are connected to the leading channel of transmission of monetary policy. Today, the expectations channel becomes the dominant channel of monetary policy. However, on one hand, the ECB has evolved since its creation and is slowly getting closer to the regime of inflation targeting. On the other hand, the post-Greenspan period could see a modification in the policy of the Fed that moves it closer to flexible inflation targeting (Bernanke's wish). So a convergence of monetary policy regimes is possible in the near future.

Notes

1 Gros *et al.* (2000); Ross (2002); De Haan *et al.* (2004). Not surprisingly, ECB's internal studies defend the opposite idea that markets are largely able to predict ECB (Gaspar *et al.*, 2001).
2 The common good of the Buba was money.
3 On 'governance' at the Fed, see also Bernanke (2004b, p. 7).
4 Contrary to the credibility framework, the myopia comes rather from the financial participants than from the government.
5 'The Fed chairman now intends his speeches and testimonies to be understood, not misunderstood' (Blinder *et al.*, 2001, p. 73).
6 It is related to the communicational theory of J. Habermas.

References

Barro, R. and Gordon, D. (1983) 'Rules, Discretion and Reputation in a Model of Monetary Policy', *Journal of Monetary Economics*, 12(1), pp. 101–21.
Bernanke, B. (2004a) 'Fedspeak', Meetings of the AEA, San Diego, January.
Bernanke, B. (2004b) 'Central Bank Talk and Monetary Policy', Remarks at the Japan Society Corporate Luncheon, New York, October.
Bernanke, B and Mihov, I. (1997) 'What Does the Bundesbank Target?', *European Economic Review*, 41, pp. 1025–53.
Bernanke, B., Reinhart, V. and Sack, B. (2004) 'Monetary Alternatives at the Zero Bound: An Empirical Assessment', Board of the Governors of the Fed, Finance and Economics Discussion Series, 2004–48.
Blinder, A. (1996) 'Central Banking in a Democracy', *Federal Bank of Richmond Economic Quarterly*, 82(4), pp. 1–14.
Blinder, A. (1999) *Central Banking in Theory and Practice* (Cambridge, MA: MIT Press).
Blinder, A., Goodhart, C., Hildebrandt, P., Lipton, D. and Wyplosz, C. (2001) 'How Do Central Banks Talk?', *Geneva Reports on the World Economy*, No. 3, *Centre for Economic Policy Research,* London.
Buiter, W. (1999) 'Alice in Euroland', *Journal of Common Market Studies*, 37(2), pp. 181–209.
De Haan, J. and Amtenbrink, F. (2002), 'A Non-Transparent European Central Bank? Who Is to Blame?', A paper given at the conference on 'Monetary Policy Transparency' held at the Bank of England, May 10.
De Haan, J., Eijffinger, S. and Waller, S. (2004) *The ECB: Centralisation, Transparency and Credibility* (Cambridge, MA: MIT Press).
Duisenberg, W. (2001) 'Introductory Statement by Mr W. F. Duisenberg, President of the ECB', press conference, (ECB, accessed on www.ecb.int), Frankfurt am Main, November 8.
ECB (European Central Bank) (2002) *Monthly Bulletin,* November (also accessed on www.ecb.int).
Ehrmann, M. and Fratzscher, M. (2005) 'Transparency, Disclosure and the Federal Reserve', *ECB Working Paper*, no. 457.
Faust, J. (1996) 'Whom Can We Trust to Run the Fed? Theoretical Support for the Founders' View', *Journal of Monetary Economics*, 37, pp. 267–83.
Faust, J. and Henderson, D. W. (2004) 'Is Inflation Targeting Best-Practised Monetary Policy?', 28th annual economic policy conference 'Inflation Targeting: Prospects and Problems', Fed of Saint Louis, October 16.

Ferguson, R. (2001) 'Transparency in Central Banking: Rationale and Recent Developments', Remarks by Governor R. Ferguson before the National Economists Club and Society of Government Ecomomists, Washington DC, September.

Ferguson, R. (2002) 'Why Central Banks should Talk', Remarks by Vice Chairman R. Ferguson at the Graduate Institute of International Studies, Geneva, January.

Gaspar, V., Perez Quiros, G. and Sicilia, J. (2001) 'The ECB Monetary Strategy and the Money Market', *ECB Working Paper*, no. 69.

Goodfriend, M. (2004) 'The Monetary Policy Debate Since October 1979: Lessons for Theory and Practice', Conference on 'Reflections on Monetary Policy: 25 Years after October 1979', Fed of St. Louis, October.

Greenspan, A. (1996) 'The Challenge of Central Banking in a Democratic Society', Remarks by Chairman A. Greenspan at the Annual Dinner and Francis Bayer Lecture of the American Enterprise Institute for Public Policy Research, Washington DC, December.

Greenspan, A. (2001) 'Transparency in Monetary Policy', Remarks by Chairman A. Greenspan at the Federal Reserve bank of St Louis, St Louis, Missouri, October.

Greenspan, A. (2003) 'Monetary Policy under Uncertainty', Remarks at a symposium sponsored by the Federal Reserve Bank of Kansas City, August.

Gros, D., Davanne, O., Emerson, M., Mayer, T., Tabellini, G. and Thygensen, N. (2000), 'Quo Vadis Euro? The Cost of Muddling Through', 2nd Report of the Center for European Policy Studies Macroeconomic Group.

Gurkaynak, R., Sack, B. and Swanson, E. (2004) 'Do Actions Speak Louder than Words? Measuring the Response of Asset Prices to Monetary Policy Actions and Statements', Fed, Finance and Economics Discussion Series, no. 2004–66, September.

Habermas, J. (1987) *Théorie de l'Agir Communicationnel*, vol. 2 (Paris: Fayard).

Hämäläinen, S. (2001) 'The ECB's Monetary Policy – Accountability, Transparency and Communication', Conference on 'Old Age, New Economy and Central Banking', September.

Issing, O. (1999) 'The Eurosystem: Transparent and Accountable or Willem in Euroland', *Journal of Common Market Studies*, 37(3), pp. 503–19.

Issing, O. (2000) 'Communication Challenges for the ECB', Opening Statement at the Center for Financial Studies, Research Conference, Frankfurt, June 26.

Issing, O. (2001) 'The Euro Area and the Single Monetary Policy', Central Bank of the Republic of Austria, Working Paper, no. 44.

Issing, O. (2005) 'Communication, Transparency, Accountability: Monetary Policy in the Twenty-First Century', *Federal Bank of St Louis Review*, 87(2), pp. 65–83.

Issing, O., Gaspar, V. Angeloni, I. and Tristani, O. (2001) *Monetary Policy in the Euro Area. Strategy and Decision-Making at the European Central Bank* (Cambridge University Press).

Kohn, D. (2005) 'Central Bank Communication', Remarks by Governor Kohn at the Annual Meeting of the American Economic Association, Philadelphia, Pennsylvania, January.

Kohn, D. and Sack, P. (2003) 'Central Bank Talk: Does It Matter and Why?', Federal Reserve System, Finance and Economics Discussion Series, no. 2003–55, Washington, DC, May.

Kydland, F. and Prescott, E. (1977) 'Rules Rather Than Discretion: The Inconsistency of Optimal Plan', *Journal of Political Economy*, 85(3), pp. 473–92.

Le Heron, E. and Carré, E. (2005) 'Credibility versus Confidence in Monetary Policy', in Randall Wray and Mathew Forstater (eds) *Money, Financial Instability and Stabilization Policy* (Aldershot: Edward Elgar).

Mankiw, G. (2001) 'U.S. Monetary Policy during the 1990s'; Conference on 'Economic Policy during the 1990s, Kennedy School of Government, June.

McCallum, B. T. (1995) 'Two Fallacies Concerning Central Bank Independence', *American Economic Review*, 85(2), pp. 207–11.

Meyer, L. (2000) 'The Politics of Monetary Policy: Balancing Independence and Accountability', Remarks by Governor L. Meyer, at the University of Winsconsin, October.

Meyer, L. (2003), 'Practical Problems and Obstacles to Inflation Targeting', Conference on 'Inflation Targeting: Prospects and Problems', Fed of Saint Louis, October.

Mishkin, F. (2004) 'Can Central Bank Transparency Go Too Far?', Reserve Bank of Australia's Conference on 'The Future of Inflation Targeting', Sydney, August.

Persson, T. and Tabellini, G. (1993) 'Designing Institutions for Monetary Stability', *Carnegie Rochester Conference Series on Public Policy*, no. 39, pp. 53–84.

Ricoeur, P. (1985) *Philosophie et Sociologie. Histoire d'une Rencontre* (Centre des Mouvements Sociaux, Paris: EHESS).

Rogoff, K. (1985) 'The Optimal Degree of Commitment to an Intermediate Monetary Target', *The Quarterly Journal of Economics*, 100(4), pp. 1169–90.

Ross, K. (2002) 'Market Predictability of ECB Monetary Policy Decisions: A Comparative Examination', *IMF Working Paper*, no. 02/233.

Scheller, H. (2004) *The European Central Bank. History, Role and Functions*, No. 51000, (Frankfurt am Main: ECB).

Svensson, L.E.O. (1997) 'Optimal Inflation Targets, Conservative Central Banks and Linear Inflation Contracts', *American Economic Review*, 87(1), pp. 98–114.

Thornton, D. (2002) 'Monetary Policy Transparency: Transparent About What?', Conference on 'Monetary Policy Transparency', Bank of England, May.

Trichet, J. C. (2004) 'Issues in Monetary Policy: Views from the ECB', Speech at the Economic Club of New York, April.

Walsh, C. (1995) 'Optimal Contracts for Central Bankers', *American Economic Review*, 85(1), pp. 150–67.

Winkler, B. (2002) 'Which Kind of Transparency? On the Need for Effective Communication in Monetary Policy-Making', München: *IFO-Studien*, No. 3, pp. 401–28.

6
The Case for Fiscal Policy

Philip Arestis and Malcolm Sawyer

The case for fiscal policy and for governments to manipulate on their budgets as appropriate with the specific objective of achieving high levels of employment arises from Kaleckian and Keynesian propositions. Put simply, the latter argue that no market mechanisms are in place to ensure that the level of aggregate demand is sufficient for high levels of economic activity (Kalecki, 1939; Keynes, 1936). Even so, many lines of argument have been developed to the effect that budget deficits and fiscal policy are ineffectual and/or have undesired (and undesirable) effects. Indeed, a great deal of work has been undertaken recently on the significance of fiscal consolidation. Countries only have to balance their budgets, run surpluses during the upswing, and expansion is in place (we have rehearsed and rejected many of these arguments in Arestis and Sawyer, 2003).

It often turns out (as argued in Arestis and Sawyer, 2004) that such analysis is conducted within a framework, which essentially assumes full employment (and hence no insufficiency of private aggregate demand). A similar view can be expressed with regard to the empirical estimation of fiscal policy when conducted in the context of a model that embeds a supply-side equilibrium (such as the non-accelerating inflation rate of unemployment – NAIRU) and some adjustment mechanism, which leads the economy to that supply-side equilibrium. An alternative perspective on the effects of fiscal policy comes from considering budget deficits from what may be termed a 'functional finance' perspective (following the terminology of Lerner, 1943; see also Forstater, 1999). In this approach, budget deficits are used to offset what would otherwise be an insufficiency of aggregate demand (relative to some desired level such as that consistent with full employment). In the 'functional finance' literature there is a general presumption that private aggregate demand is likely to be insufficient rather than excessive. However, the key notion of the 'functional finance' approach is that the budget position should be aimed at securing the desired level of economic activity, and from that perspective a budget surplus would arise when private aggregate demand was deemed to be excessive (or equivalently, when private savings are less than private investment). Budget deficits are to be used in the 'functional finance' approach when there is an *ex ante* excess of private savings over private investment. In the event that the government does not permit a budget deficit, then the Keynesian multiplier comes into operation in a deflationary direction: income falls to reduce savings to bring *ex post* savings into line with investment (which itself may be affected by declining income). The intended savings can only occur if there is a budget deficit to absorb then, and hence there are no particular difficulties for the budget deficit to be funded. In an open economy, the current account deficit provides a capital account inflow and in that sense additional savings.

The starting point for the approach here is that the effects of fiscal policy and budget deficits should be examined in the context of insufficient private aggregate demand in that the 'functional finance' approach would not advocate budget deficits in a situation of excessive private aggregate demand. The chapter starts with a number of general observations on the effectiveness of fiscal policy, which is followed by a 'functional finance' perspective that views the role of fiscal policy in terms of raising the level of aggregate demand, where it would otherwise be too low relative to what is required to achieve the desired level of economic activity. It puts forward the view that the arguments, which have been deployed against fiscal policy to the effect that it does not raise the level of economic activity, do not apply when a 'functional finance' view of fiscal policy is adopted. Two further sections complete the story: in the fourth section we discuss the possibility of fiscal policy crowding out private expenditure through its impact on interest rates, and in the fifth section a discussion of the possibility of fiscal policy crowding out private expenditure through the operation of supply-side equilibrium. A summary and conclusions section puts the argument in perspective.

Fiscal policy is effective

The general case for the use of fiscal policy and for the government budget to be 'unbalanced' (rather than in balance over some specified period of time) arises essentially from the proposition that there are no automatic market forces, which ensure a level of demand consistent with a high level of economic activity. This is a Kaleckian/Keynesian proposition relating to both the short and the long run – that is, the issue of insufficient aggregate demand is not merely one of the short run and remains an underlying problem of market economies. The proposition can be stated in a number of ways. It can, for example, be stated as a rejection of the proposition associated with Say's Law that 'supply creates its own demand'. It can be expressed in terms of *ex ante* savings and *ex ante* investment and the lack of reasons as to why equality between them would be consistent with a level of economic activity.

The main arguments that have been used against fiscal policy come from the opposing view, namely that there are factors which do ensure sufficient levels of demand to ensure high levels of economic activity. One of the major theoretical arguments as to how aggregate demand will adjust to ensure a high level of supply has come from the operation of the real balance effect (the Pigou effect): low demand generates falling prices and a rising real value of the money stock and wealth, which stimulates aggregate demand. This continues until the level of aggregate demand is (eventually) brought into line with the supply-side equilibrium. In many macroeconomic models, the level of demand has been represented by the real value of the stock of money, and in that way the Pigou effect has been given a central role, since the real value of the stock of money increases as prices decline.

But it is well known (at least since Kalecki, 1944c) that the real balance effect relies on 'external' money with net worth to the private sector and to the stock of money remaining unchanged in the face of price changes. In a world of largely bank credit money, the amount of 'external' money is relatively small: for example, in the UK, the ratio of M0 to GDP is less than 4 per cent; a price fall of 10 per cent would increase real value of M0 by the equivalent of 0.4 per cent. With a wealth effect on consumption of the order of 0.02 to 0.05 (OECD, 2000, p. 192), aggregate demand would change by the order of 0.01 per cent (for a decline of 10 per cent in the price level). As prices fall, the demand for M0 would fall and hence the stock of M0 would also fall. The empirical relevance of the real balance effect has long been doubted (though it continues to make an appearance in many macroeconomic models, notably those of a new Keynesian form).

There are strong reasons to doubt the theoretical relevance of the Pigou effect as well. When money is treated as endogenous credit money, then the stock of money is determined by the demand for money, and money does not constitute net worth. If prices were then to fall, then the demand for money would decline, and so would the stock of money, and hence the Pigou effect would not be operational. Further, since money in the form of bank deposits is an asset for its holders, it is a liability for the banks, and hence again there is no net worth for the Pigou effect to 'bite on'. Indeed, we can go further and argue that when money is endogenous, a decline in prices would have an adverse effect on those who have taken out loans (the real value of which has risen), which may well undermine rather than increase aggregate demand. Hence the theoretical reasons for the stock of money influencing the level of aggregate demand disappear.

Another adjustment mechanism to raise aggregate demand in line with supply, which is postulated, relates to the operation of interest rate policy by the central bank. In effect, if the central bank can set the policy interest rate at a level from which aggregate demand would be equal to available supply, or equivalently *ex ante* savings were equal to *ex ante* investment, then the problem is solved.

The adoption by the central bank of something akin to Taylor's rule would envisage the policy interest rate being varied in response to the rate of inflation and to the output gap. There are two particularly significant elements of this approach for our discussion of fiscal policy. The first is that this approach envisages that there is a supply-side equilibrium level of economic activity, and that the level of aggregate demand can be adjusted through interest rate changes to correspond to that equilibrium level of economic activity. The 'equilibrium' rate of interest is then seen to be that which bring aggregate demand in line with available supply (and a constant rate of inflation), and this 'equilibrium' rate of interest corresponds to a Wicksellian 'natural rate of interest'. This is particularly evident in the 'new consensus in macroeconomics' represented in the following equations:

$$Y_t^g = a_0 + a_1 Y_{t-1}^g + a_2 E_t(Y_{t+1}^g) - a_3[R_t - E_t(p_{t+1})] + s_1 \quad (1)$$

$$p_t = b_1 Y_t^g + b_2 p_{t-1} + b_3 E_t(p_{t+1}) + s_2 \quad (2)$$

$$R_t = (1 - c_3)[RR^* + E_t(p_{t+1}) + c_1 Y_{t-1}^g + c_2(p_{t-1} - p^T)] + c_3 R_{t-1} + s_3 \quad (3)$$

with $b_2 + b_3 = 1$, where Y^g is the output gap, R is nominal rate of interest, p is rate of inflation, p^T is inflation rate target, RR^* is the 'equilibrium' real rate of interest – that is, the rate of interest consistent with zero output gap which implies from Equation (2) a constant rate of inflation, s_i (with $i = 1, 2, 3$) represents stochastic shocks, and E_t refers to expectations held at time t. Equation (1) is the aggregate demand equation with the current output gap determined by past and expected future output gap and the real rate of interest. Equation (2) is a Phillips curve with inflation based on current output gap and past and future inflation. Equation (3) is a monetary-policy Taylor's rule.

However, doubts may be raised as to whether feasible variations in the rate of interest are sufficient to equate savings and investment at a high level of income. There are constraints on the extent to which interest rates can be varied (whether for reasons akin to a liquidity trap in operation, which prevent the reduction of interest rates below a particular level or for foreign exchange considerations) and there are doubts relating to the potency of interest rates to influence aggregate demand (see Arestis and Sawyer, 2004). Further, there are constraints on domestic interest rates arising from foreign exchange rate considerations and the world level of interest rates.

The second implication is that the adjustment process whereby aggregate demand is brought into line with aggregate supply does not arise from a market mechanism (such as changes in price leading to changes in real value of money supply and then changes in the level of demand), but rather rate of interest changes arising from acts of government (albeit in the form of the actions of the central bank). That consideration should immediately raise the question of the relative effectiveness of alternative policy instruments, and in this context the clearest alternative (or may be complement) to monetary policy is fiscal policy.

Fiscal policy and 'Functional Finance'

The general approach to fiscal policy, which is adopted in this chapter, is what may be termed 'Functional Finance' (Lerner, 1943). The general proposition is that the government budget position should be used to influence the level of economic activity in the economy, and specifically that a budget deficit should be used to shore up demand when there would otherwise be a low level of demand (and a budget surplus used to damp down demand when it would otherwise be excessive). Lerner (1943) put the case for Functional Finance (capitalized in the original), which 'rejects completely the traditional doctrines of "sound finance" and the principle of trying to balance the budget over a solar year or any other arbitrary period' (p. 355). 'Functional Finance' supports the important proposition that total spending should be adjusted to eliminate both unemployment and inflation.

In a similar vein, Kalecki (1944a) argued that sustained full employment 'must be based either on a long-run budget deficit policy or on the redistribution of income' (p. 135). Kalecki based his argument on the assumption that there would be a tendency for the level of aggregate demand to fall short of what was required for full employment. Then there was a need for either a budget deficit to mop up the difference between full employment savings and investment, or for full employment savings to be reduced through a redistribution of income (from rich to poor).

He also argued that 'although it has been repeatedly stated in recent discussion that the budget deficit always finances itself – that is to say, its rise always causes such an increase in incomes and changes in their distribution that there accrue just enough savings to finance it – the matter is still frequently misunderstood' (Kalecki, 1944b). He then set out for a closed economy the equality:

$$G + I = T + S \tag{2.1}$$

(where G is government expenditure, T tax revenue, I investment expenditure, and S savings) and hence:

$$G - T = S - I \tag{2.2}$$

which can be readily modified for the open economy as:

$$G + I + X = T + S + Q \tag{2.3}$$

where X stands for exports and Q for imports.

From this perspective, the budget deficit is to be used to mop up the 'excess' of private savings over investment, and the counterpart budget surplus used when investment expenditure exceeds savings (at the desired level of economic activity). It is, of course, the case that the private savings (in excess of private investment) can only in fact occur if the government runs a budget deficit. The alternative is that private savings decline (through a decline in income) until savings and investment are equal.

It follows, though, that a budget deficit is not required when there is a high level of private aggregate demand such that investment equals savings at a high level of economic activity (and a surplus would be required when investment exceeds savings at the desired level of economic activity). This can be expressed by saying that the government budget position should be set so that:

$$G - T = S(Y_f) - I(Y_f) + Q(Y_f) - X(WY) \tag{2.4}$$

where Y_f is the intended level of income (which may be thought of as equivalent to full employment or to some supply-side constraint), WY is world income (which is taken as given for the purposes of $G - T$ equation). A tendency for savings to run ahead of investment leads to the view that a budget deficit is required (in the absence of any tendency for a balance of trade surplus). But it is a shortfall of investment over savings that creates the requirement for a budget deficit: in the absence of any such shortfall (in *ex ante* terms) there is no need for a budget deficit. The analysis of budget deficits should then be undertaken in a context that at least allows for the emergence of an excess of (*ex ante*) savings over (*ex ante*) investment. In the absence of any such excess, the 'Functional Finance' view would not see any cause for a budget deficit.[1]

The case for fiscal policy rests on the proposition that there is no reason to think that the right-hand side of Equation (2.4) would equal zero. When the right-hand side is positive, then there is the requirement of a budget deficit. At the same time, this means the budget deficit can always be funded, since there is a surplus available (equivalent to the right-hand side of Equation 2.4) to fund the budget deficit. This can be summarized by saying that when a budget deficit is required, then by definition the funds to cover it will also be available. Any difficulties that might arise do not come from the budget deficit, but they may come from any current account deficit that might be involved (that is, $Q(Y_f) - X(WY) > 0$). In such circumstances it appears that the budget deficit is, in effect, funded (in part) by borrowing from abroad (to an amount equivalent to the current account deficit). But here the key problem should be seen as being that there would be a current account deficit at the income level Y_f rather than one to be identified with the budget deficit.

If there were some automatic tendency, as, for example, expressed in Say's Law, for that equality to be assured, then any case for fiscal policy in the form of unbalanced budgets would disappear. Further, if the relevant rate of interest can be manipulated through monetary policy is such a way as to ensure this equality, then again there would be little room for fiscal policy. The basic Keynesian (Kaleckian) argument is that there is no assurance that this equality will be satisfied, and hence a need for fiscal policy and for an unbalanced budget.

The general presumption of Keynesians and others has been that there is likely to be a deficiency of *ex ante* investment relative to *ex ante* savings, rather than the reverse. This does not rule out that there will be occasions (as in the late 1990s in the UK and the USA, with conditions of low unemployment) when investment runs ahead of savings. In the former case, a budget deficit is required to mop up the excess savings, while in the latter case a budget surplus results. However, the presumption that budget deficits are the more frequent outcome under the use of 'Functional Finance' does raise the problem of cumulative budget deficits and rising government debt. Lerner (1943) and others acknowledged this possibility but saw that 'No matter how much interest has to be paid on the debt, taxation must not be applied unless it is necessary to keep spending down to prevent inflation. The interest can be paid by borrowing still more' (p. 356). Lerner (1943) summarized the answers to arguments against deficit spending by saying that the national debt does not have to keep on increasing, and that even if it does, the interest does not have to be paid from current taxes. Further, interest payments on bonds are an internal transfer.

The use by the government of budget deficits to sustain aggregate demand raises the issue of the sustainability of continuing budget deficits. A frequently heard argument against the use of budget deficits is that they cannot be sustained. Here we argue that, when budget deficits are approached from a 'Functional Finance' perspective, budget deficits are indeed sustainable. The growth of government debt B is given by $dB/dt = D + rB$, where D is the primary budget deficit and r the rate of interest on government debt (this rate of interest would be somewhat below the rate of interest on government bonds since some part of the government debt is base money). The rate of change of the debt to income ratio is then given by $d(B/Y)/dt = D/B + r - g = d/b + r - g$, where g is the rate of growth of income Y, $d = D/Y$ and $b = B/Y$. For a given primary budget deficit (relative to income), the debt-to-income ratio would stabilize at $b = d/(g - r)$, which requires $g > r$. Note that in this formula, g and r can either be both in real terms or both in nominal terms, and that the relevant interest rate is the post-tax rate on government bonds.[2] As Lerner (1943), Domar (1944) and others established, a permanent primary budget deficit could be sustainable provided that the growth rate exceeds the interest rate.

However, it is the total budget deficit, including interest payments, that is relevant in the sense that it is that type of budget deficit that 'mops up' excess private savings. For a given total budget deficit (relative to income), the debt-to-income ratio stabilizes at $b = (d + br)/g$. In this context, the budget deficit is always sustainable in the sense that the debt-to-income ratio stabilizes rather than continues to grow indefinitely, provided that nominal growth is positive. It can be noted that the primary budget position may be in surplus though the total budget is in deficit in light of the interest payments. Further, when there is inflation, the budget deficit in nominal terms overstates the deficit in real terms to the extent of the decline in the value of the government debt.[3] Whenever the relevant budget deficit is the overall one, there is not (in the absence of negative nominal growth) a sustainability issue for the overall deficit.

The argument is also put that, if the government debt to GDP ratio rises, then the private sector becomes satiated with public debt and is unwilling to absorb more. This, it is argued, would also lead to a rising interest rate of government bonds as the government continues to borrow and has to persuade the private sector to accept the increasing debt. However, consider the implications of a private sector satiated with public debt – it would imply that private savings and private investment are in balance, and the private sector does not have savings it wishes to lend to the public sector. But if (*ex ante*) savings and investment are in line with each other, there is no insufficiency of aggregate demand, and no requirement for a budget deficit.

Fiscal policy is often viewed in terms of the determination of government expenditure and taxation as undertaken without specific regard to the state of private aggregate demand. The 'crowding out' argument after all assumes that there is something to be crowded out. That approach to fiscal policy suggests either that fiscal policy has no effect on the level of economic activity (since there is crowding out) or that there is a positive link between government expenditure (budget deficit) and the level of economic activity. The investigation of fiscal policy through the means of simulation of macroeconometric models is concerned (usually) with the question of what happens if government expenditure is increased, other things being equal. The results of such simulations, generally, suggest that an increase in government expenditure does have a positive effect on the level of economic activity (Arestis and Sawyer, 2003). Indeed, in the context in which these simulations are undertaken, it is somewhat surprising that positive results are obtained, since such macroeconometric models generally build in a variety of ways by which there would be crowding out – the most notable being the imposition of some form of supply-side equilibrium, usually in the form of a NAIRU, along with a mechanism that steers the economy towards that equilibrium position. If the economy operates around the supply-side equilibrium, there is, by definition, little room for manoeuvre, and indeed little need for a fiscal policy.

The approach to fiscal policy just described is not one that underlies the approach of this chapter. Indeed, we would argue that this approach has been implicit in most recent discussions of fiscal policy and 'crowding out', but does not correspond to the way in which fiscal policy should be viewed. The effects of fiscal policy (especially when it takes the form of a budget deficit) from a 'Functional Finance' perspective start from the position that budget deficits are applied when there would otherwise be a deficiency of aggregate demand (below that required for the target level of economic activity), and conversely, budget surpluses applied when there would otherwise be an excess of aggregate demand. This is not to say that fiscal policy has always (or even usually) been applied in this manner. But it *is* to argue that fiscal policy and its effects should be evaluated against this background. The evaluation of fiscal policy should not start from the presumption that there would otherwise be adequate effective demand in that all would agree that, in the context of adequate private effective demand, there is no requirement for budget deficits.

We now address two particular sets of arguments which have generally appeared under the heading of 'crowding out', to the effect that fiscal policy will be ineffective.

Crowding out mark 1: interest rates

Within the framework of the *IS–LM* analysis, a partial 'crowding-out' was seen to come from to a rise in interest rates following a fiscal expansion which shifted the *IS* curve outwards. This was based on the assumption that the money supply was exogenous and fixed by the government (or the central bank), and that the interest rate equalled the demand for and supply of money. In that context, though, it was recognized that a sufficient increase in the stock of money alongside an increase in government expenditure could prevent a rise in the interest rate, and allow the full effect on the level of economic activity of the increase in government expenditure to come through.

This argument relies on the view that monetary policy (in the form of an increase in the stock of money) does not accommodate fiscal policy, and that investment and other forms of private expenditure are sensitive to the rate of interest. It is also the case that this argument assumes that the stock of money is determined exogenously (outside the private sector). It is clear that in industrialized economies, most of what is counted as money takes the form of credit money (bank deposits). In this context, the stock of money is eventually determined by the demand for money, and the level of interest rates is not set by the interaction of the supply and demand for money, as discussed above.

Further, monetary policy no longer takes (if it ever did) the form of making changes to the stock of money (or even of targeting the rate of change of the stock of money) but rather takes the form of the setting of some key interest rate (for example, Federal Funds rate; 'repo' rate). In the context of endogenous credit money with the key interest rate set by the central bank, 'crowding out' through the operation of monetary policy would arise from the deliberate actions of the central bank. That is to say, if the central bank (presumably operating on an 'independent' basis) responds to a fiscal expansion by raising interest rates (say, on the grounds that fiscal expansion created inflationary pressures), then there would be some form of crowding out (in so far as an increase in interest rates reduces private expenditure). Its extent would depend on the size of the interest rate rise, its feed through to other interest rates, the interest rate responsiveness of expenditure, and the phase of the business cycle. The key point here is that any 'crowding out' depends on the responses of the monetary authorities: it does not occur through the response of the markets. In the short run, at least, with the key interest rate set by the central bank, any 'crowding out' comes from the discretionary actions of the central bank. The effect of a budget deficit on the general level of interest rates then depends on the reactions of the central bank to the budget deficit (or more generally, to changes that are stimulated by the budget deficit). A 'conservative' central bank that viewed a budget deficit as being to some degree inflationary (whether through a direct effect on inflation or through stimulating aggregate demand which had been perceived as inflationary) would respond to a budget deficit by raising interest rates. In contrast, a 'Keynesian' central bank whose policy decisions were co-ordinated with the fiscal policy decisions would respond by making no change to the key interest rate. It is then possible that a budget deficit will be accompanied by increased interest rates, but that would be a discretionary policy decision of the central bank and not the operation of some 'iron law'.

Others would argue that the (long-term) rate of interest is settled in the market for loanable funds, and further, that the budget deficit, being the government's demand for loanable funds, will increase demand for loanable funds and thereby the rate of interest. But the 'Functional Finance' approach views the budget deficit as filling the gap between *ex ante* savings and investment (at the desired level of economic activity). In the absence of the budget deficit, savings and investment would adjust, notably through changes in the level of economic activity. The budget deficit is required since (by assumption) the rate of interest cannot adjust sufficiently to bring *ex ante* savings and investment into line at an acceptable level of economic activity. The general expectation of the 'Functional Finance' approach is that budget deficits have no effect on interest rates (when the budget deficit is designed to 'mop up' excessive savings), and ironically this is the same conclusion as that reached by the Ricardian equivalence literature.

Crowding out mark 2: supply-side equilibrium

The second form of 'crowding out' discussed here arose from the notion that there is some form of supply-side equilibrium (such as the 'natural rate of unemployment', or the NAIRU) which is itself uninfluenced by the level of aggregate demand, and that this supply-side equilibrium acts as an 'attractor' for the level of economic activity. In effect, there are forces at work which guide the level of demand to this supply-side equilibrium. In the context of an exogenous money supply, this came through the assertion of a 'real balance' effect, with changes in the price level generating changes in the real value of the stock of money, thereby generating changes in the level of aggregate demand. In the context of endogenous money, it would come through the adjustment of the interest rate by the central bank. This could occur if the central bank adopted some form of 'Taylor's rule', under which the setting of the key interest rate depends on the 'equilibrium' rate of interest, deviation of inflation from target and deviation of output from trend level (Taylor, 1993). Monetary policy can guide aggregate demand to match supply provided that interest rates are effective in influencing the level of demand, and provided that the central bank's calculation of the 'equilibrium rate' of interest is accurate. As has been argued above, fiscal policy has an effect on the level of aggregate demand, and 'crowding out' only occurs if it assumed that the supply-side equilibrium must be attained (in order to ensure a constant rate of inflation) *and* that the level of aggregate demand would in any case be equivalent to the supply-side equilibrium. In the absence of some powerful automatic market forces or a potent monetary policy, which can ensure that the level of aggregate demand moves quickly to be consistent with the supply-side equilibrium, then fiscal policy has a clear role to play.

The supply-side equilibrium can itself by influenced by the path of aggregate demand. The size and distribution of the capital stock is a determinant of the productive capacity of the economy, and a larger capital stock would be associated with the supply-side equilibrium involving a higher level of output and employment. The level of aggregate demand (including the change in economic activity and profitability) has an impact on investment expenditure, and thereby on the size of the capital stock. The supply-side equilibrium may form an inflation barrier at any point in time, but it is not to be seen as something immutable and unaffected by the level of aggregate demand.

If the representation of the economy (economic model) is such that there are self-contained subsets of equations from which equilibrium solutions can be derived, then it is possible to speak of equilibrium positions relating to each of the subsets of equations. In particular, if there is a subset of equations that can be viewed as relating to the supply-side of the economy, then it is possible to speak of a supply-side equilibrium: and similarly for a demand-side equilibrium. The 'natural rate of unemployment' and the NAIRU appear to fall into the category of supply-side equilibrium positions. In this context, the supply-side equilibrium seems to place a constraint on the level of output or employment (more generally, the level of economic activity). In the present context, the supply-side equilibrium would appear to limit any role for fiscal policy (acting on the demand side of the economy) in that economic activity cannot be raised above the supply-side equilibrium for any length of time. However, this notion of supply-side equilibrium and the dichotomy (separation) between the supply side and demand side of the economy (which sometimes corresponds to the separation between the real side and the monetary side of the economy, as in the classical dichotomy) raises a range of issues. The first issue has been discussed in the introduction to this chapter; namely, what is the mechanism by which aggregate demand adjusts to the supply-side equilibrium. We argued there that the postulated mechanisms of the real balance effect and interest rate were ineffectual, and did not give convincing reasons for demand adjusting to supply.

The second is whether there are mechanisms on the supply side of the economy that take the economy to the supply-side equilibrium position? Little attention has been given to this. However, when the supply side is viewed as being akin to a competitive (labour) market (with the 'natural rate of unemployment' as the supply-side equilibrium), then an adjustment mechanism appears to be changes in real wages. In the expectations-augmented Phillips' curve, changes in real wages (expressed in terms of changes in nominal wages minus expected inflation) are linked with unemployment as a (negative) proxy for excess demand for labour. Real wages continue to adjust until the 'natural rate of unemployment' is attained. This approach assumes implicitly that the cause of unemployment (and indeed over-employment) arises from real wages differing from the equilibrium level. No attention is given to the level of aggregate demand, and it is assumed implicitly that the level of aggregate demand underpins the level of employment as set by the level of real wages. In the more general NAIRU approach, based on imperfect competition and wage bargaining (see, for example, Layard *et al.*, 1991), there is no obvious supply-side adjustment mechanism. Wages and prices change in response to the level of demand, but there is no mechanism at work that guides the level of real wages to its equilibrium level.[4] The adjustment in this NAIRU approach comes from the demand side alone.

The third issue can be indicated in terms of asking what the interactions are between the supply side and the demand side of the economy. It is often postulated that the relationship between these two sides of the economy in the sense of changes to one side having a long-lasting impact on the other (rather than just an adjustment process) is often seen as being non-existent. However, there are reasons for thinking this is not the case. The most cited example comes under the label of hysteresis effects in the labour market: periods of low demand and high levels of unemployment are viewed as having 'scarring' effects on the workforce and the effective supply of labour. Without dismissing such effects, in the context of the present chapter a more significant effect may come through the influence of aggregate demand on investment, and of investment on productive capacity (and hence the supply side of the economy). Fiscal policy of the 'Functional Finance' type boosts aggregate demand, and thereby has a stimulating impact on investment, which raises the future productive capacity of the economy. Further, some advocates of 'Functional Finance' have viewed public-sector investment as a form of expenditure, which can be varied according to the state of private demand,[5] and to the extent to which the budget deficit permits additional public investment there can also be a boost to future productive capacity. This, of course, would depend on the nature of the investment – for example, investment in roads or defence equipment, and the productivity of that investment. The growth rate of the economy may thereby be favourable enhanced by fiscal policy.

In Arestis and Sawyer (2005), we discuss what we term a structuralist approach to inflation. We argue that any supply-side equilibrium (which we term an inflation barrier) arose from the interaction between wage-setting and price-setting behaviour, and since the latter depended on the size of the capital stock, the supply-side equilibrium shifted as the capital stock changed. The changes in the capital stock come, of course, from investment expenditure, which in turn is influenced directly (through the government's own investments) and indirectly (through the level of demand and capacity utilization) by fiscal policy (and aggregate demand more generally).

Summary and conclusions

The levels of taxation and public expenditure, and the balance between them, vary for many reasons. Writing this at a time when the budget deficit consequences of the US administration's proposals for tax cuts for the rich are self-evident, it is not possible to forget that the fiscal stance may change for reasons far removed from the application of the ideas of 'Functional Finance'. The case we have set out in this chapter is that fiscal policy *should* be operated to secure the desired level of economic activity (and that it is a potent instrument for doing so). This 'Functional Finance' view means that any budget deficit should be seen as a response to the perceived excess of private savings over investment at the desired level of economic activity. We have argued that the 'crowding out' arguments, which have been advanced, do not take into account this view of 'Functional Finance'. The assessment of fiscal policy should relate to the circumstances in which it is intended to be employed, and then we would find that the 'crowding out' arguments do not apply.

Notes

1 One caveat to that statement is the following. A growing economy generally requires an increase in the stock of money, and within that an increase in the monetary base (M0) for which there is an increasing demand as income rises. The provision of M0 comes from a budget deficit.

2 Assuming that the budget deficit is entirely bond-financed: to the extent to which the deficit is money-financed the average rate of interest on government debt will be lower.

3 In the current context of the Stability and Growth Pact, the (on average) balanced budget requirement, the 60 per cent debt-to-income ratio and an inflation target of 2 per cent implies that the primary budget is in substantial surplus (on average), and that in real terms the total budget is in surplus to around 1.2 per cent (since there is a 2 per cent decline in the real value of the outstanding debt).

4 See Sawyer (1999) for further discussion.

5 Keynes (1980) argued for public investment to be set such that Private Investment + Public Investment = Savings, and hence that the budget deficit appeared to finance public investment. Keynes also advocated that 'in peace-time budgets through the Chancellor making a forecast of capital expenditure under all heads, and comparing this with prospective savings, so as to show that the general prospective set-up is reasonably in accordance with the requirement of equilibrium. The capital budget will be a necessary ingredient in this exposition of the prospects of investment under all heads. If, as may be the case, something like two-thirds or three-quarters of total investment will be under public or semi-public auspices, the amount of capital expenditure contemplated by the authorities will be the essential balancing factor. This is a very major change in the presentation of our affairs and one which I greatly hope we shall adopt. It has nothing whatever to do with deficit financing' (1980, p. 352).

References

Arestis, P. and Sawyer, M. (2003) 'Reinstating Fiscal Policy', *Journal of Post Keynesian Economics*, 26(1), pp. 3–25.

Arestis, P. and Sawyer, M. (2004) 'Can Monetary Policy Affect the Real Economy?', *European Review of Economics and Finance*, 3(2), pp. 9–32.

Arestis, P. and Sawyer, M. (2005) 'Aggregate Demand, Conflict, and Capacity in the Inflationary Process', *Cambridge Journal of Economics* (forthcoming).

Domar, E. D. (1944) 'The "Burden of the Debt" and the National Income', *American Economic Review*, 34(4), pp. 798–827.

Forstater, M. (1999) 'Functional Finance and Full Employment: Lessons from Lerner for Today', *Journal of Economic Issues*, 33(2), pp. 475–82.

Kalecki, M. (1939) *Essays in the Theory of Economic Fluctuations* (New York: Russell & Russell).

Kalecki, M. (1944a) 'The White Paper on Employment Policy', *Bulletin of the Oxford University Institute of Statistics*, 6(1), pp. 131–5.

Kalecki, M. (1944b) 'Three Ways to Full Employment', in Oxford University Institute of Statistics, *The Economics of Full Employment* (Oxford: Basil Blackwell).

Kalecki, M. (1944c) 'Professor Pigou on "The Classical Stationary State": A Comment', *Economic Journal*, 54(1), pp. 131–2.

Keynes, J. M. (1936) *The General Theory of Employment, Interest and Money* (London: Macmillan).

Keynes, J. M. (1980) *Activities 1940–1946 Shaping the Post-War World: Employment and Commodities, Collected Writings*, Vol. 27 (London: Macmillan).

Layard, R., Nickell, S. and Jackman, R. (1991) *Unemployment: Macroeconomic Performance and the Labour Market* (Oxford University Press).

Lerner, A. (1943) 'Functional Finance and the Federal Debt', *Social Research*, 10, pp. 38–51; reprinted in W. Mueller (ed.), *Readings in Macroeconomics* (New York: Holt, Rinehart and Winston), pp. 353–60 (page numbers refer to the reprint).

OECD (2000) *Economic Outlook* 68 (Paris: OECD).
Sawyer, M. (1999) 'The NAIRU: A Critical Analysis', *International Papers in Political Economy*, 6(2), pp. 1–40; reprinted in P. Arestis and M. Sawyer (eds), *Money, Finance and Capitalist Development* (Aldershot: Edward Elgar, 2001).
Taylor, J. (1993) 'Discretion versus Policy Rules in Practice', *Carnegie–Rochester Conference Series on Public Policy*, vol. 39, pp. 195–214.

7

Is an Increase of the Fiscal Budget at EMU Level Desirable?

*Davide Furceri**

The birth of the European Monetary Union (EMU) has determined the creation of a common currency, the Euro, but unlike other monetary unions, the EMU does not have a central fiscal authority. The role of fiscal policy is left to the responsibility of the governments of the EMU member States. The new architecture modifies the assignment of the instruments to the objectives, especially those of stabilization. The loss of the sovereignty of monetary policy and exchange rate control by the individual member states has determined the inability to use two important instruments of insurance against the risks of shocks. Moreover, the Treaty of Maastricht and the Stability and Growth Pact (SGP) could limit considerably the room of stabilizing national fiscal policies in some circumstances. In such a context, it could be important to investigate whether fiscal policy conducted by the individual governments is sufficient to insure countries against symmetric and asymmetric shocks. The results in the literature point to the fact that a transfer mechanism at the central level or an increase of the cooperation among the member states could improve substantially the capacity of the entire union to insure itself against shocks. Another important role of fiscal policy is to provide redistribution among the member states. Redistribution, in terms of income transfers from rich regions to depressed ones, might be necessary in order to guarantee a more rapid convergence towards higher living standards and in some cases could compensate individuals living in regions that are climatically and structurally disadvantaged.

The main objective of this chapter is to investigate how the birth of a central fiscal authority or the creation of a fiscal federalism could improve the action of fiscal policy in terms of the two items discussed above. In particular, our purpose is to quantify the increase in the federal budget

---

* The author would like to thank Sara Borelli, Georgios Karras, Fabio Mazzola, Paul Pieper and all participants to the 'EuroFrame 2004' and 'Developments in Economic Theory and Policy' conferences for their helpful suggestions. All errors and omissions are sole responsibility of the author.

(in fact only the 1.27 per cent of the Gross National Product (GNP) of the entire European Union (EU)) which would guarantee full insurance against symmetric and asymmetric shocks, and to show how redistribution will be affected by this increase.

The chapter is organized as follows. In the second section, we discuss the basic functions of fiscal policy in the EMU. In the third section, we present the models used to evaluate the EU budget increase that would be necessary to absorb shocks, and we estimate the redistribution effect. We present the results in fourth section and the conclusions in fifth section.

The basic functions of fiscal policy in the EMU

The three basic functions of fiscal policy are allocation, redistribution and stabilization. In principle, the allocation function can take place at both the central and subcentral levels. The provision of public goods, the correction of externalities and the regulation of the market have in general an impact at the micro level and should be insured by the local governments of the single States and/or of the single regions of the countries participating in the monetary union. This, however, does not exclude the provision of public goods that have an effect on the entire federation and that need governance at central level. The redistribution function, which is intended to generate greater equity between states, should be carried out at the central level. Oates (1968) argues that the redistributive functions of the public sector are not responsibilities of 'lower-level' governments – that is, governments which are open with respect to labour and capital markets. In presence of increasing factor mobility among the monetary union members, the governments of the single countries should not be considered 'central' in the relevant sense. As a consequence, the redistribution policies of member states could be ineffective, at both international and intranational level, making a more centralized redistributive policy necessary. The stabilization function should be provided at the central level. The principal reason is that otherwise national and regional governments would not have incentives to provide optimal stabilization.

In the existing federations (such as USA, Canada and Australia), these basic functions are carried out mainly by the central government, although local and state governments assume a different importance according to the specific cases.

The EU is characterized to having a relatively small budget. As stated above, in 2004 it was about 1.27 per cent of the entire GNP of the member states, and will be substantially stable until 2006. This budget is mainly for interregional redistributive and allocative functions. Table 7.1 shows that just less than half of the budget is spent by the European Agricultural Guidance and Guarantee Section (EAGGF), and around a third by Structural Funds and Activities (SFA). The EU revenues are drawn principally from four sources

Table 7.1 EU spending 2004

	Billions of euros	**percentage of total**
EAGGF	45.6	45.8
Structural funds	30.8	30.8
Internal policies	7.50	7.50
External actions	5.00	5.00
Administrative expenditures	6.00	6.10
Pre-accession strategies	2.90	2.90
Other	1.90	1.90

Source: European Commission (2005).

Table 7.2 EU revenues in 2004

	Billions of euros	**Percentage of total**
Agricultural duties	1.21	1.21
Custom duties	10.20	10.20
VAT-based resource	14.30	14.40
GNP-based resource	73.20	73.40
Miscellaneous	0.80	0.80

Source: European Commission (2005).

(Table 7.2): VAT revenues, GNP resources (obtained as a percentage quota of the GNP of the member states), customs duties charged on extra EU trade, and agricultural levies on imports of extra EU countries.

Looking at the trichotomy (allocation, redistribution and stabilization) it seems that the EU spending is aimed at allocative (Common Agricultural Policy) and redistributive (EAGGF, SFA) issues, while there are no fiscal instruments devoted to stabilizing income. In this context, it is important to understand how the monetary union could face symmetric and asymmetric shocks. Market forces by themselves, such as wage flexibility and labour mobility, will not be able to fulfill this task.[1] In case of symmetric shocks, only the common monetary policy could intervene. Two problems arise with the central monetary policy. The first is that the European Central Bank (ECB) could decide not to intervene, or to intervene only moderately if its action interferes with the primary objective of price stability. Second, it is generally argued that the common monetary policies have regionally differentiated effects.[2] Therefore, when the ECB acts to smooth aggregate shocks, the result could be a situation where shocks persist differentially among the member countries. In this case, the co-ordination of fiscal policies could be necessary. However, the results in the literature show that a policy mix problem arises between the common monetary policy and the decentralized fiscal policies in terms of stabilization of the shock. In particular, in case of aggregate shocks, the inefficiency in responding to shocks is increasing in the number of countries.[3]

In presence of asymmetric shocks, stabilization is, in principle, assigned to the individual governments. The Maastricht Treaty considers it the responsibility of each member state, though limited by the multilateral surveillance and by the excess deficit procedure (EDP). Moreover, the SGP affirms that each country must satisfy a set of medium-term objectives, including a budgetary position close to balance or in surplus. If the member states maintain their budget balanced in the medium term, then automatic stabilizers could be free to operate and a large amount of stabilization could be obtained. However, countries in the EMU with deficit levels close to the reference value of the 3 per cent could have difficulty to fulfilling this task. Data in Table 7.3 illustrate this aspect. Indeed, the majority of member countries have balanced budgets, with the exception of France, Germany, Greece and Netherlands. For these countries, in an unchanged scenario, there would be little room for the usual operation of automatic stabilizers and for discretionary fiscal policies to face shocks. Given the dimension of some of these countries (France and Germany), this may become a problem for the stability of the entire Union. For example, in this case, pressures could arise pushing it towards a more expansive common monetary policy.

Under these premises, a greater co-ordination of fiscal policies among the member countries might be desirable. Andersen (2002) shows that the inefficiency in responding to idiosyncratic shocks, decreases when the number of participants increases. However, the EMU institutions do not have the

Table 7.3 Deficit-GDP, debt/GDP ratios, (2003)

Country	**Deficit/GDP**	**Debt/GDP**
Austria	−1.1	65.1
Belgium	0.4	100.7
Finland	2.3	45.6
France	−4.1	63.7
Germany	−3.8	64.2
Greece	−4.6	109.9
Ireland	0.1	32.1
Italy	−2.4	106.2
Luxembourg	0.8	5.4
Netherlands	−3.2	54.1
Portugal	−2.8	60.3
Spain	0.4	50.7

Source: Eurostat, General Statistics (2004).

Note: "−" means deficit.

necessary instruments to force the member states to co-operate; they can only provide guidelines concerning the optimal behaviour for national fiscal policies. Thus an increase of fiscal budget of the European Commission, as initially argued by MacDougall (1977) and Delors (1989), could be an important instrument providing full insurance for the countries participating in the Union. Moreover, a fiscal mechanism collecting taxes and paying transfers could also increase the redistribution among the member states.

Measuring the budget of full risk-sharing

In order to measure the necessary increase in the budget to achieve full risk-sharing we shall look at this in two steps. First, we describe a model that measures risk-sharing in the current architecture of fiscal policy, and in a framework where a transfer mechanism, supported by an increase in the fiscal budget, becomes effective. Second, we introduce the transfer mechanism.

Measuring risk-sharing

Several works in the literature have estimated the ability of many federations and countries to smooth income around the potential level.[4] These works focused mainly on the ability of the fiscal budget to provide stabilization (Table 7.4).

In this chapter, we propose a model to evaluate the ability of the EMU to smooth idiosyncratic shocks through several channels, including the budget factor.

We consider N countries. Let $y_{i,t}$ be the time series of GDP for the ith country at time t. By using the Hodrick and Prescott procedure we decompose the time series in a *growth* ($g_{i,t}$) and in a *cyclical* ($c_{i,t}$) component with a smoothing parameter of 40.[5] If we regress $c_{i,j}$ on a set of explanatory variables such

Table 7.4 Budget stabilization effect

	USA	EU	Canada	UK	Germany	France	Italy
Sachs and Sala-i-Martin (1991)	38						
Von Hagen (1998)	9–10						
Goodhart and Smith (1993)	13		12–24	21–34			
Massoand Taylor (1993)			24				
Pisani-Ferri *et al.* (1993)	17				33–42	37	
Bayoumi and Masson (1995)	30		17				
Asdrubali *et al.* (1996)	13						
Obstfeld and Peri (1998)	10		13				3
Melitz and Zumer (1998)	20		14	21		19	
Fatás (1997)	11			13	10	6	
Furceri (2002)		4					

as the lagged values of the dependent variable, we can obtain a measure of risk from the variance of the error term $\varepsilon_{i,t}(\sigma_{\varepsilon}^2)$:

$$c_{i,t} = \alpha_i + \sum_{j=1}^{M} \lambda_j c_{i,t-j} + \varepsilon_{i,t} \tag{1}$$

where M is the number of lags and α_i is the country heterogeneity effect. We assume that $\varepsilon_{i,t}$'s are identically and normally distributed with mean equal to zero and variance equal to σ_{ε}^2; in symbols $\varepsilon_{i,t} \sim_{\text{i.i.d}} \mathrm{N}(0,\sigma_{\varepsilon}^2)$.

The problem with this model is that complications arise in the estimation. In fact, the lagged dependent variables are correlated with the compound disturbance. This implies that the OLS estimates are inconsistent. Thus, it is necessary to use another technique to estimate the model. The technique used in this paper is that proposed by Arellano and Bond (1991). Then, we use the residuals of this regression to compute an estimate of σ_{ε}^2.

Since the Arellano–Bond estimator is consistent, an unbiased estimator[6] of σ_{ε}^2 is provided by:

$$s^2 = \frac{\sum_{i}^{N}\sum_{t}^{T}(e_{i,t}-\bar{e}_i)^2}{NT - N - M - 1} \tag{2}$$

Successively, in order to quantify the grade of risk-sharing through different channels we decompose the GDP in different national aggregates all closely tied to the GDP: gross national product (GNP), national income (NI), disposable national income (DNI) and total consumption (C):

GDP–GNP = *net international transfers of income factors* (3)
GNP–NI = *capital depreciation*
NI–DNI = *net international transfers* (transfers less the payment of taxes)
DNI–C = *total saving*

If a shock hits the economy of one country, modifying the value of the GDP, the economic system will be able to smooth the shock if there is some counter-cyclical factor able to perform this task.

Let us consider the following equation:

$$GDP = \frac{GDP}{GNP} \cdot \frac{GNP}{NI} \cdot \frac{NI}{DNI} \cdot \frac{DNI}{C} \cdot C \tag{4}$$

If after the shock only the GDP varies, while the other aggregates are unchanged, then full stabilization has been obtained. In more detail, if the GDP varies and the GNP remains unchanged, then stabilization is achieved at the first stage by the *international net transfers of income factors*. In the same way, if the GNP also varies and the NI remains constant, then cyclical smoothing is provided by the capital depreciation. Finally, if the total consumption also changes, it means that a quota of the shock is not smoothed.

In this way it is possible to obtain a measure of stabilization for each of the factors in Equation (3). In principle, all these factors have a counter-cyclical effect. The first aggregate expresses the international transfers of the income that is earned by foreign factors in each country. The second aggregate is the capital depreciation, usually calculated as a constant part of the total amount of capital (δK). Thus, since the capital–output ratio is typically counter-cyclical in the short-run also the depreciation will be as well. The third factor is based on the mutual insurance between the countries, and in our analysis is a proxy of the fiscal budget when a transfer mechanism is operative. Finally, the fourth aggregate represents the consumption smoothing.

To measure the amount of variance reduction of the cyclical component of the original series we use the regression in Equation (1) and the formula in Equation (2) for each of the four types of income. Clearly, the cumulative variance reduction (or increase, in case of procyclical factor) is imputable to the differential term in each equation in Equation (3). Particularly important for our analysis is the third term. In fact, it measures the amount of risk-sharing by the budget factor. Once we have obtained the results from the regressions, we repeat the analysis by adjusting the measure of disposable national income by the addition of transfers and the subtraction of tax payments coming from the transfer mechanism discussed in the next section. By using this procedure, we are able to observe how the amount of risk-sharing obtained by the fiscal central budget changes by varying the marginal tax rate. Thus we can inspect the amount of budget at the EMU level (as a quota of GNP of member states) able to face asymmetric and symmetric shocks.

The transfer mechanism

A scheme of fiscal transfers to absorb asymmetric and symmetric shocks will probably be desirable in the EMU, given that it is characterized by constrained national fiscal policies, wage rigidity and low labour mobility. This scheme could serve mainly as a compensatory mechanism for the cyclical national income and could be financed by the central budget at EMU level. A mechanism based on smoothing cyclical fluctuations of national GDPs has the characteristic of being close to the fiscal mechanisms in the existing union, where part of the contribution of the member countries is proportional to the GNP. Other variables taken into account to provide insurance, such as the unemployment rate, could have some disadvantages. In fact, a typical problem with this variable is the slow process of adjustment because of factors such as labour-hoarding, which could make the transfers procyclical instead of counter-cyclical.

In principle, it is possible to list the characteristics that an ideal scheme of transfer should have and to identify at least six ideal features of a transfer mechanism:[7] simplicity, automaticity, transfers should be zero on average for long periods, transfers should be a function of serially uncorrelated shocks, the transfer mechanism should not be regressive; and the scheme should be able to offset shocks.

Although these characteristics can serve as practical guidelines in the set-up of a transfer mechanism, they cannot be satisfied simultaneously. A mechanism related to serially uncorrelated shocks with zero conditional expectation, in principle, requires techniques that are complex. And, conversely, simpler techniques in the determination of shocks and transfers could generate redistributive rather than stabilizing effects. Thus, a kind of trade-off should be considered.

Our assumptions are that the transfer mechanism aims to smooth only the cyclical component of GDP around the potential level, that the transfer mechanism is not regressive and automatic, and that it takes into account only shocks that are serially uncorrelated. The last assumption is particularly important, in fact, it avoids or at least limit strategic behaviours and moral hazard problems. Moreover, jointly with the assumption of non-regressivity it ensures that the mechanism operates for stabilization rather than redistributive purposes.

The scheme we propose collects taxes as a quota of the GNP of the member states, and pays transfers to the countries affected negatively by shocks:

$$EMU\_budget_t = \sum_i \tau . GNP_{i,t} \tag{5}$$

where τ is the marginal tax rate.

The transfers are given by the following rule:

$$T_{i,t} = 0 \quad \text{if } \varepsilon_{i,t} \geq 0 \text{ or } \frac{GDP_{i,t} - GDP_{i,t-1}}{GDP_{i,t-1}} \leq -2 \tag{6}$$

$$T_{i,t} = \frac{\varepsilon_{i,t} \sum_i \tau . GNP_{i,t}}{\sum_i \varepsilon_{i,t} \varepsilon_{i,t} < 0} \frac{n(s)_t}{n} \frac{DNI_{i,t}}{DNI_t} \text{ if } \varepsilon_{i,t} < 0 \text{ and } -2\% < \frac{GDP_{i,t} - GDP_{i,t-1}}{GDP_{i,t-1} < 0} \tag{7}$$

where $\varepsilon_{i,t}$'s are the shocks for the country *i* at time *t*, and are derived in the Appendix (see page 204). The number of countries where the negative shocks occur is indicated by $n(s)$ the DNI_i disposable national income of country *i*, and *DNI* that of the Entire EU. The transfers are a function of three elements: the relative importance of the shock for the country *i* compared to those of the other countries ($\varepsilon_{i,t} / \sum_i \varepsilon_{i,t} \varepsilon_{i,t} < 0$), the quota of the number of countries hit by negative shocks ($n(s)_t / n$)and the relative dimension of the country in terms of *DNI* ($DNI_{i,t} / DNI_t$).

The first element allows the distribution public resources in such a way that the countries with larger shocks will receive larger transfers. The second element makes possible to depurate transfers from the symmetry effect. The third element allows the generation of transfers related to the country dimension. The mechanism will not pay a country that has a decrease in the GDP of greater than 2 per cent, because this is an exceptional circumstance that allows the country to overcome the reference value of 3 per cent of the Maastricht Treaty.

Finally, we impose the condition of balanced budget at EMU level for each year:

$$\sum_i T_{i,t} + A_t = EMU\_budget_t + R_t \tag{8}$$

where the A_t and R_t are the total current expenditures and revenues in the EU.

Redistribution

Although the transfer mechanism we propose is intended to smooth both symmetric and asymmetric shocks, it is interesting to investigate the effects of these transfers in terms of redistribution.

International transfers affect and modify the value of disposable income for each member country. Then, a way to measure international redistribution could be obtained by using the following regression:

$$Y_i^* - Y^* = \alpha + \beta(Y_i - Y) + \varepsilon_i \tag{9}$$

where Y_i^* and Y_i represent, respectively, the DNI after and before taxes and transfers. The terms without subscripts indicate average values. We averaged the data over a long period of time in order to eliminate the incidence of cyclical factors. $1 - \beta$ will measure the ability of the transfer mechanism to reduce disposable national income dispersion around its mean. In fact, if $\beta = 1$ the deviations from the mean of the pre-tax and transfers income, are perfectly reflected in the deviations of the post-tax and transfers income. In other words, there is no redistribution. The smaller the value of β, the greater is the redistributive effect of the mechanism.

Results

We begin by analysing the results in terms of risk-sharing for the current institutional architecture of fiscal policy in the EMU. Table 7.5 shows the amount of shock that is absorbed by the factors in Equation (3). By analysing Table 7.5 we can see that, in the estimated model a remarkable share of shocks that hit the EMU countries are not absorbed.

Table 7.5 Variance reduction

	Percentage
Net international transfers of factors income	2.66
Capital depreciation	27.60
Net international transfers (transfers less payment of taxes)	4.31
Total saving	2.74
Not smoothed	62.70

The estimate of the non-smoothed shock is 62.7 per cent, underlining the fact that the factors in Equation (3) do not operate adequately. The only aggregate that provides a consistent amount of risk-sharing is the capital depreciation. The budget factor (transfers less payment of taxes) provides only 4.31 per cent of the total smoothing, reflecting the fact the EU (or EMU) central budget is used almost uniquely for allocative and redistributive purposes.

To see how this amount could change when a transfer mechanism is operative, we repeat the estimation of the model in Equation (1) by taking into account the net transfers generated by the transfer mechanism discussed in above. We found different grades of risk-sharing as we varied the marginal tax rate τ (Table 7.6), with an *optimal*[8] τ of 9 per cent. Substituting for this value in the transfer mechanism and repeating the estimation of Equation (1) and Equation (2) we obtain the grade of risk-sharing through different channels in the new fiscal architecture.

The results in Table 7.7 strongly support the hypothesis that a new institutional architecture of fiscal policy, with a transfer mechanism supported by an increase in the amount of budget (9 per cent of the GNP of the entire union), is remarkably effective.

We assumed that the only aggregate that is changed is DNI. In practice, we have modified DNI by the transfers and by the contribution in terms to the EMU budget in terms of GNP. Thus the first two factors and the associated degree of risk-sharing are unchanged. We also assumed that consumption smoothing remains the same. This is because we have no data for the new consumption deriving from the new DNI. Another way to proceed could be to assume that the economy does not change the quota of DNI allocated to consumption. Results in the literature assuming this restriction show that the consumption smoothing remains almost unchanged.[9]

The international net transfers now play a key role in absorbing exogenous shocks; in fact, they alone smooth 55.4 per cent of the shock. The quota of shock that is not absorbed is only 11.6 per cent. In principle, this amount is small enough to be absorbed by the market forces (labour mobility and wage flexibility). From the results concerning the two frameworks considered in the analysis, it emerges that the institution of a fiscal federalism can significantly help the EMU member countries to face both symmetric and asymmetric shocks (see Figures 7.1–7.4).

Table 7.6 Percentage of unsmoothed shock with different τ

	$\tau = 0\%$	$\tau = 8\%$	$\tau = 9\%$	$\tau = 10\%$
Percentage of unsmoothed stock	62.7	23.7	11.6	17.8

Table 7.7 Variance reduction (%) when $\tau = 9\%$

	Percentage
Net international transfers of factors income	2.66
Capital depreciation	27.60
Net international transfers (transfers less payment of taxes)	55.40
Total saving	2.74
Not smoothed	11.60

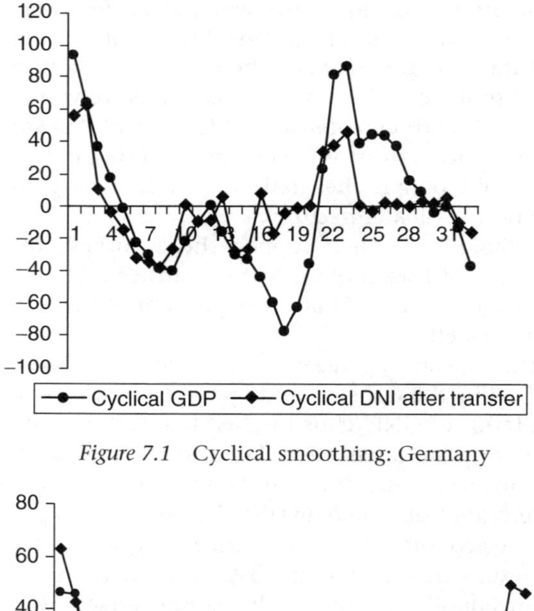

Figure 7.1 Cyclical smoothing: Germany

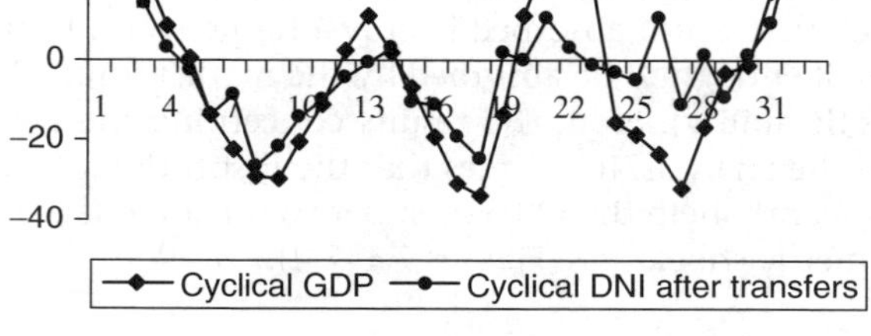

Figure 7.2 Cyclical smoothing: France

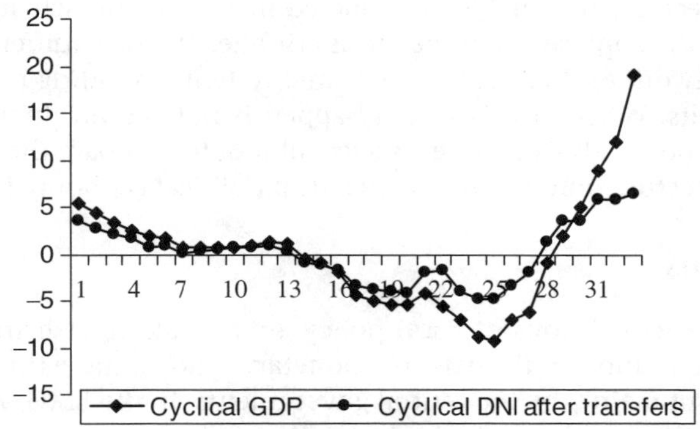

Figure 7.3 Cyclical smoothing: Ireland

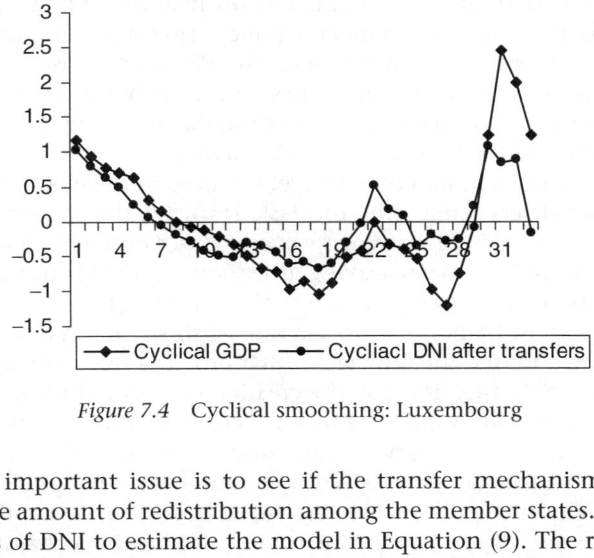

Figure 7.4 Cyclical smoothing: Luxembourg

Another important issue is to see if the transfer mechanism is able to increase the amount of redistribution among the member states. We use the new values of DNI to estimate the model in Equation (9). The results show that the amount of redistribution resulting from the transfer mechanism is $1 - \beta = 18$ per cent. This value is low compared to the other results found in the literature,[10] but it is not surprising. In fact, we must remember that this mechanism was uniquely designed to absorb shocks. Probably, by imposing different (fewer) restrictions in the determination of shocks and transfers we shall obtain greater redistribution and smaller stabilization.

To conclude, it is important to remark that the analysis also has (at least) two irresolvable weaknesses. First, the use of past data does not guarantee that the gain in terms of risk-sharing with the new architecture will be as large; and second, the analysis conducted in the second scheme is typical grounds for the application of the Lucas critique. The new (different) institutional framework could alter the economic system, providing no robustness for our results. Whether this would happen is not certain. In any case, we believe that our analysis represents a useful tool to compare the two institutional architectures and to provide practical political economy indications.

Conclusions

The three basic functions of fiscal policy are allocation, redistribution and stabilization. In most of the existing monetary unions, these three functions are carried out mainly by the central governments. In the EMU, with no central fiscal authority, the entire budget is devoted to allocative and to redistributive purposes. The main problem with this framework of political economy is the inability of the economic system to manage both symmetric and asymmetric shocks.

In a situation of symmetric shocks, the only instrument that could provide insurance is the common monetary policy. However, although the ECB could act to smooth aggregate shocks, the different transmission mechanisms among the EMU member states will probably produce a situation where shocks persist differentially. Thus stabilization is mainly assigned to the fiscal policy of the individual member states.

If single nations maintain their budget balanced in the medium term, then automatic stabilizers could fulfill this task. However, the data on the deficit–GDP ratio show that the reference value of 3 per cent represents a serious limit for the largest countries, leaving little room for stabilizing fiscal policies.

The results of this chapter confirm these findings. In fact, they show that in the current framework, the amount of shock that is not smoothed is 62.7 per cent, and that the only factor that provides risk-sharing is the capital depreciation. In this situation the creation of a central fiscal authority or a transfer mechanism, supported by an increase in the fiscal budget of the EMU, could become necessary. In particular, we found that, in presence of a transfer mechanism, an increase in the central budget by up to 9 per cent of the GNP of the entire EU enables the facing of asymmetric and symmetric shocks. Another appealing feature of the proposed mechanism is that, although it was not designed for redistributive purposes, this helps to reduce inequalities among the member countries by up to 18 per cent of the DNI.

Appendix

Following Hodrick and Prescott (1997), we decompose the GDP time series y_t in two terms, the cyclical component c_t and growth component g_t:

$$y_t = c_t + g_t \quad \text{for } t = 1 \cdots\cdots T$$

The c_t are the deviations of y_t from g_t and are assumed equal to zero over a long period of time.

The c_t are calculated using the Hodrick–Prescott filter with a parameter of smoothness equal to 40.The criterion of choosing λ (the smoothness parameter) equal to 40, is to determine a cyclical component that varies moderately (less than 2 per cent). For example, in correspondence of this value, Hodrick and Prescott have found that the standard deviation of the cyclical component of US GNP is only the 1.56 per cent. In this way, we stabilize only moderate shocks. Greater shocks (≥2 per cent) permit single-member states to overcome the limit on the 3 per cent on the ratio Deficit/GDP.

In order to guarantee that the components that we have found are serially uncorrelated we regress c_t for each i against its three lagged terms:

$$c_t = \alpha + \beta.c_{t-1} + \gamma.c_{t-2} + \delta.c_{t-3} + \zeta_t$$

where ζ_t is the error term distributed as a White Noise.

The residual from this regression ε_t are transitory and not significantly serially correlated.

Notes

1 Layard *et al.* (1991); Vinals and Jimeno (1996).
2 Arden *et al.* (2000); Guiso *et al.* (2000); Ramaswami and Slok (1998).
3 Andersen (2002).
4 Asdrubali *et al.* (1996), Bayoumi and Masson (1995), Crucini and Hess (2000), Fatás (1997), Furceri (2002), Goodhart and Smith (2001), Masson and Taylor (1993) , Melitz and Zumer (2000), Obstfeld and Peri (1998), Sachs and Sala-i-Martin (1991), von Hagen J. (1998).
5 For the reason $\lambda = 40$ was chosen, see the Appendix.
6 Maddala (1971).
7 For a detailed discussion about these characteristics see Hammond and von Hagen (1995).
8 The marginal rate generating the greatest variance reduction in the cyclical component.
9 Furceri (2002).
10 See Sachs and Sala-i-Martin (1991), for example.

References

Andersen, T.R. (2002) 'Fiscal Policy Stabilization in a Monetary Union with Inflation Targeting', CEPR Discussion Papers, no. 3232.

Arden, R., Cook, S. Holly, S., and Turner, P. (2000) 'The Asymmetric Effects of Monetary Policy: Some Results from a Macroeconometric Model', *The Manchester School*, 68, pp. 419–41.

Arellano, M. and Bond, S. (1991) 'Some Tests of Specification for Panel Data: Monte Carlo Evidence and an Application to Employment Equations', *Review of Economic Studies*, 58, pp. 277–97.

Asdrubali, P., Sorensen, B.E., and Yosha, O. (1996) 'Channels of Interstate Risk-sharing: US 1963–1990', *Quarterly Journal of Economics*, 144, pp. 1081–110.

Bayoumi, T. and Masson, P.R. (1995) 'Fiscal Flows in the United States and in Canada: Lessons from Monetary Union in Europe', *European Economic Review*, 39(2), pp. 253–74.

Bayoumi, T. and Prasad E. (1997): 'Currency Unions, Economic Fluctuations, and Adjustment: Some New Empirical Evidence', *IMF Staff Papers*, no. 44 (1), pp. 36–57

Crucini, M.J. and G.D. Hess (2000) 'International and Intranational Risk Sharing', in Hess, G.D. and Van Wincoop, E. (eds), *Intranational Macroeconomics* (Cambridge University Press), pp. 37–59.

Delors, J. (1989) 'Report of the Committee on the Study of Economic and Monetary Union', European Commission Report.

Fatás, A. (1997) 'EMU: Countries or Regions? Lessons from The EMS Experience', CEPR Discussion Paper, no. 1558.

Furceri, D. (2002) 'Risk-sharing and Institutional Architecture of Stabilization Policies in the EMU: Methodological Aspects and Empirical Evidence', *Rivista di Politca Economica*, November–December, pp. 175–210.

Goodhart, C.A.E and Smith, S. (1993) 'Stabilization', *European Economy, Reports and Studies*, 5, pp. 417–56.

Guiso, L., Kashyap, A.K., Panetta, F., and Terlizzese, D. (2000) 'Will a Common European Monetary Policy Have Asymmetric Effects?', Economic Perspectives of Federal Reserve Bank of Chicago, pp. 56–75.

Hammond, J. and von Hagen J. (1995) 'Regional Insurance Against Asymmetric Shocks: An Empirical Study for the European Community, *The Manchester School*, 66, pp. 331–353.

Hodrick, R.J. and Prescott, E.C. (1980) 'Postwar U.S. Business Cycles: An Empirical Investigation', Discussion Paper, no. 451, Carnegie Mellon University.

Layard, R., Nickell, N.S. and Jackman, R. (1991) *Unemployment, Macroeconomic Performance and the Labour Market* (Oxford: Oxford Economic Press).

MacDougall, D. (1977) 'Report of the Study Group on the Role of Public Finance in European Integration', European Commission Report.

Maddala, G. (1971) 'The Use of Variance Components Model in pooling Cross Section and Time Series Data', *Econometrica*, 39, pp. 341–58.

Masson, P.R and Taylor M. (1992) 'Common Currency Areas and Currency Unions: An Analysis of the Issues', CEPR Discussion Paper, no. 617.

Mélitz, J. and Zumer, F. (2000): 'Regional Redistribution and Stabilization by the Central Government in Canada, France, the UK and the US: A Reassessment and New Tests', CEPR Discussion Paper, no. 1829.

Obstfeld, M. and Peri, G. (1998) 'Regional Non-Adjustment and Fiscal Policy', *Economic Policy*, April, pp. 207–59.

Oates, W. (1968) 'The Theory of Public Finance in Federal System', *Canadian Journal of Economics*, 1, pp. 37–54.

Pisani-Ferry, Jean, Italianer, A. and Lescure, R. (1993) 'Stabilization Properties of Budgetary Systems: a Simulation Analysis', The Economics of Community Public Finance, *European Economy*, no. 5, pp. 511–38.

Ramaswami, R. and Slok, T. (1998) 'The Real Effects of Monetary Policy in The European Union: What Are The Differences?', IMF Staff Papers, no. 45, pp. 374–96.

Sachs, J. and Sala-i-Martin, X. (1991) 'Fiscal Federalism and Optimum Currency Areas: Evidence for Europe from the US', NBER Working Paper, no. 3885.

Vinals, J. and Jimeno, J. (1996) 'Monetary Union and European Unemployment', CEPR Discussion Paper, no. 1485.

Von Hagen, J. (1998) 'Fiscal Policy and Intranational Risksharing', CEPR Discussion Paper, no. 126.

8
How Sensitive Is the Dollar to Economic Policy?

Elias Karakitsos

A common feature of all traditional exchange rate models is that the value of the currency is determined as a derived demand from the underlying assets. This is true of early models that emphasized the current account as a key determinant of exchange rate movements (see, for example, Meade, 1951), later models that placed the emphasis on the capital account, and even models that integrated the current account as a long-term constraint in an otherwise short-term determination within the capital account (see, for example, Mundell, 1960, 1963; Fleming, 1962; Dornbusch, 1976; Dornbusch and Fisher, 1980). In these models, economic policy (both fiscal and monetary) would influence the value of the currency by altering other macroeconomic variables, such as GDP and short-term (or long-term) interest rates, which affect the derived demand for foreign currency. Thus, in these models, economic policy has an indirect effect on the currency. But most empirical euro–dollar models are unstable in the sense that the influence of variables such as (short- or long-term) interest rate differentials change over time from statistically significant to statistically insignificant, and sometimes from positive to negative.

This chapter argues that this instability inherent in all currency models based on the small, open economy paradigm or the two-country model is because the US dollar is a reserve currency, which through the ever increasing use of hedging techniques has developed into a separate asset class from its underlying assets; it is no longer the product of a derived demand. From this perspective the chapter builds on earlier attempts (see Frowen and Karakitsos, 1998; Arestis and Karakitsos, 2004, 2005) to show that this instability disappears if the exchange rate is determined within a structural model in which the economic policy of the two countries involved plays centre stage – it has a direct rather than an indirect effect on the currency. Hence the relevant variables in affecting, say, the value of the euro–dollar rate are the fiscal and monetary policies pursued by US and EU policy-makers.

An appropriate framework for such an analysis is a game-theoretic approach in which the instability can be characterized as a shift of the equilibrium from a 'Stackelberg-leader' to a 'Stackelberg-follower' case. Once this is taken into account game-theoretic framework and the shift of equilibrium, the resulting euro-dollar model is stable. Such a framework is appropriate because the dollar is a reserve currency that has developed into a separate asset class. In this framework, the exchange rate, as an important part of the transmission mechanism of monetary policy, is an equilibrium outcome that is consistent with the investors' portfolio objectives.

The second section discusses why neither the current account nor the capital account are determinants of the dollar. The third section shows how the long-run condition that the current account should balance, should be modified in the case of a reserve currency. The fourth section utilizes this game framework, in which the dollar has developed into a separate asset class from its underlying assets, to explain the behaviour of the dollar since the 1990s. The chapter also argues that the dollar has now entered a long process of reversal since its fall over recent years. The conclusions are summarized in the last section.

The role of the current and capital accounts in dollar determination

The deficit in the US current account, which records transactions in goods and services, has widened progressively since the recession in the early 1990s, hitting 6.2 per cent of GDP in the fourth quarter of 2004, an unprecedented deficit in the last fifty years (see Figure 8.1). In the 1980s, the current account was also in deficit, but it narrowed with the dollar depreciation

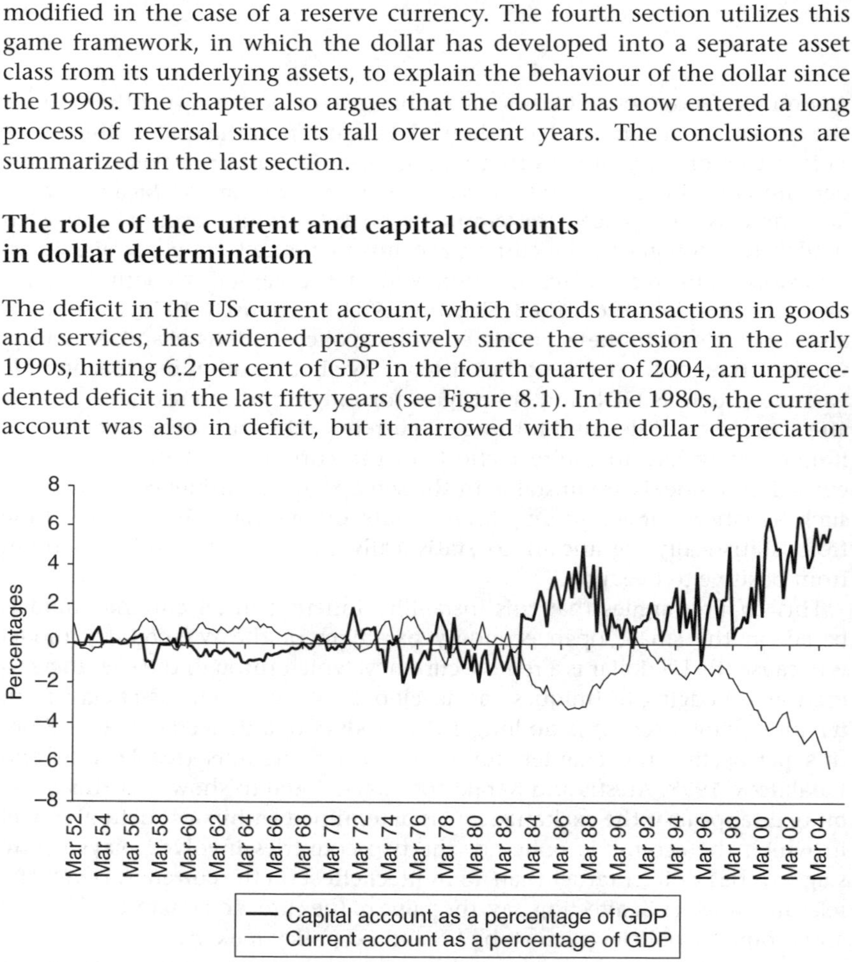

Figure 8.1 US balance of payments

following the Plaza Accord in 1985 and was closed with the recession of 1990–1. Many gloomy forecasts for a continuous dollar weakness rely on the ballooning current account deficit. But this is a myth, as the current account deficit is not a dollar determinant. If this were the case, then the dollar could have fallen at any time between 1995 and 2001 when the current account deficit widened, while it was on an appreciating trend at that time. Nor does any particular level of the deficit trigger dollar depreciation. For example, in the 1980s, the current account deficit was ignored until it hit 3.2 per cent of GDP. If this is a level that triggers dollar depreciation, then the dollar should have started falling in 1999. There is in fact no particular deficit level that triggers dollar depreciation. In the 1980s, the dollar began to fall after the concerted foreign exchange intervention following the Plaza Accord. Unfortunately, and in spite of such a popular belief, the current account is not a dollar determinant. Nor, for that matter, is the capital account. This myth is based on a flawed analysis of the financing of the current account deficit the fact that ignores the fact that the dollar is a reserve currency.

Under free floating, the capital account, which records transactions in assets and foreign direct investment (FDI), is the mirror image of the current account and represents the way the current account deficit is financed. The discrepancy, if any, between the current account and the capital account reflects changes in foreign exchange reserves, which on occasion may arise from central bank intervention in the foreign exchange market.

The financing of the current account deficit, has so far not been a problem, since the surplus in the capital account has exceeded the deficit in the current account. For example, since the recession of the early 1990s, when the current account started to widen, the average surplus in the capital account was 2.8 per cent of GDP, outstripping the deficit in the current account by 0.5 per cent. But is this sustainable, if the current account deficit keeps growing? Dollar bears would answer in the negative, but this is where the flaw lies.

In the small open economy paradigm, and therefore for any currency other than the dollar, a growing current other account deficit is not sustainable because the external debt is in foreign currency. A country with a surplus in its current account will invest the proceeds in the Rest of the World (ROW) by buying tangible assets, or will be willing to lend to ROW by accumulating ROW financial assets. A country with a current account deficit will sell its tangible assets to ROW or borrow from ROW in ROW currency. If confidence in the ability of the economy to service its external debt is shaken, the currency will fall and the country in question become insolvent, as its debt will soar by the degree of currency depreciation.

Therefore, in theory, while a deficit in the current account can be financed in the short run either by a corresponding surplus in the capital account or by running down foreign exchange reserves, this cannot go on for ever. In the long run, the current account must be zero, because otherwise it implies that domestic residents can sell their assets for ever or borrow indefinitely from overseas to finance their excess expenditure over their income. Clearly, this cannot last forever, as domestic residents will ultimately run out of assets, or foreign residents will lose their appetite for acquiring such assets. Hence, in the long run the current account must be balanced. But this is true about any currency, except the dollar.

So what is the difference with the USA? Because the dollar is a reserve currency, the US debt is simply domestic rather than foreign. This means that any crisis in the USA must come from lack of confidence in its ability to service its domestic debt. But this is not possible! Although foreign residents hold almost half of the US Federal government debt, this is smaller than any other G7 economy. The US corporate debt is not large compared with other G7 countries (less than 50 per cent of US GDP), and moreover foreign residents hold only a quarter of this. Hence there is no compelling reason why, in the last three years, foreign residents should have lost their confidence in the ability of the USA to service its debt. Thus the dollar weakness of the early 2000s could not have been caused by fears of US insolvency. Nor is it justified that foreign investors would lose their confidence in the near future, as the debt levels are still very small. Therefore other factors must have caused the dollar to fall. The growing current account deficit has not played a part and therefore it would not cause continuous dollar weakness in the future.

Although there is no insolvency issue, is there a risk that foreign residents might lose their appetite to for lending to the USA? Can such fear account for the dollar weakness since 2001? The accumulation over time of the US current account deficits (the external imbalance) measures the degree of the US indebtedness. Figure 8.2 shows the ROW net worth, defined as ROW

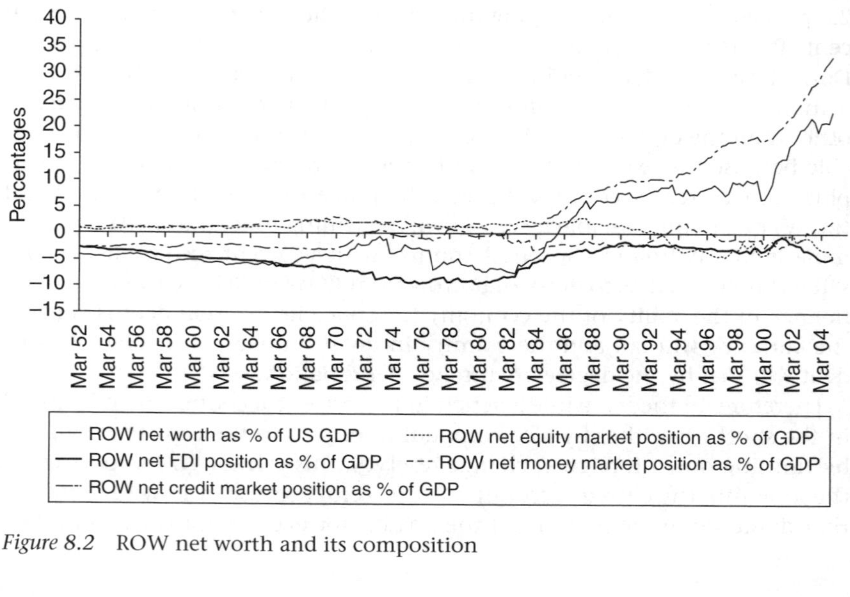

Figure 8.2 ROW net worth and its composition

holdings of US assets less US holdings of ROW assets, and its composition. The ROW net worth measures the indebtedness (if positive) or creditworthiness (if negative) of the US economy. The USA became for the first time a net debtor to the rest of the world at the end of 1985, and this debt has continued to grow ever since. At the end of the fourth quarter of 2004 the US net debt to ROW was of the order of 23 per cent of US GDP, or US $2.7 trillion.

The ROW net worth consists of ROW holdings of US money market instruments, credit market instruments, equities, FDI and miscellaneous assets, less the corresponding US holdings of ROW assets. By far the biggest component of ROW net worth is the net credit market position (ROW holdings of US government and corporate bonds, less US holdings of ROW bonds). At the end of the fourth quarter of 2004 the net credit market position of ROW was 33 per cent of US GDP, the net money market position was 2.3 per cent of GDP, while the net equity market position was −4.3 per cent of GDP and the net FDI position was −4.6 per cent (see Figure 8.2). The US government as well as the corporate sector have been borrowing heavily from ROW by issuing bonds. A cursory look at Figure 8.2 shows that the net FDI position has been negative since the 1950s. The conclusion from the FDI figures is that in the thirty years to 1983, the USA was buying ROW companies via the surpluses in the current account. Since 1983, it has been borrowing from ROW to buy ROW companies. Is this a problem? Clearly, not! If foreign residents are willing to lend to the USA to buy their own companies, they must be doing so because they believe that they would be more profitable under US rather than domestic management.

A detailed analysis of the composition of ROW net worth shows that only a small part of US borrowing is devoted to buying foreign companies; the rest is financing the excess expenditure over its income. Hence, the overall conclusion is that the USA has been borrowing from ROW by issuing bonds partly to buy ROW companies, but mainly to finance the excess expenditure over its income. However, to some extent the USA is importing products from its own factories abroad. Is there a risk, therefore, that foreign residents will lose their appetite for holding US assets in the future?

Japan and China together hold 20 per cent of the total federal debt, which is nearly half of what foreign residents hold of US Treasuries (see Table 8.1). If China or Japan lost their appetite for holding US Treasuries then the price of bonds would fall and the yields would rise. But what would the effect be on the dollar? In the small open economy paradigm and in the two-country model, the demand for foreign currency is a derived demand consisting of a demand for the underlying assets. Thus the demand for foreign currency stems from the demand for imports, demand for foreign assets (deposits, bonds and equities), demand for foreign property and, finally, demand for foreign direct investment. The supply of foreign currency stems from the demand for exports, foreign demand for domestic assets (deposits, bonds and equities), foreign demand for domestic property and, finally, demand

Table 8.1 Federal debt and its finance

	Federal govt debt (Billions dollars)	Foreign holdings of US treasuries (Billions dollars)	Foreign holdings of US treasuries (Percentage of total)	Japan: holdings of US treasuries (Billions dollars)	Japan: holdings of US treasuries (Percentage of foreign total)	China: holdings of US treasuries (Billions dollars)	China: holdings of US treasuries (Percentage of foreign total)	Japan and China holdings of of US treasuries (Billions dollars)	Japan and China holdings of US treasuries (Percentage of foreign total)	Japan and China holdings of US treasuries (Percentage of fed. debts)
Minimum govt debt (Jun 2001)	3,251	983	31	301	31	73	7%	374	38	11
Latest month (Dec 2004)	4,396	1,900	43	714	38	187	10%	901	47	20
Difference	1,144	917	12	413	7	114	2%	527	9	9

for foreign direct investment in the domestic economy. Hence, in the traditional theoretical models, if foreigners decided to reduce their holdings of US Treasuries the dollar should also fall. However, in practice that was true until the 1990s, but since then the currency has developed into a separate asset in itself. This is justified by the fact that the foreign exchange market has an estimated volume of nearly US 1.5 trillion, according to the latest BIS Report on the foreign exchange market see Table 2, BIS 2005. Such a large volume is not justified from the volumes of the underlying assets. Hence the sheer volume of the foreign exchange market stands as evidence that it has developed into a separate asset class from the underlying assets. This has become possible because of the widespread use of hedging techniques that have managed to separate the demand for the underlying assets from the demand for currency.

Although there would be no direct effects on the dollar from a drop of US Treasuries by foreign residents, there would still be indirect effects. Other things being equal, the higher bond yields would lower growth in the US economy and this might affect the true variables that affect the dollar, such as the priorities the policy-makers assign to the targets of economic policy. Hence the strict condition that the current account should balance in the long run, which is true of all currencies, should be replaced in the case of the dollar, because it is a reserve currency, with the condition that domestic borrowing by the Federal government and the private sector, taken together, should not be so high as to create a high risk of insolvency. Nor should the proportion of foreign holdings of US assets be very high.

Hence neither the current account nor the capital account is a dollar determinant, but the opposite is true: the dollar is a determinant of the current account. A current account deficit requires either a fall in the dollar or slower US growth relative to its main trading partners for a considerable period of time, or a combination of the two, if the deficit is to disappear. Hence the justification of the premise 'the dollar is our currency, but it is your problem'. To a large extent, the deficit reflects faster US growth relative to its main trading partners. For example, the US grew at double the rate of the EU and triple the rate of Japan between the 1991 recovery and the peak of the business cycle at the end of 1999. Even since then, in the aftermath of the bursting of the Nasdaq bubble, the USA grew nearly 1 per cent faster than the EU or Japan. In some periods, such as 1995–2001, the US current account deficit was aggravated by a loss in US competitiveness.

A game theoretic approach to euro–dollar exchange rate

Two features are important in setting up a valid alternative to the bankrupt small open economy or two-country framework of dollar exchange rate determination. The first is that, since the 1990s, the dollar has become increasingly a separate asset class from the underlying assets: it is no longer the product of a derived demand. The second feature is that the exchange rate, as an important part of the transmission mechanism of monetary policy, should be an equilibrium outcome that is consistent with the investors' portfolio objectives. These features entail an appropriate game-theoretic framework, in which the equilibrium outcome depends on the policy actions of both policy-makers (players), and where the interactions of such decisions are modelled explicitly.[1] Hence the relevant variables affecting, say, the value of the euro–dollar rate are the fiscal and monetary policies pursued by US and EU policy-makers. This is so because policy-makers in each country pursue policies that attempt to reach the best possible outcome (optimum) in terms of such target variables as inflation and growth, through manipulating the level of interest rates, tax rates or discretionary government spending (in other words, monetary and fiscal policy). But the exchange rate plays an important part in the way fiscal and monetary policies affect the target variables of inflation and growth, and therefore its value is determined in the middle of that process.

The condition that the exchange rate is consistent with investors' portfolio objectives ensures the stability of the economic and financial system, and therefore the success of the policies pursued. For example, tight monetary policy with the objective of curbing inflation would be more effective if the currency appreciates, since it is expected to reduce imported inflation. If investors endorse such a policy as optimal, then the currency would appreciate. On the other hand, easy monetary policy with the objective of promoting growth would be more effective if the currency depreciates, because gains in competitiveness would boost exports and reduce imports. Again, if investors endorse such a policy as optimal, then the currency would depreciate.

In this framework, the policy decisions of one country may affect favourably or adversely economic magnitudes in the other country, where the outcome depends on the state of each economy in the business cycle. If the business cycles are not synchronized, then the policy decisions of one country will affect the other country favourably. For example, whenever the US business cycle is not synchronized with that of the euro area, the resulting equilibrium is stable, simply because there is no conflict: one player's interest dictates a strong currency, while the other's dictates a weak currency. By contrast, whenever there is synchronization of the business cycles, there is conflict in that it is in both players' interests to have either a weak or a strong currency. In the latter case, investors impose the equilibrium that enhances US welfare even if that is detrimental to the euro area in the short run, since this implies that the world economic and financial system is stable. Two reasons indicate that the equilibrium that enhances US welfare implies a stable system. First, the effect of US monetary and fiscal policy on the euro area is bigger than the effect of euro area policies on the USA (that is, a bigger 'beggar thy neighbour' policy effect). Second, the euro area is more vulnerable than the USA to supply shocks, such as the price of oil (see Karakitsos, 1988a, 1988b).

It can be shown that, in this framework,[2] the dollar is strong when the US economy is either overheated or cools down, but inflation continues to rise because of inertia. In this phase of the business cycle the Fed wants to cap inflationary pressures and assigns a higher priority to combating inflation than to promoting growth. On the other hand, the dollar is weak when the economy is either in recession or in the recovery phase of the business cycle, where there is spare capacity. In this phase of the business cycle, the Fed wants to promote growth through exports and the policy priority is higher than that of fighting inflation. In the early 2000s the dollar was weak because the USA wanted an export-led recovery, but in the second half of the 1990s the dollar was strong because the USA was growing faster than its potential, thereby creating inflationary pressures. The equilibrium outcome in which the dollar is either strong or weak is different. It can be proved that the strong dollar is derived as 'Stackelberg-leader' equilibrium, and the weak dollar as 'Stackelberg-follower' equilibrium.[3]

The implication of this game-theoretic framework is that what matters for the dollar is the USA and not its relative position with regard to its main trading partners. Hence popular variables, such as (short or long) interest rate differentials, growth differentials, money supply differentials and, inflation differentials, which emanate from the small open economy or the two-country model, may lead to erroneous conclusions about dollar movements. The models that involve such variables are usually unstable, in the sense that the impact of these variables on the euro–dollar exchange rate changes over time from statistically significant to statistically insignificant, and sometimes from positive to negative. The model instability is caused by a shift in the equilibrium from Stackelberg-leader to Stackelberg-follower. Once this game framework has been taken into account, and the shift of the equilibrium between Stackelberg-leader and Stackelberg-follower, the resulting dollar–euro model is stable. Moreover, the Stackelberg game framework does not imply that the traditional variables should be used for the USA only. Instead, what is important is that the dollar should move in such a way so that the US economy can benefit under all circumstances. If this is not the case, then not only is the USA, but also ROW, at risk, as the economic and financial system would be unstable.

The stability issue clarifies why the ECB in some periods is unable either to stem the euro's dip or its rise. In the post-bubble environment, a rate cut by the ECB does not have the desired effect of restraining the euro's rise, in view of the euro area's business cycle being synchronized with that of the USA. Since the bursting of the bubble in 2000, both the USA and the euro area are struggling to recover, and a weak currency is desired by both. In the absence of intervention, the only stable equilibrium is the one that favours dollar weakness, and this is the one that markets impose. The equilibrium with a weak dollar is stable, because it would lead to a US-led world recovery, whereas a dollar rise (and consequently a euro fall) would not help the rest of the world to recover, and perhaps not even the euro area itself. In this respect, the experience of France in the early 1980s is pertinent. At that time, the rest of G7 pursued deflationary policies to fend off the inflation effect of the second oil shock, while the socialist French government pursued expansionary policies to fight the recession. In the event, France was forced after a short time to reverse its policies, as they led to instability because of a currency crisis. In the period between the end of the Asian–Russian crisis (1998) and the bursting of the equity bubble (2000) the ECB, and prior to that the Bundesbank, was again unable to stem the euro's fall, in spite of tight monetary policy, because its business cycle was again synchronized with that of the USA. By contrast, whenever the US business cycle is not synchronized with that of the euro area, the resulting equilibrium is stable, simply because there is no conflict – one player's interest dictates a strong currency, while the other's dictates a weak currency. This was the case between 1994 and 1998, when the USA was overheated, but the euro area was operating with spare capacity.

The above analysis suggests that the variables affecting the value of the dollar are: (i) US fiscal policy; (ii) US monetary policy; (iii) the priorities that the Fed assigns to the targets of economic policy; and (iv) the risk of insolvency, along with the risk that foreign residents' appetite for US assets may dry up. Figure 8.3 shows that the level of the Federal debt stands as a proxy of the insolvency risk, along with the risk that foreign residents' appetite for US assets may dry up. Clearly, the higher the Federal debt is, the higher are both risks, and therefore the lower the value of the dollar. Hence declining Federal debt is consistent with a stronger dollar. Figure 8.4 shows that the insolvency and appetite risk also depends on the Federal budget deficit.

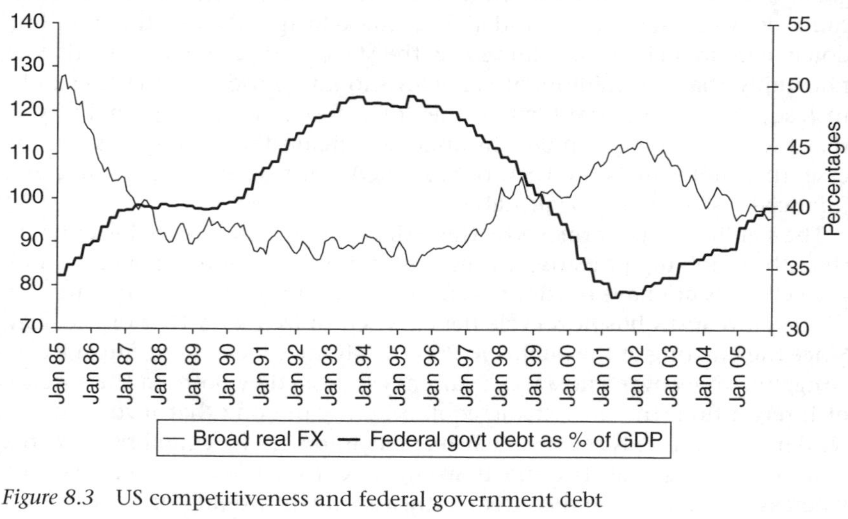

Figure 8.3 US competitiveness and federal government debt

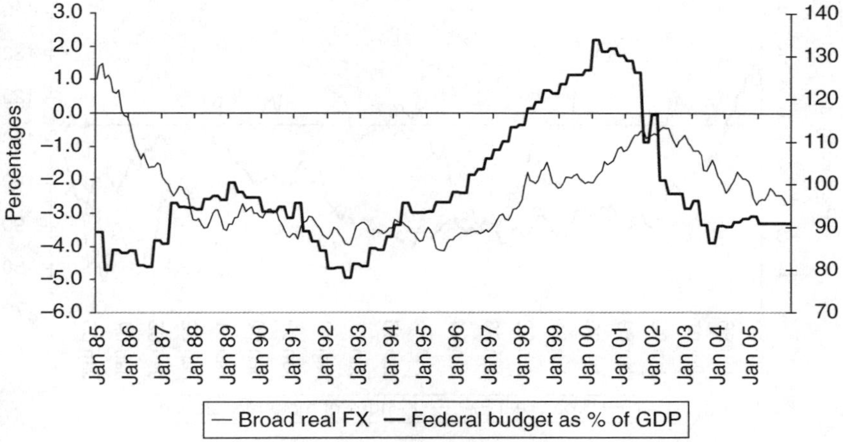

Figure 8.4 Federal budget and broad real exchange rate

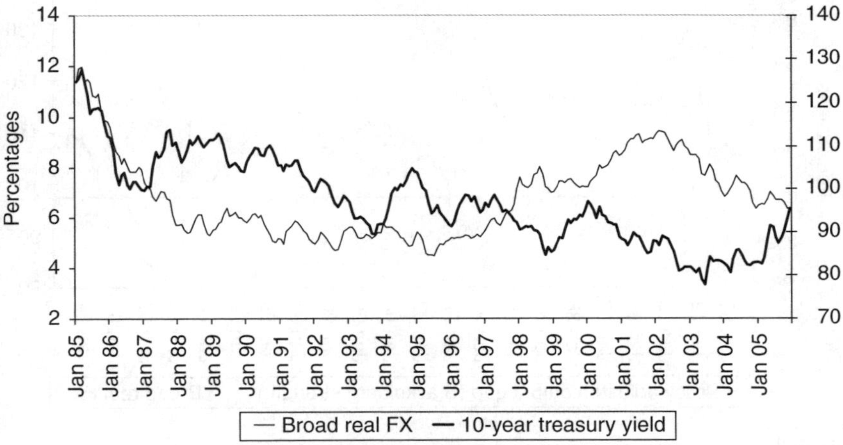

Figure 8.5 Ten-year note yield and broad real exchange rate

The higher the budget deficit, either because of easy fiscal policy or because of exogenous factors that cause slower growth, the lower the value of the dollar. Hence a dwindling budget deficit leads to a stronger dollar. Figure 8.5 shows that the insolvency and appetite risk also depends on US Treasury yields. The higher the 10-year Treasury yield the higher are both risks, and therefore the weaker the dollar.[4] Figure 8.6 shows that the value of the dollar depends on the stance of monetary policy: the tighter the stance of

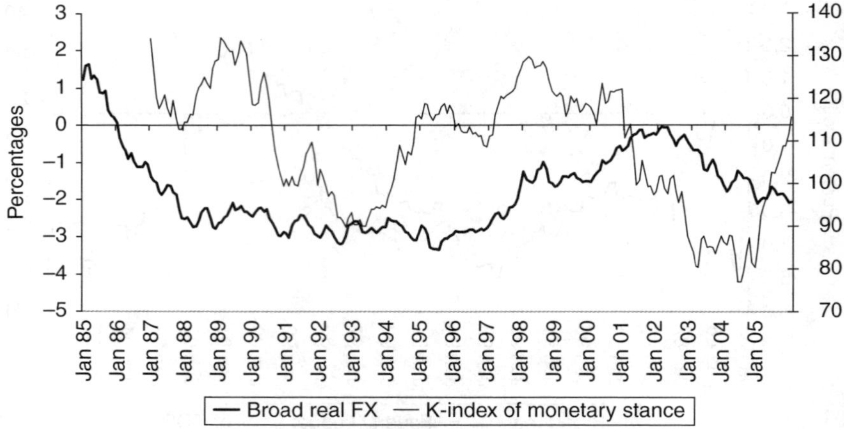

Figure 8.6 Stance of monetary policy and US competitiveness

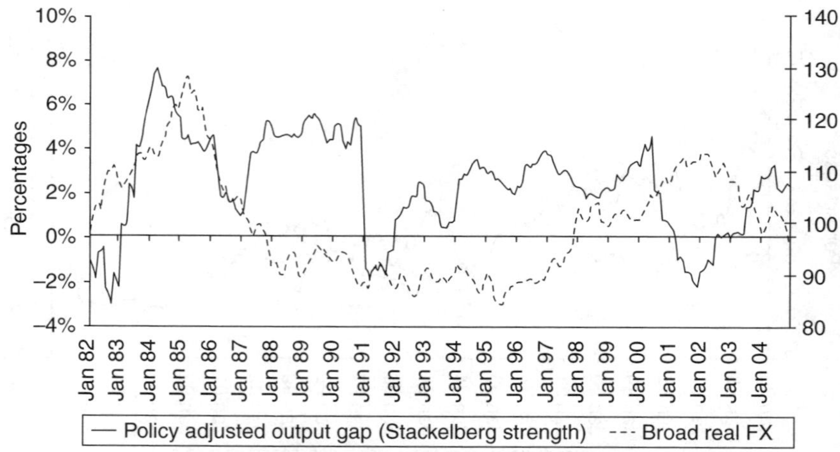

Figure 8.7 US competitiveness and policy adjusted output gap

monetary policy, the stronger is the dollar. The stance of monetary policy is judged by an index, which is a weighted average of domestic and external monetary conditions, with the weights reflecting the importance of domestic demand and exports to GDP. Domestic monetary conditions are measured by the deviation of the real Fed funds rate from its neutral level, while external monetary conditions are measured by the deviation of the real effective exchange rate from its neutral level.[5] Finally, Figure 8.7 shows that the dollar depends on the policy-adjusted output gap. The larger the policy-adjusted output gap, the more importance the Fed is assigning to the inflation target. The adjusted policy output gap is a weighted average of the excess of growth over potential output growth and inflation with the weights reflecting the priorities that the Fed assigns to these two targets of economic policy.

An account of the recent dollar behaviour

In this framework, it is easy to explain why the dollar fell in the early 2000s, and why this may be a turning point. Fiscal policy turned into an easy stance in the aftermath of the bursting of the equity bubble, and this increased the deficit and reversed the falling trend of Federal debt. Both factors contributed to the dollar fall, as the insolvency and appetite risks increased. Monetary policy turned into an easy stance at the end of 2000, as inflation peaked and the economy slowed dramatically, falling into recession in 2001. Easy monetary policy also contributed to the dollar's slide since 2001. At the end of 2000, the Fed also switched its priorities on inflation and growth. The high priority of combating inflation that had been in place in the aftermath of the Asian–Russian crisis was replaced by a high priority of protecting the economy from the deflationary forces that emerged with the bursting of the equity bubble. This change in the priorities of the Fed, along with a rapidly weakening economy, produced a sharp fall in the policy adjusted output gap, which with a lag-caused dollar weakness. Despite easy fiscal policy, bond yields fell, as the Fed relaxed monetary policy, and this put a cushion on the extent to which the dollar has fallen since 2001.

The majority of these factors suggest that the dollar has turned around putting an end to a three-year falling dollar trend. First, fiscal policy became tighter in fiscal year 2005, and this should stabilize, both the Federal budget deficit and the Federal debt as a percentage of GDP. In time, this should reverse the falling dollar into an up-trend. The Fed started raising interest rates in June 2004, but the pace has so far been rather slow. The stance of monetary policy has not yet shown any reversal, as the higher interest rates have been offset by higher inflation and the weakening dollar. However, at the beginning of February 2005, Greenspan characterized the low long-term interest rates as a 'conundrum', and this pushed bond yields up. The FOMC statement at the end of March 2005, effectively announced a change in the priorities the Fed assigns to inflation and growth. The Fed has restored a high priority to combating inflation, and assigned a low priority to promoting growth, as the stubbornly high oil price has pushed up inflationary pressures in the economy. On the other hand, growth has exceeded potential output for nearly two years. In time, the change of policy priorities would also help to reverse the dollar weakness.

Although the real dollar (or competitiveness) has already turned around at the time of writing, a clear up-trend will take quite some time to emerge. The bottoming-out process may take more than a year, with large swings in the dollar that will make the market doubt that the dollar in fact has turned around. Nevertheless, economic fundamentals suggest that the dollar has bottomed-out not only with respect to the main currencies such as the euro, the yen and the pound sterling, but also against the main commodity currencies such as the Australian and the Canadian dollars, and the currencies of emerging countries. The extent to which the dollar will rebound depends on how its four main determinants move in the near future, which depends on the stance of economic policy (both fiscal and monetary) and developments in the two main policy targets of growth and inflation, which at the time of writing are heavily influenced by the oil price.

The risks are not balanced. If the price of oil keeps rising or remains stubbornly higher than we have assumed, then the Fed would rein in even faster than we have assumed and the economy fall into recession in 2006. The US economy will drag the world economy down and the price of oil will collapse. In this case the dollar would resume its downward trend, as the US would again seek to get out of the recession with an export-led recovery.

If the price of oil subsides in the summer and stays low, without recovering to above US$50 per barrel in the winter, as we have assumed in the main scenario, then the Fed funds rate will rise less than expected in the main scenario. Hence, this risk does not make any qualitative difference to the main scenario; it simply reinforces the conclusion that the dollar has bottomed-out, although the up-trend will become apparent next year.

Conclusions

Many gloomy dollar forecasts rely either on the assumption that the already huge current account deficit will continue to widen, as the USA is growing at a faster pace than its main trading partners, or on the assumption that foreign residents' appetite for US assets will dry up. However, neither the current account nor the capital account is a dollar determinant, as the dollar is a reserve currency. Hence, the condition that the current account should balance in the long run holds true for all currencies except the dollar. Nevertheless, this does not imply that the USA can run an ever-growing current account deficit, as this would increase the risk of insolvency and the risk that the appetite of foreign residents for US assets might ultimately dry up. But these risks are better measured by the Federal budget deficit, the Federal debt and Treasury yields rather than the current account deficit.

The small open economy and the two-country model, upon which most gloomy dollar forecasts rely, cannot easily explain why the dollar fell after 2001. Both models are likely to continue to be misleading in the future, as they rely on variables that do not have a stable relationship with the dollar. Instead, our game-theoretic approach has identified a stable dollar relationship with the variables that affect its value. Fiscal and monetary policy, the priorities on the policy targets of economic policy and the risk related to insolvency and appetite for US assets are the major determinants of the real dollar.

In this framework, it is easy to explain the ups and downs of the dollar in the 2000s. Following the burstings of the bubble in 2000 and the ensuing recession, fiscal policy turned from tight to easy providing a huge fiscal stimulus of the order of 6.5 per cent of GDP in the three years to 2004. This resulted in a deficit in the Federal budget, which reversed the falling trends of the Federal debt. Monetary policy which was tight untill the end of 2000 to fight inflation, turned easy to combat the recession. The reversal in the stance of monetary policy reflects a switch in the Fed's priorities between inflation and growth. All these factors have combined to produce a weakening dollar since 2001.

Since mid-2004, all these have been progressively reversed once more and they herald the beginning of dollar strength, provided the economy remains near capacity and inflationary pressures continue to build up.

Given that fiscal policy has become tighter, the stance of monetary policy will become even more so in the months ahead, and the priorities of the Fed on inflation and growth have changed, the real dollar (or competitiveness) has already turned around, but a clear up-trend will take quite some time to emerge. The bottoming-out process may take more than a year, with large swings in the dollar that will make the market doubt that the dollar has turned around. Nevertheless, economic fundamentals suggest that the dollar has bottomed out not only with respect to the main currencies such as the euro, the yen and the pound sterling, but also against the main commodity currencies such the Australian and the Canadian dollars and the currencies of emerging countries.

Notes

1 Although game theory has been used extensively in microeconomics, the only applications at the macro level have been in the area of macro policies in an interdependent world (see the seminal papers by Hamada (1974, 1976, 1979), Cooper (1985) and applications by Canzoneri and Gray (1983), Becker (1986) and Sachs *et al.* (1983)).
2 See Frowen and Karakitsos (1998), Arestis and Karakitsos (2004, 2005).
3 The relevant proofs can be found in Frowen and Karakitsos (1998), and Arestis and Karakitsos (2004, 2005).
4 This is interesting, as in the two-country model a higher bond yield would be more likely to lead to dollar appreciation than depreciation.
5 Neutral level of a variable is defined as the level that corresponds to the rate of growth of the potential output.

References

Arestis, P. and Karakitsos, E. (2004) *The Post-Bubble US Economy: Implications for Financial Markets and the Economy*, Basingstoke: Palgrave Macmillan.

Arestis, P. and Karakitsos, E. (2005) 'A Policy-Game Framework for the Dollar–Euro Exchange Rate', Working Paper Series no. 2, Cambridge Centre for Economic and Public Policy, University of Cambridge.

Bank for International Settlement (2005) *OTC Derivatives Market Activity in the Second half of 2004*, May (Basel: BIS).

Becker, R. G., Dwolatzky, B., Karakitsos, E. and Rustem, B. (1986) 'Optimal Policy Design with Non-linear Models: The Multi Agent Case', *Journal of Economic Dynamics and Control*, 10(1), pp. 27–36.

Canzoneri, M. and Gray, J. (1983) 'Two Essays on Monetary Policy in an Interdependent World', Discussion Paper Series no. 219, *Federal Reserve Board International Finance*.

Cooper, R. N. (1985) 'Economic Interdependence and Co-ordination of Economic Policies', in R. W. Jones and P. B. Kenen (eds), *Handbook of International Economics*, vol. II (London: Elsevier Science Publishers).

Dornbusch, R. (1976) 'Expectations and Exchange Rate Dynamics', *Journal of Political Economy*, 84(4), pp. 1161–76.

Dornbusch, R. and Fisher, S. (1980) 'Exchange Rates and the Current Account', *American Economic Review*, 70(5), pp. 960–71.

Fleming, J. M. (1962) 'Domestic Financial Policies Under Fixed and Under Flexible Exchange Rates', *International Monetary Fund Staff Papers*, 9(4), pp. 369–79.

Frowen, S. F. and Karakitsos, E. (1998) 'A Strategic Approach to the Euro Prospects', *Public Finance*, 53(1), pp. 1–18.

Hamada, K. (1974) 'Alternative Exchange Rate Systems and the Interdependence of Monetary Policies', in R. Z. Aliber (ed.), *National Monetary Policies and the International Financial System* (University of Chicago Press).

Hamada, K. (1976) 'A Strategic Analysis on Monetary Interdependence', *Journal of Political Economy*, 84(4), pp. 677–700.

Hamada, K. (1979) 'Macroeconomic Strategy and Co-ordination Under Alternative Exchange Rate Regimes', in R. Dornbusch and J. A. Frankel (eds), *International Economic Policy* (Baltimore, Md.: Johns Hopkins University Press).

Karakitsos, E. (1988a) 'Asymmetrical Effects of Monetary Policy between the US and Europe', *Journal of Economic Dynamic and Control*, 12(1), pp. 79–85.

Karakitsos, E. (1988b) 'An Analysis of the Asymmetrical Effects of Fiscal Policy Between the US and Europe', *Oxford Bulletin of Economics and Statistics*, 50(3), pp. 279–303.

Meade, J. E. (1951) *The Theory of International Economics, Vol. 1: The Balance of Payments* (Oxford University Press).

Mundell, R. A. (1960) 'The Monetary Dynamics of Adjustment Under Fixed and Flexible Exchange Rates', *Quarterly Journal of Economics*, 74(2), pp. 227–57. Reprinted in R. A. Mundell (1968) *International Economics* (New York: Macmillan).

Mundell, R. A. (1963) 'Capital Mobility and Stabilisation Policy Under Fixed and Flexible Exchange Rates', *Canadian Journal of Economics and Political Science*, 29(4), pp. 475–85.

Sachs, J. (1983) 'International Policy Co-ordination in a Dynamic Macro-Model', NBER Working Paper Series no. 1166, Washington, DC: National Bureau of Economic Research.

9

The Pattern of Inward FDI Geographical Distribution: Can Developing Countries Base Their Development on Those Flows?*

Jesus Ferreiro, Carmen Gomez and Carlos Rodriguez

Developing economies have been recommended strongly since the 1980s by international organizations (WB, WTO, IMF, UNCTAD) to rely primarily on foreign direct investment (FDI) as a source of external funds and as an engine for growth. It is argued that FDI is superior to other types of capital flows, acting as a kind of 'good cholesterol', because it offers to the host country not just less volatile financial resources but also a bundle of important assets for growth: access to modern technology, and know-how. This recommendation has been general to all the developing economies, without taking into account their structural differences. The success of some Latin-American and South-East Asian economies would be examples to be imitated.

However, empirical studies show how the generation of long-term positive effects of FDI inflows is, basically contingent on some conditions, and besides the amount of flow, the stability of the flow and effective generation and diffusion of spillovers. With these caveats in mind, the objective of this chapter is twofold: first, to analyse from a long-term perspective the stability of the FDI inflows in developing countries, and, second, whether there has been an even distribution of FDI inflows among the developing countries.

FDI as a potential engine for growth and development

Inward FDI (except that funded by affiliates' profits and borrowing in the host country) is a source of external resources that allows host economies to invest more than they save. But, while this is important, the main contribution of inward FDI to the growth of host economies is not the amount of capital flows received but rather the consequent supply of

* This work is within the remit of the research project financed by the University of the Basque Country (Project code: 1/UPV 00032.321-H-15295/2003).

elements considered as determinants of long-term growth: namely, technology and knowledge. The more effective working of foreign subsidiaries and the induced improvements in efficiency of local firms (rivals, suppliers and customers) lead to higher competitiveness among host countries and to higher rates of economic growth in the long run.

FDI is considered to be an important determinant of endogenous growth, because it is a way of augmenting the existing stock of knowledge in the recipient country through labour training, skills acquisition and diffusion, and the introduction of alternative management practices and organizational arrangements. In sum, FDI is expected to be a potential source of productivity gains via spillovers to local firms. In this sense, inward FDI raises economic growth by promoting technological diffusion from developed world to host countries. FDI offers know-how and technology that are proprietary to the investor – that is, the multinational enterprise (MNE), ('ownership advantages' according to Dunning, 1993) because they rely on the most advanced methods of production and organization. Therefore MNEs are seen as natural and powerful vehicles of technology transfer to less developed economies[1] (UNCTAD, 1992).

However, these positive consequences of inward FDI depend on the existence of a number of conditions and assumptions – among them, first, that FDI flows must be more stable than portfolio flows; and, second, that FDI must supply these competitive advantages through spillover effects[2] that help to create a stable long-term path of development in which the host economy can compete with other economies at a similar or higher level of development.[3]

The rising dependence of developing countries on FDI inflows

This positive view of the consequences for growth and development has led most developing countries to rely on FDI inflows, and the work and spread of foreign subsidiaries, as catalysts for the desired structural transformation and modernization of their productive structures. For these developing countries, it is assumed that FDI inflows have a number of advantages compared to portfolio flows: a higher stability, the ability to create employment, the ability to generate external resources because of the higher export propensity of foreign subsidiaries, the improved efficiency in the working of the markets where domestic suppliers and rivals firms operate, and, finally, the supply of competitive advantages. In sum, inward FDI helps to solve two of the main constraints suffered by developing countries: the lack of financial resources and of competitive advantages that allow them to compete with the most advances countries or with economies with a similar level of development.

With regard to the question of the stability of FDI flows, there is a belief, based on the experience of the debt crisis of the 1980s, and the subsequent Mexican and Asiatic financial crisis in the 1990s, that, in comparison with short-term capital flows, FDI is the most secure and stable source of funds for developing countries (Dadush *et al.*, 2000; Lipsey 2001). The basic assumption is that FDI reflects a long-term compromise of the investor when s/he owns 10 per cent or more of the shares of the affiliate. Furthermore, these funds do not generate debt and cannot be withdrawn quickly. Nevertheless, this is a more complicated issue. First, the distinction between FDI and portfolio investment is currently weaker than it was some decades ago because of the development of derivatives and hedge-funds, which allow foreign investors to liquidate their immobile assets with local funds (Claessens *et al.*, 1995). Second, reinvested earnings obtained from foreign affiliates operations are considered to be FDI flows; and these may be another source of volatility inducing FDI fluctuations, since their amount depends on the business cycle in the host economy. Third, there is also evidence that FDI inflows arrive in waves, generating volatility in the flows (Singh, 2004), especially when there are specific international mega mergers and acquisitions operations, as has been the case in the most recent years.

Another argument supporting confidence in the long-term stability of FDI flows is the significant growth of FDI inflows in developing countries during the 1990s that has increased the ratio of FDI inflows to other capital inflows.[4] However, the evolution of this ratio is not a direct effect of the growth in FDI inflows: indeed, it is mainly explained by the fall in portfolio investment and other private, short-term capital flows.

Figure 9.1 shows the evolution of the net flows of direct and private portfolio investment in developing countries since 1982. Since the early 1990s, FDI inflows to developing countries have grown at an enormous rate, a

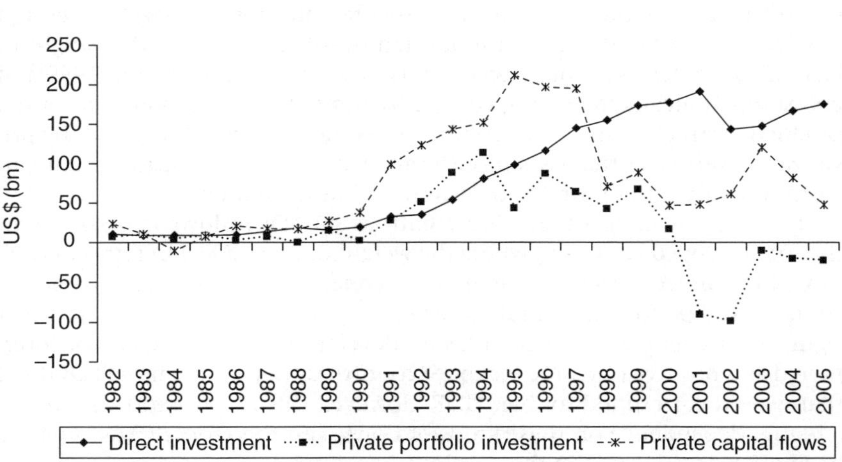

Figure 9.1 Net capital flows in other emerging market and developing countries (billions of US dollars)

Source: IMF *World Economic Outlook* databases.

phenomenon related directly to the growth in FDI flows on a worldwide basis, as we shall see later. During the early years of the 1990s the growth in FDI inflows was in parallel with the increase in other capital flows, with the outcome being that the net private capital flows to these economies reached unparalleled level. However, since the late 1990s, after several currency crises affecting some Latin-American countries, South-East Asia, Turkey and Russia, the net private portfolio flows fell dramatically, leading to negative net private flows in developing economies. In fact, the rise in FDI inflows since the late 1990s have only partially offset the fall in portfolio flows. Therefore, the importance given by developing countries to inward FDI seems to be a side effect of the fall in the portfolio flows.

This conclusion is reinforced if we analyse the distribution by groups of countries of the net capital flows to developing countries. As can be seen from Table 9.1, since 2000 net private portfolio flows have fallen in all the regions, reaching negative figures. The only exceptions are the economies of Central and Eastern Europe, which maintain positive net portfolio flows.

Nevertheless, in all regions the dependence of developing countries on foreign direct investment has increased dramatically. As can be seen from Table 9.2, with the only exception being the Central and Eastern Europe economies, the share of direct investment in total private capital flows has increased rapidly, reaching in all regions percentages well above 100 per cent. In any case, it is evident that the increase in that share is not only caused by the increase in direct investment flows but largely by the fall in other private capital flows.

The rising dependence of developing economies on FDI inflows is shown clearly in Figure 9.2. Since the early 1990s, the percentage of net FDI inflows in GDP has risen in the developing countries reaching figures close to 4 per cent of GDP in the year 2000. Even more significant is the rise in the weight of FDI inflows in terms of total investments, reaching 16.6 percent in 1999 and 2000, which means increasing control by transnational corporations of the productive structure in those economies, a process linked directly to the privatization processes that took place in many developing countries, mainly in Latin America, and Central and Eastern European countries.

The dependence of developing countries on FDI inflows is higher than that of developed countries, where the weight of inward FDI in terms of GDP or GFCF is much lower. This higher dependence is also reflected when we compare the performance indices for both groups of economies.[5] At a first sight, the higher performance index for developing countries could be interpreted as a positive outcome for those countries: they attract more FDI flows than would correspond to their GDP. However, this higher ratio also means a higher dependence on these kinds of flows, and therefore of MNEs whose head offices are located in the developed economies.

Furthermore, the evolution of the performance index is much more volatile in the developing countries. It is remarkable in fact that despite the

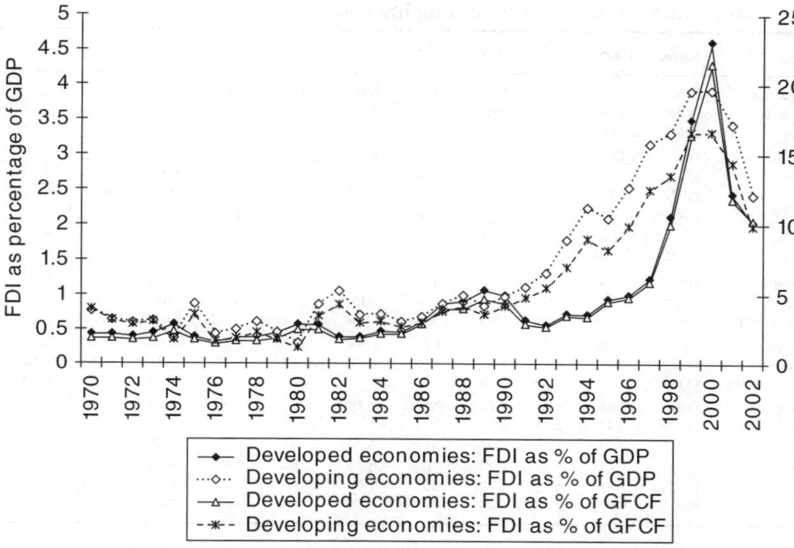

Figure 9.2 FDI as percentage of GDP and GFCF in host economies

Source: UNCTAD *Handbook of Statistics* on-line (www.unctad.org).

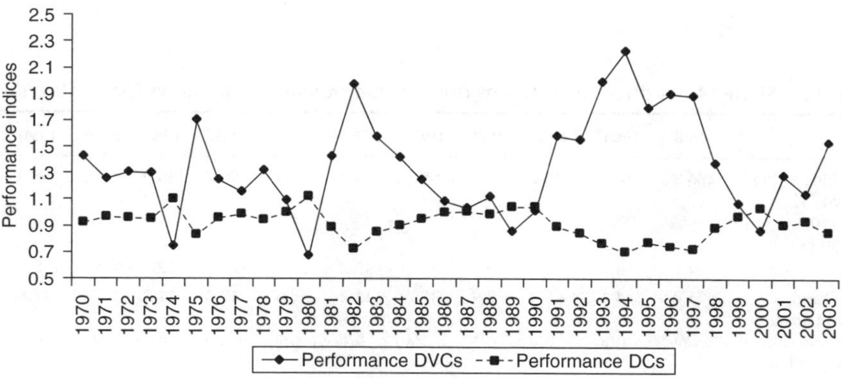

Figure 9.3 Performance indices in developing countries (DVCs) and developed countries (DCs)

Source: UNCTAD *Handbook of Statistics* on-line (www.unctad.org).

Table 9.1 Net private capital flows to developing countries (billions of US dollars)

Region	Flows	1980	1981	1982	1983	1984	1985	1986	1987	1988	1989	1990
EMDC, including selected advanced economies	DIN	7.51	13.0	10.7	10.4	9.97	10.1	10.6	13.1	18.5	15.6	19.1
	PCFN	5.96	50.0	23.2	10.7	−11.7	4.52	16.5	14.4	12.5	27.2	29.3
	PPFN	0.8	2.65	6.86	9.7	4.62	8.57	3.09	7.52	2.37	18.1	−1.85
Africa	DIN	0.79	0.35	1.38	0.9	0.65	0.2	1.41	1.47	1.71	2.5	1.94
	PCFN	3.2	9.44	8.33	4.6	2.54	0.5	4.38	−0.65	7.75	−0.62	1.64
	PPFN	−0.44	0.21	0.99	−0.28	1.08	0.05	−0.34	−0.31	−0.17	−0.01	−0.19
Central and Eastern Europe	DIN	0.04	0.15	0.09	0.09	0.16	0.13	0.14	0.13	0.38	0.96	1.17
	PCFN	3.6	4.38	−0.92	−2.95	−0.41	1.18	−2.44	0.97	3.23	3.51	6.59
	PPFN	0	0	0	0	0	0	0.15	0.28	1.18	1.33	0.55
Commonwealth of Independent States and Mongolia	DIN	n/a	n/a	n/a	n/a	n/a	n/a	n/a	n/a	n/a	n/a	n/a
	PCFN	n/a	n/a	n/a	n/a	n/a	n/a	n/a	n/a	n/a	n/a	n/a
	PPFN	n/a	n/a	n/a	n/a	n/a	n/a	n/a	n/a	n/a	n/a	n/a
Developing Asia including selected advanced economies	DIN	3.0	4.31	3.71	4.25	4.2	3.07	4.24	6.63	7.28	5.67	9.5
	PCFN	18.9	22.3	19.9	17.6	6.77	11.8	13.9	5.79	−3.87	6.65	11.9
	PPFN	0.29	1.34	1.09	1.1	0.34	5.89	1.15	1.13	−1.56	−0.05	−1.63
Middle East including selected advanced economies	DIN	−1.44	0.25	−0.23	0.64	1.18	1.39	1.05	−0.69	−0.15	−0.58	0.53
	PCFN	−41	−25.1	−15.6	7.23	−12.0	0.7	4.22	7.23	1.44	10.4	−2.86
	PPFN	−0.03	−1.38	0.33	8.1	2.72	3.53	2.35	6.38	1.57	11.6	2.07
Latin-America	DIN	5.62	8.44	6.28	5.03	4.29	5.88	3.98	5.72	8.8	7.34	6.63
	PCFN	36.5	46.0	15.9	−9.36	−1.69	−2.0	0.84	9.89	3.97	1.6	12.2
	PPFN	0.99	2.48	4.44	0.77	0.49	−0.9	−0.22	0.04	1.35	5.18	−2.64

Source: IMF, *World Economic Outlook* database, September 2004.

Notes: n/a – /not available; EMDC – emerging markets and developing countries; DIN – direct investment, net; PCFN – private capital flows, net; and PPFN – private portfolio flows, net.

Table 9.2 Share of net direct investment flows in net private capital flows (percentages)

	1980	1981	1982	1983	1984	1985	1986	1987	1988	1989	1990	1991
EMDC including selected advanced economies	126.0	26.0	46.2	97.4	−85.5	223.7	64.4	90.7	148.0	57.4	65.0	41.6
Africa	24.7	3.7	16.6	19.5	25.7	40.2	32.2	−225.8	22.1	−402.4	118.3	136.5
Central and Eastern Europe	1.0	3.4	−9.4	−2.9	−37.7	11.2	−5.8	13.3	11.7	27.3	17.8	−25.1
Commonwealth of independent States and Mongolia	n/a	n/a	n/a	n/a	n/a	n/a	n/a	n/a	n/a	n/a	n/a	n/a
Middle East	3.5	−1.0	1.5	8.8	−9.8	199.4	24.8	−9.6	−10.5	−5.5	−18.5	2.1
Latin America	15.4	18.4	39.4	−53.7	−253.1	−294.0	474.1	57.8	221.7	457.5	54.3	49.7
Developing Asia	15.89	19.29	18.61	24.16	61.97	25.97	30.44	114.5	−187.9	85.18	79.71	47.66

Source: IMF, *World Economic Outlook* database, September 2004.

Notes: n/a–not available; EMDC – Emerging markets and developing countries; DIN – direct investment, net; PCFN – private capital flows, net; PPFN – private portfolio flows, net.

1991	1992	1993	1994	1995	1996	1997	1998	1999	2000	2001	2002	2003	2004	2005
36.0	38.8	53.9	80.9	103.0	116.0	145.0	155.0	173.0	177.0	191.0	143.0	148.0	167.0	175.0
86.4	116.0	148.0	119.0	173.0	197.0	195.0	70.5	88.1	46.6	47.8	61.2	120.0	81.6	47.5
31.0	54.2	92.0	93.2	25.4	86.3	63.3	41.9	66.6	16.1	−91.3	−99.6	−11.0	−21.3	−23.4
2.67	1.15	2.84	2.97	1.66	3.11	7.91	6.62	8.95	8.04	23.8	13.1	13.6	14.4	15.5
1.96	−2.55	−0.46	7.39	3.8	4.45	12.3	8.33	12.2	5.64	13.5	11.9	14.8	16.6	13.7
0.73	2.36	1.18	3.58	3.08	2.86	7.01	3.72	8.69	−1.74	−8.37	−0.55	−0.08	1.4	1.11
3.19	4.01	4.9	4.41	13.0	10.4	11.6	19.2	22.6	23.9	24.2	25.1	14.9	22.7	24.7
−12.7	5.17	12.9	−14.8	28.7	23	20.2	27.2	36.7	39.1	12.1	55.3	51.5	53.2	49.3
0.38	2.25	8.59	4.05	6.13	1.9	5.4	−1.39	5.65	3.08	0.46	1.51	7.0	9.25	10.0
n/a	1.02	1.76	1.37	3.26	4.89	5.94	5.34	4.33	2.43	4.63	3.92	3.81	5.72	5.95
n/a	2.76	9.01	−8.65	9.47	−3.85	19.6	7.24	−6.13	−12.6	−1.68	−9.16	15.2	−19.2	−5.79
n/a	0	3.77	−11.7	−11.2	−0.09	17.6	7.73	−3.05	−6.04	−9.21	−8.23	−4.98	−7.88	−8.22
17.7	17.9	32.5	44.5	54.4	53.4	56.5	56.1	66.4	67.4	60.5	53.8	70.0	77.2	77.5
37.2	25.3	49.4	68.1	96.6	119.0	37.6	−52.2	8.58	−4.54	9.58	25.4	52.8	79.8	8.61
2.11	12.9	25.9	20.9	22.9	32.5	6.68	8.13	56.1	19.8	−56.9	−59.6	5.55	12.0	−1.85
1.06	1.49	3.21	4.31	5.66	4.57	5.26	5.78	5.27	6.39	7.82	5.84	13.4	8.78	12.2
49.9	31.4	20.2	19.7	4.8	−1.04	7.76	13.3	−0.56	−20.6	−7.88	−23.6	−14.0	−45.5	−32.5
9.92	11.0	2.95	6.13	0.77	0.98	−2.74	−2.08	−2.31	−0.26	−7.93	−15.6	−16.7	−33.3	−27.5
11.3	13.3	8.7	23.3	24.8	39.6	57.7	61.9	65.8	69.0	70.2	41.7	31.8	38	39.3
22.7	54.3	57.1	47.5	29.8	54.8	97.4	66.6	37.3	39.6	22.2	1.4	0.02	−3.28	14.2
17.9	25.7	49.6	70.3	3.75	48.2	29.4	25.8	1.47	1.27	−9.38	−17.1	−1.71	−2.77	3.03

1992	1993	1994	1995	1996	1997	1998	1999	2000	2001	2002	2003	2004	2005
33.3	36.4	67.9	59.3	59.0	74.3	219.9	196.8	379.8	400.0	234.3	122.6	204.5	369.2
−45.0	−622.1	40.2	43.7	69.9	64.3	79.5	73.5	142.7	176.7	110.3	91.7	86.6	113.4
77.6	38.1	−29.8	45.3	45.3	57.3	70.7	61.6	61.2	200.3	45.4	28.9	42.8	50.1
37.1	19.5	−15.8	34.4	−126.9	30.3	73.7	−70.6	−19.4	−274.9	−42.8	25.0	−29.8	−102.7
4.7	15.8	21.9	118.0	−439.2	67.8	43.6	−936.1	−31.0	−99.2	−24.7	−96.1	−19.3	−37.5
24.4	15.2	49.1	83.1	72.3	59.2	92.9	176.4	174.1	316.0	2978.1	138287.0	−1159.7	276.9
70.72	65.84	65.35	56.32	44.76	150.1	−107.5	773.8	−1485	631.6	211.9	132.66	96.72	900.3

huge growth in FDI flows since the 1970s, the performance indices have hardly changed: the indices for developing countries were 1.43 in 1970 and 1.54 in 2003, and 0.93 and 0.85, respectively, for developed countries. From a long-term perspective, it seems clear that the growth in FDI inflows has been quite similar to the growth of GDP since the 1970s for both groups of economies. If FDI were to play a more active part in the growth and structural transformation of developing economies, inward FDI should grow at a faster rate than GDP. However, the experience poses serious doubts as to whether that it might happen in the near future.

The uneven distribution of FDI among developing economies

The increase in net FDI inflows to the developing countries has not been evenly distributed among these developing economies, as Figure 9.4 shows. In the 1980s, two regions (Asia and Latin America) concentrated more than 90 percent of FDI in developing economies. This share fell in the 1990s to 78.4 per cent because of the boost of direct investment in the former socialist economies of Central and Eastern Europe. It is worth noting that, in that period, when a huge increase in worldwide FDI flows took place, the share of the poorest region, Africa, fell to only 4.3 per cent. Since 2000, the regional distribution of net FDI inflows in developing economies is more even, because of the fall of the shares of Latin America and Asia, and the increases of the shares of African and Central and Eastern Europe countries.

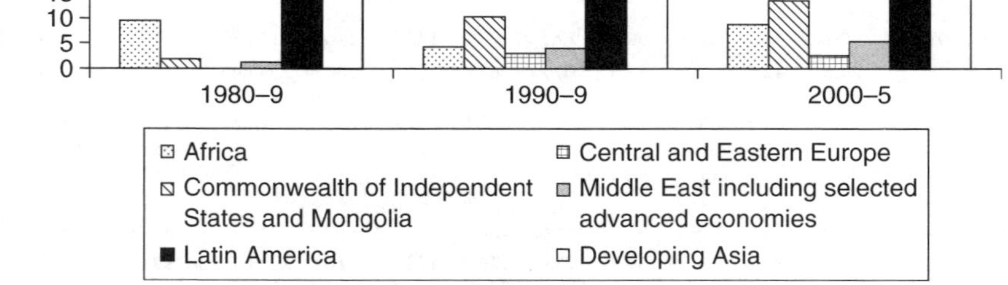

Figure 9.4 Share of net FDI inflows in developing economies (percentages)

Source: IMF, *World Economic Outlook* database, September 2004.

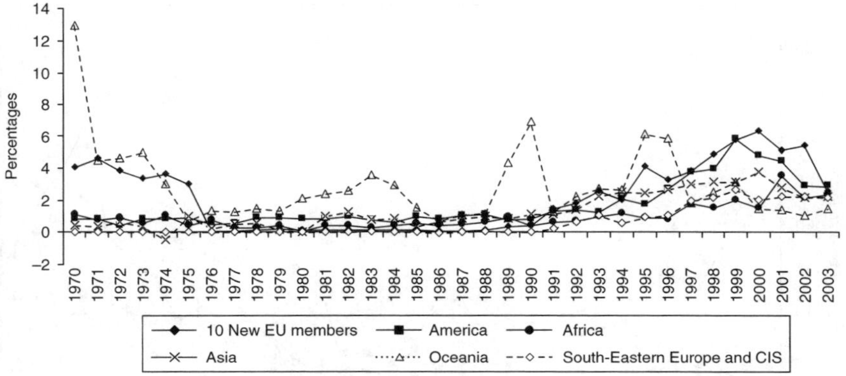

Figure 9.5 FDI inflows as percentage GDP in developing countries
Source: UNCTAD *Handbook of Statistics* on-line (www.unctad.org).

The uneven distribution of inward FDI in developing countries mirrors the different degrees of dependence of the developing regions on FDI inflows. Figure 9.5 shows the weight of FDI inflows in the GDP of the host economies. From a long-term perspective, the rise in the FDI importance for Latin America and the ten new members of EU from Central and Eastern Europe stands out. But most interesting is the case of Asia that, despite that it has become in the nineties the first receiver of FDI flows, has maintained rather stable the weight of FDI inflows in her GDP. That outcome is the result of the high rate of growth of Asian economies, higher than those of the other developing regions and even higher than that of developed economies.[6]

On the other hand, since 2000, a deep fall in the amount of FDI inflows has been registered in the case of Latin America[7] and the new EU members. Behind this outcome we can find, in the Latin-American economies, the crisis of Argentina and exhaustion of the privatization process, and in the Central and Eastern economies the end of the privatization processes and rising competition in the attraction of FDI flows exerted by South-Eastern European economies that offer better conditions (that is, lower wages) for the location of FDI[8]. In parallel, the economies of Asia, Africa and South-East Asia have enjoyed a stable or rising share of FDI inflows in their respective GDPs. Those developing economies therefore have been the least affected by the fall in world FDI flows registered in recent years.

In terms of the weight of FDI inflows in the formation of see gross fixed capital (Figure 9.6), it is clear there is a rising dependence of developing economies on foreign investment. In fact, only in Oceania has the inward FDI lost weight. Nevertheless, it is remarkable how, again, Asian countries have the lowest weight of FDI inflows. Considering the fast growth of the

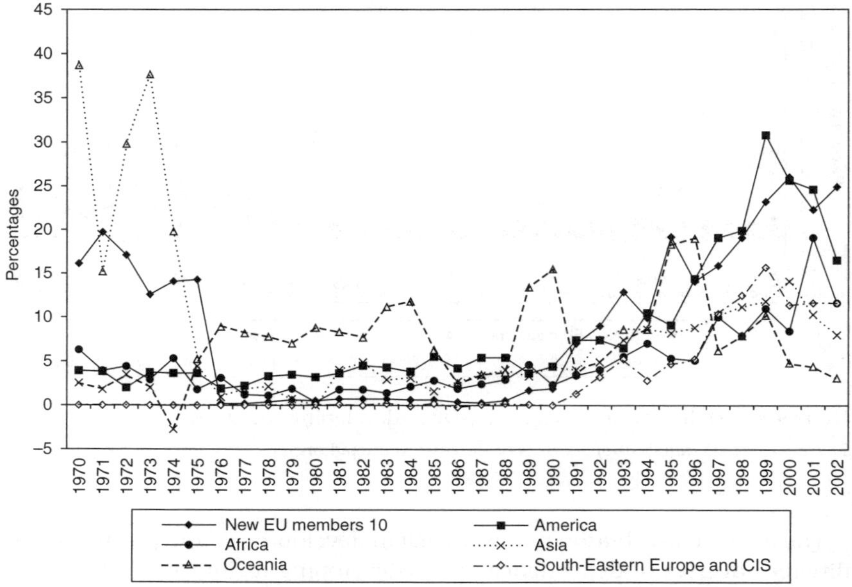

Figure 9.6 FDI inflows as percentage of GFCF in developing economies
Source: UNCTAD *Handbook of Statistics* on-line (www.unctad.org).

regions, it is clear that FDI inflows, despite their importance, are not the (only) engine of growth in the region.

Although developing economies are increasingly dependent on FDI inflows for their strategies and targets of growth and development, despite the huge growth in world FDI inflows registered since 1990, the share of these economies in world FDI flows has not increased, as shown in Figure 9.7. The share of developing countries in 2003 is only 2.3 points above that of 1970. During the whole period analyses, only in eleven years has the share ever been higher than 30 per cent.

As mentioned above, FDI inflows in developing economies have had a very volatile evolution. In fact, this volatility is clearly related to the cycles in world FDI flows. Developing countries do not profit very much when there is an FDI boom or a growth above trend. Much more often the reverse is true—the peaks regarding developing countries' shares in FDI have occurred when world FDI is below trend.[9] Booms and busts in FDI flows go hand in hand in intensity with those occurring between developed countries, but this does not happen between developing countries. This explains why the share of developing countries in world FDI flows grows when world FDI falls, and falls again inexorably when the latter recovers.

Even more striking is the fact that the gap between developed and developing countries in terms of FDI inflows per capita has significantly widened,

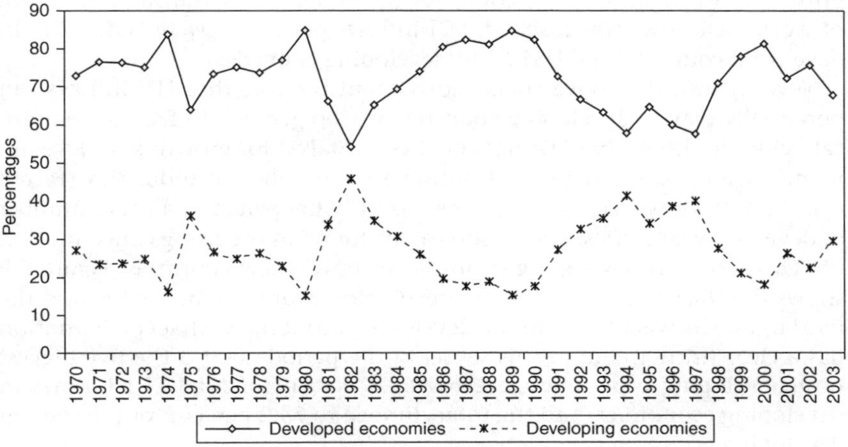

Figure 9.7 Share of FDI inflows of world FDI inflows (percentages)
Source: UNCTAD *Handbook of Statistics* on-line (www.unctad.org).

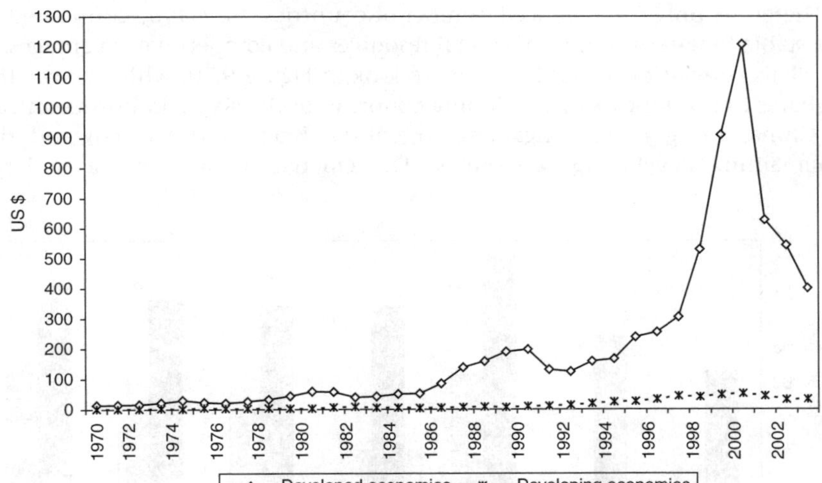

Figure 9.8 FDI inflows per capita in developed and developing economies (US dollars)
Source: UNCTAD *Handbook of Statistics* on-line (www.unctad.org).

as shown in Figure 9.8. In 1970, the FDI inflows per capita amounted to US$ 14 in developed countries and US$ 2 in developing countries. In 1990, those figures were US$ 197 in developed countries and US$ 9 in developing countries, and in 2003 the figure were US$ 400 in developed countries but only US$ 33 in developing countries (in 2000, when the highest record of world FDI flows was reached, FDI inflows per capita were US$ 1,207 in developed countries and US$ 52 in developing countries).

Nevertheless, the above conclusions about the role that FDI inflows can potentially play in developing countries are too general. In fact, the empirical evidence shows that FDI has acted as a catalyst for growth and development, raising productivity and output in a number of industries (Farrell *et al.*, 2004). However, that outcome has only happened in a small number of developing countries. The reason can be found in the rising concentration of FDI inflows in developing countries in only a few countries. Figure 9.9 shows the shares in FDI inflows in developing countries for the ten and the five largest receivers of FDI in the developing economies. That concentration has a clear rising trend: in this sense, in the period 2000–3 the five biggest host developing economies received 62.8 percent of total FDI inflows in developing economies, and the total climbed to 74.2 percent for the top-ten developing economies.

A related problem is the fact that the composition of these groups of favoured economies has not been stable. The fact is that since 1970 only four economies have been ranked among the top ten, although their absolute ranks have varied. These are: Brazil, Hong Kong, Mexico and Singapore. Therefore, only for a reduced number of countries can FDI be considered as a stable long-term source of capital resources and competitive advantages.

This conclusion is reinforced if we look at Figure 9.10, which shows the shares in FDI inflows in developing countries of the six main host countries (China, Hong Kong, Singapore, Argentina, Brazil and Mexico) and the remaining developing economies. The emergence of China as a large

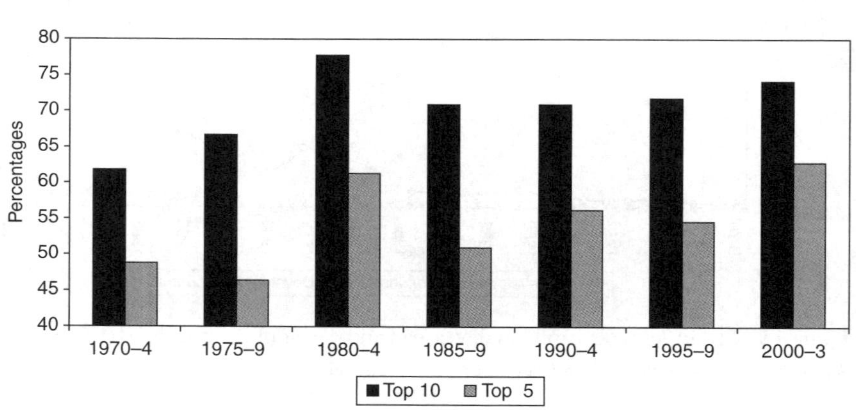

Figure 9.9 Share of FDI inflows in developing countries for the top ten and top five developing countries percentages

Source: UNCTAD *Handbook of Statistics* on-line (www.unctad.org).

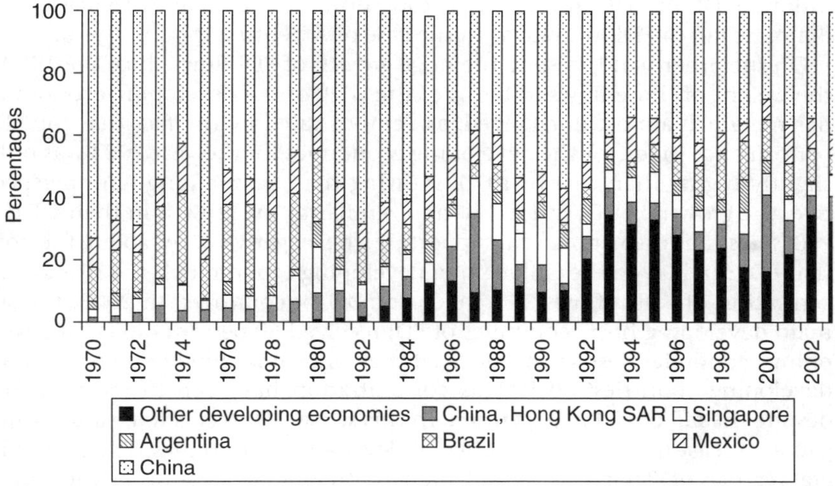

Figure 9.10 Distribution of FDI inflows in developing countries (percentages)
Source: UNCTAD *Handbook of Statistics* on-line (www.unctad.org).

receiver of FDI in the 1980s has led to a dramatic fall in the share of the other developing countries. In 2003, China and Hong Kong concentrated 40.6 per cent of FDI in developing countries whilse the share of the 'other developing economies' was only 39.5 per cent.[10] We must consider the fact that, according to data from UNCTAD, in 2003, the GDP of the above-mentioned six developing economies amounted to only 40 per cent of the GDP of developing countries, and China and China Hong Kong amounted to 21.8 per cent of the GDP of the developing economies.

Conclusions

Despite the generalized recommendations for developing countries to rely on foreign direct investments as an engine for long-term growth and development, an analysis of the geographical distribution of world FDI inflows since the 1970s does not support that argument. It is true that the ratio of FDI inflows/other capital flows has risen in recent decades. However, that ratio is mainly explained by the fall in the other private capital flows. In fact despite the growth in absolute FDI inflows to developing economies, the forecast for 2005 is that the net private capital flows to those economies will be quite similar to the flows of 1990. Therefore, the increase in absolute FDI inflows has not led to more foreign private capital resources for developing countries. This is a source of potential future problems for developing countries: their rising dependence on FDI, as shown in the ratios of FDI inflows/GDP or FDI inflows/GFCF, can show its dark side in the case of a dramatic fall in FDI inflows, as in the case of Argentina in recent years.

On the other hand, despite the huge growth of FDI flows since the 1980s, the weight of those flows in terms of the GDP of the developing economies has remained almost unchanged, as demonstrated by the fact that the FDI performance index for the developing economies for the year 2003 was only slightly higher than that of 1970, showing that, from a long-term perspective, the growth in FDI inflows is quite similar to the growth in their GDP.

Besides, another argument supporting the negative view about the role that FDI can play in the whole set of developing economies is the rising concentration of FDI inflows in a small number of countries. In 2003, the six main developing host economies of FDI received 60 percent of FDI in developing economies despite the fact that they only amounted to 40 per cent of developing countries' GDP. This concentration has risen in recent years, despite the fall of FDI in Argentina. In this sense, FDI seems to be a zero-sum game, at least from the perspective of developing economies. The more liberal regimes of FDI in the Central and Eastern European countries and China that took place in the 1990s may have had a negative effect on other developing economies, with a few exceptions in Latin America (for example, Brazil and Mexico) and in East Asia. In this sense, new liberalization processes in economies with current restrictions to FDI inflows, as in the case of India, can again have a negative effect on most developing countries.

Notes

1. The empirical testing of the effects of FDI inflows is much more controversial. Macroeconometric studies, using cross-section, time series or panel data, provides conflicting results not only regarding the existence of a significant link between FDI and growth or the sign of this relationship, but also about the causal relationship between these variables (Carkovic and Levine, 2002; Navaretti *et al.*, 2004; Xiaoying and Xiaming, 2005).
2. Again, another controversial issue in the empirical findings (Hadad and Harrison, 1993; Aitken and Harrison, 1999; Görg and Greenaway, 2001; Navaretti *et al.*, 2004).
3. For a summary of the doubts about the long-run consequences of inward FDI, see ECLAC (2004).
4. This high share of FDI in the total capital inflows is not, according to Hausmann and Fernandez-Arias (2000), necessarily a symptom of good health ('good cholesterol') since that ratio is lower in developed countries.
5. The UNCTAD FDI performance index is calculated for a country as the ratio between the country's share in world FDI divided by its share in world GDP.
6. In 1992, the GDP of Asian developing countries was 10.4% of world GDP and 57.4% of developing economies' GDP. In 2002, those figures amounted, respectively, to 13% and 65.4% (Source: UNCTAD *Handbook of Statistics* on-line (www.unctad.org).
7. The FDI inflows in Latin America registered an increase of 44% in 2004. Despite this positive outcome, and according to ECLAC reports, the problems of the countries of the region that make them poor prospects for attracting FDI (leading to a persistent fall of the share of Latin America in world FDI flows) still persist (ECLAC, 2005).

8. The fall in privatization-related FDI inflows would be explained not only by the exhaustion of the privatization process but also but the conflicts amongst foreign investors and host governments (quite striking in Argentina) that led to renegotiations between governments and foreign investors regarding the conditions of operation of foreign subsidiaries (Ramamurti, 2004).
9. For example, during the FDI boom of the 1980s (1986 to 1987) when world FDI was growing at more than 50% annually, developing economies' share dropped from 26.1% in 1985 to 17.6% in 1987. During the last boom of FDI in the late 1990s, when it was growing again at an annual rate above 50% during 1998–2000 (the year FDI flows reached the highest figure ever – US $1,400 billion) developing countries' shares dropped from 40.7% in 1997 to 18.2% in 2000. In the same vein, it can be said in general that developing economies' shares recover when FDI flows decline. In 1975, developing economies' shares increased to 36.2%, when FDI flows increased by only 3.8%. The record in developing countries' shares (46%) was achieved in 1982 when FDI flows declined – 14.6%; again in 1994, the share climbed to 41.7% when FDI flows dropped from 33% to 14%. Finally, developing economies are recovering in the first years of the twenty-first century (from 18.2% in 2000 to 30.7% in 2003) coinciding with the worst crisis for FDI flows (an average fall of more than 25% annually).
10. This figure has risen slightly, mainly because of the fall of FDI in Argentina.

References

Aitken, B. and Harrison, A. (1999) 'Do Domestic Forms Benefit from Foreign Investment? Evidence from Venezuela', *American Economic Review*, 89, pp. 605–18.

Carkovic, M. and Levine, R. (2002) 'Does Foreign Direct Investment Accelerate Economic Growth?', Mimeo, University of Minnesota, Minneapolis.

Claessens, S., Dooley, M. P. and Warner, A. (1995) 'Portfolio Capital Flows: Hot or Cold?', *World Bank Economic Review*, 9 (1), pp. 153–74.

Dadush, U., Dasgupta, D., and Ratha, D. (2000) 'The Role of Short-Term Debt in Recent Crises', *Finance and Development*, 37 (December), pp. 54–7.

Dunning, J. H. (1993) *Multinational Enterprise and the Global Economy* (Workingham: Addison-Wesley).

ECLAC (2004) *Foreign Investment in Latin America and the Caribbean 2003* (Santiago de Chile: ECLAC).

ECLAC (2005) *Foreign Investment in Latin America and the Caribbean 2004* (Santiago de Chile: ECLAC).

Farrell, D., Remes, J. K. and Schulz, H. (2004) 'The Truth About Foreign Direct Investment in Emerging Markets', *The McKinsey Quarterly*, 1.

Görg, H. and Greenaway, D. (2001) 'Foreign Direct Investment and Intraindustry Spillovers: A Review of the Literature', GEP Research Paper, 2001/37, Leverhulme Center for Research on Globalization and Economic Policy, Nottingham.

Haddad, M. and Harrison, A. (1993) 'Are There Positive Spillovers from Direct Foreign Investment? Evidence from Panel Data for Morocco', *Journal of Development Economics*, 42, pp. 51–74.

Hausmann, R. and Fernandez-Arias, E. (2000) 'Foreign Direct Investment: Good Cholesterol?', Inter-American Development Bank Working Paper No. 417, Washington, DC.

IMF (2004) *World Economic Outlook*, Washington, DC: International Monetary Fund.

Lipsey, R. E. (2001) 'Foreign Direct Investors in Three Financial Crises', NBER Working Paper No. 8084, January.

Navaretti, G. B. and Venables, A. J. (2004) *Multinational Firms in the World Economy* (Princeton, NJ: Princeton University Press).
Ramamurti, R. (2004) 'Developing Countries and MNEs: Extending and Enriching the Research Agenda', *Journal of International Business Studies*, 35, pp. 277–83.
Singh, A. (2004) 'IED, Globalización y Desarrollo Económico: Hacia la Reforma de las Reglas del Juego Nacionales e Internacionales', *Ekonomiaz*, 55, pp. 14–39.
UNCTAD (1992) *World Investment Report: TNC as Engines of Growth* (New York Geneva: United Nations).
Xiaoying, L. and Xiaming, L. (2005) 'Foreign Direct Investment and Economic Growth: An Increasingly Endogenous Relationship', *World Development*, 33, pp. 393–407.

10

Financial Deregulation and Capital Flows in Latin American Countries

Eugenia Correa and Gregorio Vidal

Latin American (LA) countries have been changing with an increasing new focus on free market philosophy, liberalization and policies that are more open. Ideas on repressed financial markets, and the need to free them with the objective of increasing savings and investment have been at the forefront of debate among the LA political and financial authorities. The history of the last thirty years (since the early 1970s) can be easily summarized under the banner of financial deregulation.

Strangely enough, LA financial markets were not repressed, they were merely regulated. The relationship between credit, investment, banks and firms acquired specific historical modalities, and the regulation of these relationships allowed the further development of the market, competition and accumulation. Foreign debt, short maturity and variable interest rates opened the door that led to deep transformations of the LA countries, with intense implications in the domestic financial systems.

The stable financial relations among local firms and banks were broken and, with this, local currency disruption and failure, as well as new credit, institutions and domestic financial relations emerged. After the Argentinean financial crisis and Brazil's financial problems that produced stressful financial markets in 2002, an important lesson followed: the participation of large foreign banks in local markets could not stabilize the exchange rate or the real interest rate and also could not, alone, restore the investors' confidence.

In this chapter, some of the transformation trends of the major LA economies financial systems are studied, as well as the characteristics of two waves of bank crises. Finally, the new foreign banks in the main LA countries and the new financial structure are analysed.

Instability, financial flows and creditors: the forces for change

During the 1970s, the LA countries were net receivers of loan capital coming from a new wave of expansion by the transnational banks. The rapid growth

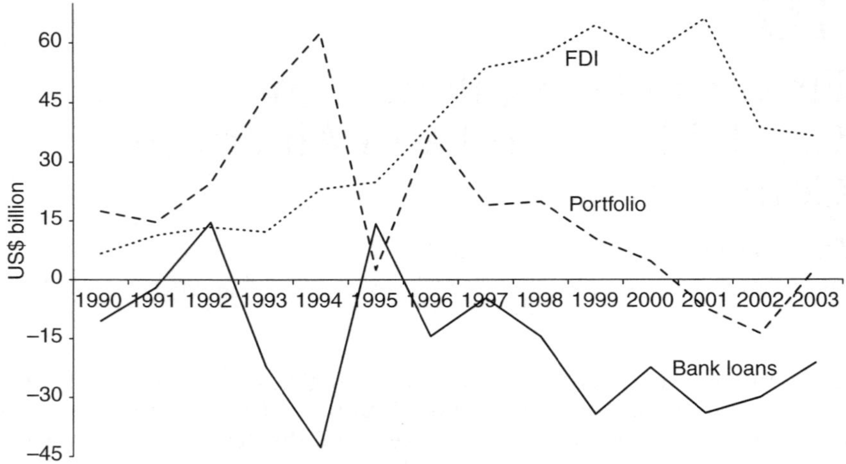

Figure 10.1 LA countries private net flows, 1990–2003

Sources: International Monetary Fund (1999, 2001) and IMF *World Economic Outlook* database April 2005 (available at http://www.imf.org).

of domestic banks' credit in the developed countries, and the international credit from these markets to developing economies, achieved the allocation of funds in Latin America (between 1970 and 1981) of almost US$200 billion (Girón, 1995). LA foreign debt doubled in only four years (1978–1981) as a result of Paul Volcker's successive increases in interest rates to tame US inflation. That provoked a recession lasting almost throughout the 1980s. In short, banks stopped principal refunding and interest capitalization, and as a result the debt crisis simply exploded (Correa, 1992).

For the LA financial systems, foreign debt meant large foreign banks doing internal business, so that local banks had to face new financial competition conditions. Consequently, during the 1970s, LA banks associated with foreign banks made loans from the international markets to LA governments in an attempt to cope with that competition. Trends in private capital inflows are shown in Figure 10.1. Therefore, since the end of the 1970s the following financial changes in main LA countries took place:

1 Foreign currency deposits authorization (Argentina, Colombia, Costa Rica, Chile, Venezuela, Uruguay and Peru);
2 Public bonds issues, which opened the way to fiscal deficit financing on the open market. The issue of public bonds during the 1980s modified monetary policy and interest rates regulation (Argentine, Brazil, Chile, Mexico, Peru and Uruguay);

3 Interest rate liberalization linked LA countries to the international financial markets (Argentina, Brazil, Chile, Mexico, Uruguay and Venezuela);
4 The establishment and growth of foreign non-bank financial firms, leasing companies, factoring, investment societies, insurance companies, and so on (Argentina, Brazil, Chile, Mexico, Uruguay and Venezuela).

During the 1980s, when loan flows were no longer voluntary, the largest LA financial firms faced increasing difficulties: a growing risk in their balance sheets of foreign currency positions; capital outflows that eventually depleted international credit lines; and, together with their governments, these banks ceased to have voluntary access to the international market. The IMF stabilization programmes in the 1980s had these results:

1 Major state participation as lender of last resort in the financial sector in the form of lender of last resort to rescue the main bond market debtors, firms and banks (Argentina, Chile, Mexico, Uruguay, Bolivia and Venezuela);
2 Privatization processes and local stock market allocations of shares in national firms (Argentina, Mexico, Chile);
3 Debt swaps for firms' assets and foreign investment with discounts (Argentina, Brazil, Chile and Mexico);
4 Interest rates, bank deposits in the Central Bank, and other credit deregulations (Argentine, Chile, Brazil, Mexico);
5 The decline of development banks.

LA capital inflows were modified again in the 1990s, essentially because of new US financial market deregulation. Those inflows came from the new expansion and market position strategies of institutional investors (Correa, 1998). Institutional investors channelled funds towards some LA countries, profiting from, among others, the following four conditions:

1 Government bonds offered attractive returns (at least in Argentina, Brazil and Mexico);
2 Incorporation of local firms to the stock market was very significant in Mexico, Chile, Argentina, Brazil and Venezuela;
3 Domestic financial firms were interested in doing business with investment banks and brokers, enabling the former to participate in securitization, bond issues and allocation, as well as interest rate arbitrage;
4 Patrimonial diversification in search of larger yields and lower risk.

Capital inflows through portfolio investments benefited mainly the earnings of private firms that had recently been admitted to the stock market, or from recently privatized enterprises. In both cases, their stock was creating markets and looking for prices that had generated extraordinary returns for market

Table 10.1 LA countries: net capital transfers

Years	Net capital inflows	Debt interest and FDI returns net outflows	Net capital transfers
		(US$ bn)	
1980	30.9	18.9	12.0
1990	16.1	34.2	−18.1
1995	61.1	40.8	20.2
2000	53.6	53.6	0.0
2001	51.8	54.7	−2.9
2002	10.3	51.2	−41.0
2003	21.4	55.8	−34.4
2004	−12.5	65.3	−77.8

Source: ECLAC, 2004, table A-13.

makers. LA emerging markets' profitability was limited for the first time towards 1994, when the US Federal Reserve System again increased interest rates. In 1995, foreign direct investment (FDI) returns and debt interest outflows achieved more than US$40 billion, as shown in Table 10.1. Again the Mexican financial crisis triggered market changes, but FDI inflows were very significant during the second half of the 1990s. Those developments can be explained almost entirely by the LA privatization processes.

However, negative net capital transfers appeared again in the early twenty-first century (see Table 10.1), along with net FDI returns, which increased (ECLAC, 2001; 2003a; 2004) despite the fact that FDI annual inflows were reduced over that period (see Table 10.2). In fact, financial services, indispensable for FDI privatization and acquisitions, were offered by the increasing presence of foreign financial firms and commercial banks, as well as investment banks and insurance companies (Vidal, 2001). So, from the wave of bankruptcies during the 1990s, some foreign financial conglomerate positioning has developed within the largest economies.

Successive bank crises

The new financial competition, transformation in capital markets following liberalization, the appearance of new profitable structures, as well as the IMF inspired fiscal balance constraints with the consequent fall in public expenditure, have led to a serious erosion of national bank systems. Stressful banking systems and local currency weaknesses led to successive bank crises in the region (see Table 10.3). The liberalization trajectory and financial deregulation created weak conditions within the LA financial systems. Domestic banks did not have the opportunity to expand their cross border

Table 10.2 LA countries FDI inflows and return

	FDI annual inflows	FDI annual returns
Years	(US$ bn)	
1970	1.7	1.9
1980	6.1	4.6
1990	7.8	7.0
1993	13.2	10.2
1994	27.8	13.6
1995	29.8	14.6
1996	43.4	15.4
1997	65.2	20.1
1998	72.1	20.9
1999	86.5	17.2
2000	76.9	23.3
2001	69.1	19.9
2002	44.5	17.2
2003	34.9	21.2
2004 (e)	48.9	28.8

(e) estimation

Source: ECLAC, database on line (hhtp://www.eclac.cl/badestat), April 2005.

activities at the speed that their economies demanded, mainly in a situation characterized by massive capital outflows, in some cases high and sustained FDI outflows, growing debt service conditions, and even internationalized domestic flows. In fact, larger economies could not find or develop growing sources of foreign currency inflows within the level their interest rates and external liabilities required. This was so because of the declining terms of trade, the FDI high returns and the high real interest rates of the foreign debt (Kregel, 2004, is a representative example).

The first wave of bank crises during the 1980s (see Table 10.3), such as those in Argentina, Chile, Mexico, Peru and Uruguay, were associated with the financial liberalization processes and debt crises. This first wave is explained by:

- a sudden half to banks balance expansion, imposed by the difficulties to continue with the refinancing of past loans
- the temporal impossibility to continue with the internationalization of local capital
- local currency devaluation with partial bank balance sheet dollarization and, most importantly
- the government and the banks were prevented from participating and exploiting the voluntary foreign credit market.

Table 10.3 LA countries: bank crises

Country	Year	Country	Year
Argentina	1980	Guatemala	1990
	1989	Haiti	1991
	1995	Jamaica	1994
	2002	Mexico	1982
Bolivia	1986		1994
	1994	Panama	1988
Brasil	1994	Nicaragua	1990
	2001	Paraguay	1995
Chile	1981	Peru	1983
Colombia	1982		1990
Costa Rica	1994	Uruguay	1981
Ecuador	1995		2002
El Salvador	1989	Venezuela	1994

Source: Lindgren *et al.*, 1996.

It was then evident how the liberalization process in underdeveloped countries required a lender of last resort in dollars, not only in local currency, even before reaching great advances towards capital account opening and deregulation. This lender of last resort could be the US Federal Reserve System, the US Treasury, the IMF, one large bank or a group of large private banks. The financial systems of the LA countries had a double currency circulation as a structural characteristic but, with financial liberalization and deregulation, this characteristic became dependent on the international financial markets, especially on the institutional investors and credit rating agencies.

The second wave of bank crises in the region, during the 1990s, meant massive bank bankruptcies for several countries, the introduction of government assistance and high fiscal costs. Asian, African and Eastern Europe countries had similar experiences with LA countries. In several of these countries, the crisis precipitated a process of foreign control of their financial system. According to IMF data, foreign control increased over a period of only a few months. For example, in Central Europe it represented 8 per cent in 1994 but, by 1999, it had increased to more than 56 per cent. In LA, excluding Brazil and Mexico, it went from 13 per cent to 45 per cent during the same period.

Financial stabilization and foreign banks

In population, production, trade and financial assets, LA countries have a relatively small percentage in world tables, but this is not the same in terms of FDI, as can be seen from Table 10.4. In spite of FDI growth and the wide

Table 10.4 LA countries in the world, 2004 (Percentage of world figures)

Population	8.4
Extreme poverty (a)	6.7
GDP	7.5
Exports	4.2
Reserves (less gold) (b)	6.2
Equity markets capitalization (b)	1.9
Private and public bonds (b)	1.6
Bank assets (b)	1.9
Bonds, equity and bank assets (b)	1.8
FDI inward stock (b)	7.9

Sources: World Bank. World Development indicators database (http://www.worldbank.org), April 2003; International Monetary Fund, Global Financial Stability Report (http://www.imf.org), April 2005; IMF, *World Economic Outlook* (http://www.inf.org), April 2005.

Notes: (a) 2001; (b) 2003.

external liberalization of all mayor economies, resulting in a fast growth in foreign trade and capital flows, the LA economies have not expanded in tandem. In the early part of the twenty-first century, LA economies are even growing below the levels achieved during the 1990s. In spite of Latin America's relatively marginal position in worldwide financial markets, these have been the setting for the rapid expansion of global banks, as can be seen from Figure 10.2.

Efforts towards a financial reform in LA countries proposed as a stabilizer by the IMF are just a change in financial firms' ownership, including systemic risk deposit banks, for foreign banks. Of course, as on other occasions, it has been said that these reforms would decrease financial costs and give more confidence to depositors, as well as enable development and a way out of poverty (World Bank, 2000).

Among the twenty-five largest banks in LA countries, a good number have foreign investments, or they have become foreign bank subsidiaries (see Table 10.5). The exceptions are the largest Brazilian banks. The Spanish BBVA and BSCH banks had the largest expansion in the region (Vilariño, 2001). They have the largest number of branches, with an investment of almost US$13 billion controlling thirty banks in ten countries with assets greater than US$153 billion, or almost 10 per cent of LA bank assets. In addition, they participate in the pension funds management of almost 45 per cent of total funds (Mathieson and Roldós, 2001).

The IMF has been confronted with a number of criticisms made in recent years because it has encouraged countries into a growing liberalization and

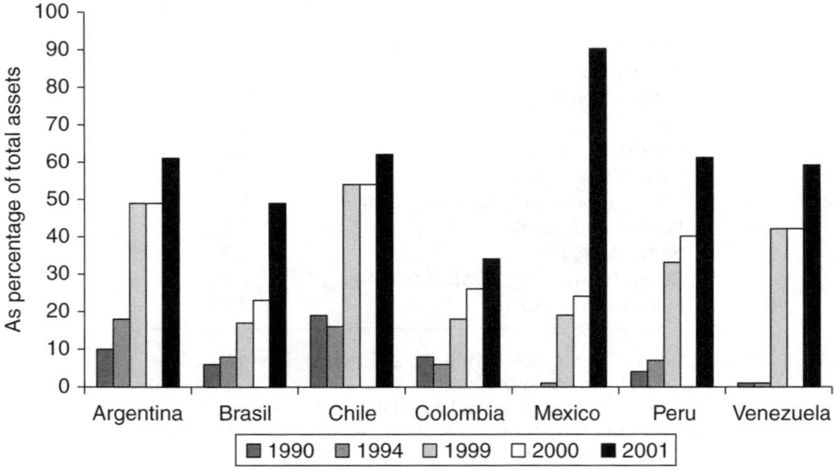

Figure 10.2 LA foreign banks assets
Source: ECLAC (2003), p. 118.

financial opening processes. That has led them to a path of financial and economic instability, bank crises, stagnation or slow economic growth, increase in poverty growing denationalization of the whole economy. Until now, foreign bank subsidiaries in Argentina and Mexico, at least, have shown that they are not interested in expanding and deepening national markets, but are taking advantage of a position that guarantees them profitability above that achieved in their own home countries. They do not want to face currency mismatching against their returns or their stockholders, but want to transfer currency mismatching costs to deposit insurance or to any other supporting mechanism that finally transfers the risk to taxpayers, or simply want to transfer losses to depositors.

Therefore, new episodes of financial fragility are unavoidable, even under wide expansion of foreign financial firms' conditions. LA governments have fewer opportunities to stop the deeper consequences of these external shocks when deposit banks are mainly foreign banks' subsidiaries. On the other hand, LA countries have not yet been able to verify that these subsidiaries would bring with them a large volume of financial resource at more competitive prices, or whether depositors would see their savings grow with attractive interest rates.

Conclusions

LA major economies began a financial system transformation in the early 1970s with changes in net capital transfers towards positive flows, and for

Table 10.5 LA countries, top 25 banks' main shareholders, 2004

Position	Bank	Host country	Assets (US$ millions)	Shareholders	Participation %
1	Banco do Brasil	Brazil	73,181	National Treasury	71.80
				Previ	13.70
				BNDES	5.80
				Foreign Capital	1.00
				Pension Funds	1.20
				Local Investors	4.80
				Local Enterprises	1.70
2	Bradesco	Brazil	56,728	Cidade de Deus (Brazil)	24.45
				BES	3.24
				Credit Agricole	3.26
				Deutsche Bank	0.43
				Sanwa Bank	1.28
				Bradesco Fundation	9.51
				BBVA (Spain)	4.44
3	Caixa Econômica Federal CEF	Brazil	53,652	Brazilian Goverment	100.00
4	BBVA Bancomer	Mexico	43,803	BBVA-Spain	99.55
5	Banco Itaú	Brazil	39,510	Investimetnos Itaú S.A.	47.70
				Local Investors	52.30
6	Banamex Citibank	Mexico	38,511	Citigroup (USA)	99.50
7	Unibanco	Brazil	25,722	Grupo Moreira Salles (E. Johnston)	29.54
				Caixa Geral de Depósitos	12.42
				Commerzbank	11.44
				The Dai-Ichi Kangyo Bank Ltd	2.71
				Float PN/Unit	6.92
				Float GDS	32.29
				Float ON	3.58
8	Santander Serfín	Mexico	23,648	Santander Central Hispano (Spain)	71.10
				Bank of America-USA	24.90
9	Santander Banespa	Brazil	22,042	Santander Central Hispano(Spain)	98.00
10	ABN-Amro Bank	Brazil	19,295	ABN AMRO BANK N.V. (Canada)	50.70
				ABN AMRO BRASIL	45.9
11	Banorte	Mexico	18,194	Gónzalez Barrera and Family	41.10
				Gruma Group	10.9
				JPMChaseBank (Invesment Fund)	nd
				Darby Overseas Investment ltd	nd
12	Stantander Santiago	Chile	17,895	Santander Central Hispano (Spain)	84.00
13	HSBC (before Bital)	Mexico	15,970	Hong Kong Shangai Bank(England)	100.00
14	Banco de Chile	Chile	15,141	Private Local Capital	nd
15	Banco de la Nación Argentina	Argentine	13,451	Argentine Government	100.00
16	Banco del Estado de Chile	Chile	12,517	Chile Government	100.00
17	Banco Safra	Brazil	11,991	Family Safra	nd
18	Votorantim	Brazil	11,225	Votorantim Financas	100.00
19	HSBC Bank Brasil	Brazil	10,408	Hong Kong Shangai Bank(England)	99.00
20	Banco de Crédito e Inversiones	Chile	9,624	Empresas Juan Yarur S.A.C.	53.50
21	Citibank	Brazil	9,600	Citibank (USA)	nd
22	Nossa Caixa	Brazil	8,865	Brazil Local Government	nd
23	Scotiabank Inverlat	Mexico	7,895	ScotiaBank (Canada)	91.00
24	Banco de la Provincia de Buenos Aires	Argentine	7,652	Argentine Local Government	nd
25	Galicia y Buenos Aires	Argentine	7,229	Private Local Capital	nd

Note: nd = no data available.

Sources: *Review America Economia* (http://www.americaeconomia.com) and Latintrade (http://www.latintrade.com).

some years the region was a net capital receiver; that stage ended with the debt crisis in 1982. Foreign debt opened the door to new financial competition and deregulation. Since then, LA countries have experienced dollarization and financial crises. During the 1980s, LA countries changed again to negative net capital transfers and began a second stage of financial liberalization. The monetary and fiscal policies encouraged by the IMF, the new government bond markets, and budget constraints, all combined culminated in international exposure and the determination of domestic interest rates by forces outside the LA regimes. In the 1990s, a third stage of financial liberalization emerged. Institutional investors and investment banks initiated an expansion and LA countries became positive capital receivers again. Capital inflows through portfolio investments profited mainly private firms, which had been incorporated in the stock markets, or from recently privatized enterprises. In both cases, their stocks were creating markets and prices that generated extraordinary returns for institutional investors and investment banks. The negative net capital transfers appeared again in the second half of the 1990s, this time not only because of debt interest, but mainly because of portfolio and FDI returns. Those were the years of a new wave of bank crises and rapid growth of foreign banks. A new stage in financial transformation emerged with the immense significance of foreign global financial conglomerates in the major LA countries. The lack of financing in local currency for local investment has been characteristic, even though the profits of the foreign banks have either remained the same or even increased. These difficult years of successive bank and financial crises may not yet have reached their demise in the LA region.

References

Correa, E. (1992) *Los mercados financieros y la crisis en América Latina*, 1st edn (Mexico: Instituto de Investigaciones Económicas-UNAM).

Correa, E. (1998) *Crisis y desregulación financiera*, 1st edn (Mexico: Siglo Veintiuno).

ECLAC (2001) *Balance preliminar de la economía de América Latina y el Caribe 2001* (Santiago de Chile: CEPAL).

ECLAC (2003a) *Balance preliminar de la economía de América Latina y el Caribe 2003* (Santiago de Chile: CEPAL).

ECLAC (2003b) *La inversión extranjera en América Latina y el Caribe 2002* (Santiago de Chile: CEPAL).

ECLAC (2004) *Balance preliminar de la economía de América Latina y el Caribe 2004* (Santiago de Chile: CEPAL).

Girón, A. (1995) *Fin de siglo y deuda externa: historia sin fin* (Mexico: Instituto de Investigaciones Económicas, UNAM).

International Monetary Fund (1999) *International Capital Markets*, International Monetary Fund, Washington, DC, September.

International Monetary Fund (2001) *International Capital Markets*, International Monetary Fund, Washington, DC, August.

Kregel, J. (2004) 'Do We Need Alternative Financial Strategies for Development in Latin America?', Paper presented at the IV Seminario de Economía Financiera: *Cooperación, instituciones y asimetrías financieras en América Latina* sponsored by Universidad Nacional Autónoma de México, Instituto de Investigaciones Económicas y Posgrado de Economía, Mexico, October.

Lindgren, C.J., García, G. and Saal, M. (1996) *Bank Soundness and Macroeconomic Policy*, 1st edn (Washington, DC: International Monetary Fund).

Mathieson, D. and Roldós, J. (2001) 'The role of foreign banks in emerging markets', Paper presented at the IMF–WB–Brookings Institution Conference, Washington, DC, April.

Vidal, G. (2001) *Privatizaciones, Fusiones y Adquisiciones. Las Grandes Empresas en América Latina*, 1st edn (Barcelona: Anthropos).

Vilariño, A. (2001) 'La presencia de los bancos españoles en la economía mexicana', *Información Comercial Española*, 795, pp. 101–11.

World Bank (2000) *Global Development Finance 2000* (Washington, DC: World Bank).

11

The Impact of Multinational Banking on Domestic Banking

Claude Gnos and Louis-Philippe Rochon

Post-Keynesians have made endogenous money a central argument in their theory of output. Indeed, production cannot be undertaken if access to finance, usually meaning bank credit, does not exist. Such access is needed if wages are to be paid, and inputs of production purchased. In a monetary economy, therefore, money is created at the demand of borrowers, supplied by banks.

But with the notion of endogenous money firmly entrenched in the post-Keynesian theoretical literature, it is time to go beyond it and to look at a number of policy issues that surround it. One of these issues is that of possible discrimination confronting many potential borrowers who see their access to credit denied, for a variety of reasons. The burning question, therefore, from a post-Keynesian perspective, is whether this matters.

Our first impression is that it does. If production is tied to access to credit, the composition of output and the distribution of income can be affected if a whole class of borrowers can be denied credit. Yet this is particularly what some claim has been happening in recent years as the liberalizing of finance, under the guises of the Washington Consensus, led to an unprecedented phenomenon: the growing importance of foreign banks in many countries – and, in particular in Latin America.

By now, many agree that the Washington Consensus is not proving to be the panacea it promised to be. In fact, many adherents are encouraging another round of discussion for a second-generation Washington Consensus. While these reforms may include such areas as the environment and social issues, it is clear that the general direction or the overall ideological orientation will probably not change. In addition, it will most probably address directly the issue of financial liberalization, as opposed to 'interest rate liberalization,' which is currently in the Washington Consensus. In other words, the underlying economic ideology will remain the same, which, from a post-Keynesian perspective, amounts to very little change.

Post-Keynesians form a consensus of their own. Indeed, this post-Keynesian consensus rejects the Washington Consensus, claiming that it is an attempt to apply strict free-market – read neoclassical – rules to developing countries. And perhaps more so than in developed countries, applying policies based on wrong economic theory can be, as J.M. Keynes warns us in the opening chapter of the *General Theory* (1973, p. 3), disastrous. Institutions, effective demand, income distribution and an observation of the real world are the cornerstone of any successful policy of growth.

Despite the criticism raised against the Washington Consensus from the perspective of growth and trade in particular, we believe there is yet another perspective that has largely been ignored by post-Keynesians, and that is the rise of foreign banks in local or domestic economies. Indeed, for many emerging economies, one of the more striking structural changes that has taken place since the 1990s has been the rapid expansion of multinational banks. One of the direct results of the opening of capital accounts, the elimination of barriers to international capital flows and a general relaxation of barriers to entry, was the multinationalization of the banking system and of banking activities, which in turn is supported by such international institutions as the IMF and the World Trade Organization (WTO).[1] The irony, of course, is that while these policies have been adopted to regulate and stabilize financial markets in emerging economies, financial and banking crises have become more pronounced. Hence it appears as though the 'globalization of banking' has contributed to making the world's financial markets more fragile, and not less so.

We wish to look at this argument more closely. Indeed, as the theory of endogenous money indicates, employment and money are linked through the supply of bank loans from the banking system. Hence, should post-Keynesians be wary of a domestic banking sector that increasingly is being controlled by foreign interests? Does this pose any threat to the domestic economy? Does it make the banking sector and the local economy more or less stable? Such are the questions to which we would like to find suitable answers.

In this chapter, we consider several topics. In the next section, we look at data concerning the rise of multinational banking in selected countries in Latin America and give a general overview of this trend. The following two sections seek to explain this rise and to evaluate the benefits and costs of multinational banks, based on arguments in the current literature. In the fifth section, we propose a post-Keynesian critique of this literature and some possible policy implications, and the sixth section concludes.

Multinational banking: the case of Latin America

Many economists have taken an interest in the stability of the banking system in emerging economies, especially in the wake of a number of banking and financial crises since the 1980s. After the adoption of the Washington Consensus and its emphasis on financial liberalization, there has been a disturbing increase in multinational banks in emerging economies, and in Latin America in particular. We say 'disturbing', because we do not believe that this trend is a comforting one. In fact, we do not believe that relinquishing any sizeable control of a country's financial industry to foreign interests can lead any gains. This is based on purely economic arguments, as we shall argue below. Moreover, we believe that it also exports to developing countries one of the most problematic elements of developed countries: namely, the unequal influence of financial interest. This point is developed more fully in the final section of the chapter.

To be clear, this trend is not limited wholly to American banks. Indeed, Canadian, Spanish, Swiss and UK banks all enjoy an expansion of their national banks in a number of emerging-economy countries.[2] The pace of foreign penetration into the banking system has increased dramatically since the mid-1990s, and since the year 2000 in particular.

Between 1990 and 2002, the increase of foreign banks in Latin American, and indeed in *all* emerging economies, was nothing but remarkable. In particular, in the second half of the 1990s, there was a dramatic increase of foreign involvement, either by a measure of participation in domestic banking, or more directly by ownership and control of the domestic banking industry. According to the Bank for International Settlements (2003), foreign banks in 2001 accounted for 47 per cent of total loans and 43 per cent of total deposits, up from 38 per cent and 36 per cent in 2000. Table 11.1 shows the percentage of foreign ownership of bank assets, bank equity, bank deposits and total bank loans for selected Latin American countries in 2001. As can be seen, there is a marked difference in the degree of foreign ownership of the domestic banking system. Nevertheless, the data shows that, for certain countries, multinational banking can reach nearly 75 per cent of total banking activity. On average, it is close to 50 per cent. But Table 11.1 only masks the enormous changes that have taken place since the mid-1990s. In fact, in Table 11.2, there are figures that show the tremendous increase in international banking and its growth between 1994 and 1999, based on IMF data. The conclusion is undeniable: 'For many emerging markets, one of the most striking structural changes in their financial systems during the 1990s has been the growing presence of foreign-owned financial institutions, especially in the banking system ... In some Latin American countries, almost one-half of total bank assets are controlled by foreign institutions' (IMF, 2000, p. 152).

All over Latin America, the foreign banks are expanding quickly. As Tables 11.1 and 11.2 show, however, Brazil remains an exception in the region. While the presence of foreign banks has increased since the implementation of the Real Plan, foreign control remains *relatively* low. But foreign ownership of banks has almost tripled since before the Real Plan. The reason for the relatively lower share of foreign involvement in Brazil is because many of bank assets are under government control. Moreover, there

Table 11.1 Foreign participation in domestic banking systems, selected Latin-American countries, 2001

Countries	Foreign ownership of total bank assets %	Foreign ownership of total bank equity %	Foreign ownership of total bank deposits %	Foreign ownership of total bank loans %
Argentina	53.1	43.1	46.4	46.5
Brazil	28.3	30.1	16.3	24.4
Chile	59.3	54.1	44.5	44.9
Colombia	22.7	24.4	19.9	22.6
Mexico	75.9	74.8	76.2	72.9
Peru	57.9	55.2	59.4	55.9
Venezuela	45.3	49.3	45.3	48.5

Source: Salomon Smith Barney, *Foreign Financial Institutions in Latin America*, 28 November 2001.

Table 11.2 Foreign participation in domestic banking systems, *selected Latin-American countries, 1994–9*

Countries	Foreign control 1994 %	Foreign control 1999 %
Argentina	17.9	48.6
Brazil	8.4	17.7
Chile	16.3	53.6
Colombia	6.2	17.8
Mexico	1.0	18.8
Peru	6.7	33.4
Venezuela	0.3	43.9

Source: Bank for International Settlements.

are a number of well-capitalized private banks in Brazil compared to other Latin-American countries. But the proposed privatization of several state banks and the recent entry of European banks have nevertheless had an important impact and pave the way for a possible greater role of foreign banks in the future. In this sense, Brazil will not be shielded for ever from the rapid increase in foreign banks.

That foreign ownership of domestic banks is a real phenomenon is undeniable. But it does lead to a number of questions that we shall attempt to address here. We see three questions that need to be scrutinized more closely. These are:

(i) What conditions led to the penetration of foreign banks into local economies, in particular in Latin America?
(ii) Does this change the structure of bank lending? By this we mean, does the increased presence of foreign banks lead to a crowding-out of local borrowers or smaller borrowers?
(iii) Does the increased presence of foreign banks tend to stabilize or destabilize the banking system? Is there more systemic risk as a result?

Of course, the overall issue is whether this increase in foreign ownership of emerging markets' banking systems is problematic. There are two sides to this question as policy-makers debate the merits of opening emerging market banking and financial sectors. Washington Consensus-type policies and the possibility that an increased Washington Consensus might pave the way to greater integration is an issue that needs to be addressed urgently by policy-makers.

Since the adoption of the Washington Consensus, which corresponded to the rise in globalization, financial deregulation and economic liberalization policies have taken centre stage. As a result, many barriers to the free flow of capital have been eliminated. With the rise of these policies, financial institutions found profitable the possibility of expanding to other countries, and this intense competitive pressure led to the increased multinationalization of the industry-seeking potential new borrowers.

Many countries have in the past had regulatory policies and substantial barriers to entry, that prevented foreign ownership of the domestic banking system, especially in emerging markets. Examples of such barriers include number of branches, controls over permissible activities and strict limits to the percentage of foreign ownerships of domestic banks. Indeed, as Eichengreen and Mussa (1998) show, many emerging economies have eliminated a number of such barriers especially since the early/mid-1990s, specifically to attract foreign banks.

However, with the advent of banking crises and the instability that followed, coupled with the increased emphasis on a greater openness to foreign trade and investment, which the Washington Consensus embodies, for example, it was deemed necessary to stabilize the banking system by attracting 'sound' and 'efficient' banks. This was a quick solution, and one that many believed would bring much-needed stability. Hence domestic banking crises were the catalyst for the removal of these so-called barriers to entry: domestic banks faced severe financial situations, poor balance sheets and low capitalization. At the heart of these policies was the belief that allowing foreign banks to enter was a better (cheaper) way of rapidly restructuring and recapitalizing domestic banks following an important crisis (IMF, 2000, p. 158; see also Lindgren *et al.*, 1996).

Foreign banks, on the other hand, facing increased competition from financial deregulation in their own countries, were quick to take advantage of the situation. Indeed, the globalization of financial services implies increasingly that large banks face competition from non-bank sources of credit and other financial services at home, which has put considerable pressure on their domestic profits. In other words, what large foreign banks were looking for, emerging markets were ready to supply. Yet, despite their strong desire to find new markets, it is only recently that the barriers to entry into emerging economies have been removed.

Many studies have analysed the reasons why multinational banks choose to enter emerging economies. These have to do with factors in both the country of origin and the host country. For example, current account balances, the exchange rate, current levels of interest rates relative to the USA (reflecting country and devaluation risk) are certainly among the important ones in the host economy (see, among other studies, Goldberg and Saunders, 1981; see also Weller, 2001, for a discussion), as are economic growth and the presence of other multinational banks. Claessens *et al.* (2000) find evidence that foreign banks choose countries with lower taxes and higher per capita income (see also Yamori, 1998). Focarelli and Pozzolo (2000) find similarly that the presence of foreign banks is greater when the expected rate of growth is stronger, and when the existing banking system in the emerging economy is weaker.

The benefits of multinational banking

In an important sense, the rapid increase of foreign banks in the late 1990s in Latin America and other emerging economies is a clear sign that the debate over the benefits and costs of such policies is over. Indeed, the consensus seems to be that the benefits of the multinationalization of the banking industry largely outweigh the costs. This debate is seen strictly in terms of efficiency in a narrow, neoclassical sense. In this sense, analysis is done in terms of comparative advantage: foreign banks are 'successful' banks, and they can therefore export to emerging economies the skills, expertise and knowledge that they have accumulated in the past. In this sense, proponents argue, the benefits can be far-reaching, which will in turn lead to enhanced stability.

Capital restructuring and recapitalization are seen as being the dominant benefits of allowing foreign banks into the domestic economy, as these banks will bring much-needed capital that will quickly re-establish 'sound market fundamentals'. This will in turn benefit all market participants, including domestic or local banks. Once local banks are capitalized more strongly, they would be better able to withstand certain shocks.

It is also argued that foreign banks bring market competition, which forces local banks to re-evaluate their lending practices. Competition is seen as generally having a positive influence. Policy recommendations are therefore based on efforts to encourage 'sound' foreign banks to open branches in local economies, to encourage competition and efficiency, and this in turn will encourage local banks to follow suit and also become 'sound' banks. This should then lead to better, stronger banks all around, and better market discipline. By becoming 'better' banks, local banks will develop the skills necessary to lend to 'better' borrowers, thereby reducing the possibility of default. Since it is argued that banks face credit rationing, better-disciplined banks will be able to allocate a given supply of credit to better borrowers. This should lead to a more stable banking and financial system.

In addition, many have argued that banks that tend to enter emerging economies are 'solid and respectable' banks that bring a degree of expertise and thus respectability to the emerging banking system through spillover effects. Foreign banks are believed to have a comparative advantage in evaluating credit risks, and are able to pass on this knowledge to local banks, thereby benefiting the industry as a whole. They bring new technology, enhanced services and skilled banking personnel, and will encourage domestic banks 'to introduce similar improvements. These new financial products can provide better opportunities for portfolio diversification and intertemporal trade' (IMF, 2000, p. 163). This is seen as a win–win solution for both the banks and the local economy: 'better' banks with better knowledge and technology coupled with local bankers with a better knowledge of the needs of the local economy. The argument also applies to better prudential supervision.

A last benefit that is generally recognized is that foreign banks come with their own lender-of-last-resort. In difficult times, it is believed that foreign banks will be able to tap into the resources of the parent corporation and access additional funding and capital when needed. At critical times, therefore, foreign banks would be able to 'ride the wave' and smooth out the troughs of crises. The parent corporation would be ready to supply their branches with the necessary funds to keep them well capitalized and ready to meet the requirements of a crisis.

In the end, this should lead not only to 'better' banks, but also to better pricing, improved quality of lending, and more credit through increased credit supply. Competition therefore lowers prices and increases supply. As supply of credit increases, there are more loans, more output, more investment and stronger economic growth. This is especially true since foreign banks are better-equipped for detecting potentially bad borrowers, and evaluating and pricing credit risks. The entry of multinational banks generally increases the stability of the local banking system.

The costs of multinational banking and the changing composition of bank supply

But these views on the benefits of multinational banks are not universally shared. While we would argue that the vast majority of economists possibly agree with the situation as described above, it is safe to assume that post-Keynesian economists would generally disagree with it. Indeed, post-Keynesians would argue that the above analysis misses the point completely.

One of the leading heterodox critics of multinational banking, Weller (2001), has persistently argued strongly against the perils they pose. As Weller points out (1998, p. 1), 'the spread of global banking has contributed to the financial instability of many nations and led to the disruption of domestic credit markets'.

Despite the elimination of barriers to entry as early as the start of the 1990s, foreign bank penetration was slow until the mid-1990s, as can be seen from Table 11.2 on page 181 shows. This reflects in part the potential negative effects of foreign banks on the domestic banking system (IMF, 2000). As was argued above, however, these concerns were quickly abandoned as foreign ownership increased throughout the 1990s and well into the 2000s, and the urgent need for foreign capital increased. We would argue that many developing countries probably did not have the necessary time to evaluate properly the effect that multinational banks would have. Indeed, faced with financial crises and unstable banking sectors, they opted for a short-term solution. The instant effect of allowing foreign banks to enter is the instant recapitalization of local banks, thus creating an illusion of stability.

Post-Keynesian theory has much to offer this literature and in fact is able to challenge directly one of the more fundamental conclusions of this debate. In fact, if money is endogenous, then the supply of credit cannot be raised simply by the presence of foreign banks. Bank credit is provided at the exclusive demand of bank borrowers. Hence, bank supply can only increase provided there are more creditworthy borrowers willing to enter into debt: the increase in the number of banks does not translate automatically into an increase in the number of creditworthy borrowers. Hence the recapitalization and restructuring of the banking industry in developing and emerging markets does not in itself lead to higher credit. In fact, from a post-Keynesian perspective, assuming that the number of creditworthy borrowers does not change, the entry of foreign banks may lead to a 'crowding-out' effect. By this we mean that foreign banks may be better able to attract 'good' borrowers, leaving local banks scrambling to find such borrowers. If this is the case, as we shall see below, the implications may in fact be more *instability*.

There is some evidence that foreign multinational banks follow their multinational clients (Clarke *et al.*, 1999; Clarke *et al.*, 2001). After all, as Clarke *et al.* (2001, p. 11) argue, 'multinational enterprises are expected to be customers of larger banks'. This is not surprising, and it is not surprising either that the trend in multinational banking followed greater economic integration. As multinational corporations are increasingly opening factories in emerging economies, banks will follow their clients to finance their operations.

Moreover, as foreign banks set up shop in emerging markets, they will also be able to attract the larger local firms. Because of their better reputation, large 'blue-chip' corporations prefer banking with 'blue chip' (reputable) banks. This implies that foreign banks will be able to capture the 'best' part of the market or the more creditworthy borrowers, both foreign and domestic. This is evidenced by Belaisch *et al.* (2000) who have argued that, since foreign banks rely on the assessment and quantification of risk, smaller local (non-oligopolistic) banks are disadvantaged, the lending of which depends more on developing long-term relationships with the clients. In this sense, the increase in multinational banking leads to an oligopolization of credit supply:

> To the extent that they lend to small borrowers, large banks are likely to employ standardized methods for assessing creditworthiness based on readily available information. For smaller banks, it may pay to grant loan officers greater latitude to use idiosyncratic borrower information, most of which is not easily quantified or transferable, in assessing creditworthiness. This flexibility makes it easier to create and maintain a relationship between small banks and small borrowers. (Clarke *et al.*, 2001, p. 21; see also Focarelli and Pozzolo, 2000)

This practice, known as 'cherry-picking', suggests therefore that foreign banks will lend only to the more profitable industries and borrowers – both domestic and foreign – thereby leaving the riskier borrowers to local banks. In this sense, foreign banks are able to pick and choose their borrowers, and do not contribute to the improvement of local banks' balance sheets, but will often lead to their worsening: 'Foreign banks are viewed as focusing their lending on wealthy individuals and the most creditworthy corporates ... Experience in the early stages of financial liberalizations ... in many countries suggests that this is not an unwarranted concern' (IMF, 2000, pp. 163, 164; see also Demirgüç-Kunt and Detragiache, 1998). Clarke *et al.* (2001, p. 20) found evidence to this effect. Clarke *et al.* (2000) conclude that foreign banks devote almost twice as much of their loan portfolio to manufacturing firms.

So, if the demand from creditworthy borrowers does not change, a shift from local to foreign banks by the larger firms will lead to a crowding-out effect, and local banks will lose an important source of lending. This in turn can lead to two possible outcomes, each contributing to the instability of the local banking system.

On the one hand, local banks will face a decline in their bank supply. As their more creditworthy customers move to multinational banks, local banks will be crowded out of the loan market, which will translate not only into a decline in their loans, but also in their profits. Indeed, in an extensive study using bank-level data from eighty countries for the period 1988–95, Claessens *et al.* (2000) have shown that multinational banking has led to a general decrease in the profits of local banks. Weller (2001, p. 11) points precisely to this scenario in Korea, Hungary and Poland (see also Euh and

Baker, 1990; Anderson and Kegels, 1998; and Weller, 2000). With depressed profits and capital structures, local banks are thus less likely to be able to raise the necessary capital, thereby paving the way for increased foreign entry in the future.

On the other hand, or in fact perhaps as an eventual result of the first scenario, local banks may react by increasing their supply of credit, and this is perhaps the more problematic of the two scenarios. As their balance sheets deteriorate, local banks may be forced to react to increased competition by lending to riskier borrowers, or by financing riskier projects, thereby increasing the overall risk to the lending pool (Darity and Horn, 1998). This is especially true if existing local banks already have weak or deteriorating capital positions. Riskier projects or borrowers are seen as the only possible way of rebuilding their capital position.

In an alternative scenario, local banks may lend to not only riskier projects, but also to projects that are more short-term and speculative in nature, which could then translate into financial and speculative bubbles.

Either way, the supply of 'good' credit will fall, thereby threatening the future growth of the economy and the stability of the overall banking system. If this is a direct result of international competitive forces, then competition can be seen as a double-edged sword. Indeed, far from encouraging stability, it can lead to instability, especially in less regulated markets. Local banks are unable to lend to 'good' borrowers and must therefore rely on riskier borrowers and finance riskier projects.

In addition, we would argue that the usual explanation of market discipline is displaced. In line with Keynes' most fundamental insights into modern capitalist economies of production, the greater threat to banking crises, we would argue, is the lack of effective demand. Banks' balance sheets are weakened because too many borrowers are unable to reimburse their debt. If this is characteristic of a few borrowers only, then it could be argued that local banks might indeed lack the knowledge to distinguish bad borrowers from good. Such banks may not be able to quantify risk appropriately. But we suspect that this is not the case. Rather, when this is spread over the general population, then the problem becomes a lack of effective demand, which is insufficient to generate the revenues and profits necessary for borrowers to meet their contractual agreements with the banks. This is a generalized problem that cannot be solved by markets alone, and even less by encouraging foreign banks to enter local economies. In other words, proponents of financial liberalization are providing policy solutions to the wrong problems. The proper policy response would be to ensure a proper 'macro-financial environment' – to use Keynes' expression – and place the emphasis on the need for governments to ensure sufficient growth in effective demand to allow borrowers to repay their bank loans.

Finally, increased international banking can in fact be destabilizing, as foreign banks can be more susceptible of withdrawing funds in times of crisis and tightening credit. Known as 'cut and run' strategies, some studies have shown that foreign banks may decide to withdraw from crisis-stricken countries, thereby contributing to increased instability. Indeed, at times of country-wide crisis, foreign banks are just as susceptible to losing capital. This was the case in Asia after the 1997 crisis, and was also what occurred during the Argentinian crisis, when Scotia Bank of Canada ended its lending operations in Argentina in 2002. Other banks followed suit, thus precipitating the crisis to its highest level.

The overall conclusion therefore is that increased numbers of foreign banks lead to more unstable and less capitalized local banks, which may eventually turn to foreign ownership as a possible way of salvaging what remains. Thus multinational banks lead to more multinational banks.

Post-Keynesian critique and policy recommendations

Post-Keynesians generally consider only the relationship between credit and output. Yet the structure or composition of this supply of credit has generally been ignored. But the increase in numbers of multinational banks, especially in Latin America, raises some important questions. Indeed, if we are interested in credit output relationships, should we not consider who is supplying the credit, to whom and for what purposes? This enters micro territory, which post-Keynesians generally neglect, but remains crucial, we believe, to our analysis. In other words, are there any potential negative side effects to greater banking and financial integration?

More importantly, the increase in the numbers of American and other foreign banks and firms extends the American brand of capitalism to other regions, and with that the advantages and costs of this particular institutional arrangement. In a very large measure, the same concerns can be argued with other forms of financial liberalization. For example, dollarization as part of a more general movement towards greater financial openness suffers from a similar criticism. In this sense, there are many parallels to be drawn between dollarization and the Washington Consensus. In the case of dollarization, former Treasury Secretary Lawrence Summers once argued that 'to the extent that dollarization helped to consolidate or expand our large role in Latin American markets, it might help to ensure that we continued to benefit disproportionately from their future growth' (US Senate, 1999). At the core of this debate over the multinationalization of banks, in a political economy sense, is the same logic.

The above analysis of the benefits of foreign banking is discussed strictly in terms of a neoclassical view of markets. From a post-Keynesian – or horizontalist – perspective, however, the supply of credit is not constrained *ex ante* and depends first and foremost on the availability of good borrowers, on the one hand, and on the expected growth of effective demand in the future, on the other which allows firms to realize their profit goals and reimburse banks (Rochon, 2005). Indeed, banks lend to creditworthy customers and are concerned chiefly with the reimbursement of debt. This fundamental behaviour of banks is the same in all markets, both developed and developing: loans create deposits. What needs to be done, from post-Keynesian perspective, is to improve the prospects that all borrowers will be in a position to reimburse banks.

In this sense, policy prescriptions must take place on two levels. In the first instance, policy-makers must be able to propose specific policy proposals that address the direct issue of multinational banks. However, on another, and just as important, level, the issue of growth and effective demand must be addressed simultaneously. In other words, reforming the banking system cannot take place in a vacuum – that is, without a thorough discussion of general growth strategies. While the latter is beyond the immediate scope of this chapter, many post-Keynesians have proposed specific growth strategies for developing countries.

But what we can say is that if indeed the emphasis is on effective demand and growth, then this implies that government has a role to play. We cannot separate the health of the banking system from effective demand and economic growth, and the potential role the government can play. From a post-Keynesian perspective, we must focus on economic growth that will ensure the level of effective demand, the necessary profitability of firms, and the reimbursement of debts to banks. In the main means that the government's budget has a part to play. It also means that government should not disregard income distribution – not only to combat inequality of wealth but also, as Keynes put it in his concluding notes to the *General Theory* (1973, pp. 372–84), to raise the propensity to consume and thus stimulate demand.

On the former issue of banks, however, policy proposals can take place on many fronts, from limits on the percentage of foreign ownership of local banks, to restrictions on foreign banks altogether. Whether these would prove beneficial or not remains to be seen, but from our perspective, such policies miss the boat. The issue is not whether to allow foreign banks to enter (although we would most certainly favour restrictions on their percentage and presence). We believe that if post-Keynesians are to have some impact, then policies must be realistic. In this sense, advocating a complete ban on foreign banks may prove difficult to sell and implement.

Rather, we think that if such deregulation and liberalization are inevitable, given the powers that be, the proper policy response from a post-Keynesian perspective is to advocate the regulation of foreign banks. As emphasized above, foreign banks usually gain important profitable market shares in emerging countries, and thus benefit from some oligopolistic power, thanks to their relationships with foreign companies implemented in these countries, and to their reputation. One proposal we would advocate is to reinforce the fair competition that liberalization in this way paradoxically jeopardizes. This could be achieved through diverse measures compelling foreign banks to diversify to whom they lend, and restricting the amount lent to any of the borrowers (as a percentage of the needs of the latter).

What we need therefore is to allow foreign banks to enter, but governments must have in place established rules of conduct and controls that will direct foreign banks to allocate a given percentage of their loan portfolio to smaller and local borrowers, and give local banks the opportunity of supplying credit to 'good' borrowers. Indeed, in doing this, the government would ensure that local interests are being addressed, with regard to both local borrowers and banks.

Conclusion

Given the discussion above, we believe that it is time to 'reform the reforms'. Indeed, post-Keynesians should push for deep reforms in any post-Washington Consensus discussion that would contain policy proposals to liberalize further the financial markets of emerging economies. In particular, given the topic addressed in this chapter, we believe that one of the important factors that needs to be addressed is the composition of credit supply, both in terms of *who* supplies credit and *to whom* it is supplied.

The policy proposals contained here are just as important, we believe, both before and immediately after a crisis. In fact, in the aftermath of a crisis, when the economy is at its most fragile, a policy of sound banking practices including small, medium and large firms, domestic and foreign, must be a priority of banks and governments alike. This, we believe, along with proper fiscal policies for sustained growth, will enhance the stability of the banking system and of the economy as a whole.

Notes

1 A 'multinational' bank is wholly different from an 'international' bank. While the latter is a bank that accepts deposits in one country and lends in another, the former is a bank of one country that has a branch in another country, accepting deposits and lending to local individuals and firms.
2 Canadian and Spanish banks are the most globalized (see McCauley *et al.*, 2002).

References

Anderson, R. and Kegels, C. (1998) *Transition Banking: Financial Development of Central and Eastern Europe* (Oxford University Press).

Belaisch, A., Kodres, L., Levy, J. and Ubide, A. (2000) 'Euro Area Banking at the crossroads', Unpublished paper, Washington, DC: IMF, May.

Berg, A. and Borensztein, E. (2000) 'The Pros and Cons of Dollarization', IMF Working paper WP/00/50, Washington, DC.

Clarke, G., Cull, R., D'Amato, L. and Molinari, A. (1999) 'The Effect of Foreign Entry on Argentina's Domestic Banking Sector', Unpublished paper, Washington, DC: World Bank.

Clarke, G., Cull, R., D'Amato, L. and Molinari, A. (2000) 'On the Kindness of Strangers? The Impact of Foreign Entry on Domestic Bnks in Argentina', in S. Claessens and M. Jansen (eds), *The Internationalization of Financial Services: Issues and Lessons for Developing Countries* (Boston, Mass.: Kluwer Academic Press).

Clarke, G., Cull, R., Peria, M. and Sánchez, S. (2001) 'Foreign Bank Entry: Experience, Implications for Developing Countries, and Agenda for Further Research', World Bank discussion paper.

Claessens, S., Demirgüç-Kunt, A. and Huizinga, H. (2000) 'How Does Foreign Entry Affect the Domestic Banking Market?', *Journal of Banking and Finance*, 25(1), May, pp. 391–911.

Darity, W. and Horn, B. (1998) *The Loan Pushers: The Role of Commercial Banks in the International Debt Crisis* (Cambridge, Mass.: Harper & Row, Ballinger).

Demirgüç-Kunt, A. and Detragiache, E. (1998) 'Financial Liberalization and Financial Fragility', World Bank Policy Research Working Paper No. 1917, Washington, DC.

Edwards, S. (1989) *Real Exchange Rates, Devaluation, and Adjustment* (Cambridge University Press).

Eichengreen, B. and Mussa, M. (1998) 'Capital Account Liberalization – Theoretical and Practical Aspects', IMF Occasional Paper No. 172 (Washington, DC).

Euh, Y. and Baker, J. (1990) *The Korean Banking System and Foreign Influence* (London: Routledge).

Focarelli, D. and Pozzolo, A. (2000) 'The Determinants of Cross-border Shareholding: An Analysis with Bank-level Data from OECD Countries', Paper presented at the Federal Reserve Bank of Chicago Structure Conference, May.

Goldberg, L.G. and Saunders A. (1981) 'The Multinational Bank: A Financial MNC?' *Journal of Banking and Finance*, **5**, pp. 33–63.

IMF (2000) 'International Capital Markets Developments, Prospects, and Key Policy Issues', *World Economic and Financial Surveys*, September (Washington, DC).

Keynes, J.M. (1973) *The General Theory of Employment, Interest and Money*, in D. Moggridge (ed.), *The Collected Writings of J.M. Keynes*, Vol. VII (London: Macmillan).

Lindgren, C.-J., García, G. and Saal, M. (1996) *Bank Soundness and Macroeconomic Policy*, Washington, DC: IMF.

McCauley, R, Rudd, J. and Wooldridge, P. (2002) 'Globalising International Banking', *BIS Quarterly Review*, March (Switzerland), pp. 41–50.

Rochon, L.-P. (2005) 'Endogenous Money, Central Banks and the Banking System: Basil Moore and a Return to Horizontalist Roots', in M. Setterfield (ed.), *Essays in Honour of Basil Moore* (Cheltenham (UK) and Northampton (USA): Edward Elgar, forthcoming).

Weller, C. (1998) 'Global Banking', *Foreign Policy*, 3(9), May, pp. 1–3.

Weller, C. (2000) 'Financial Liberalization, Multinational Banks and Declining Real Credit: The Case of Poland', *International Review of Applied Economics*, 14(2), Spring, pp. 193–212.

Weller, C. (2001) 'The Supply of Credit by Multinational Banks in Developing and Transition Economies: Determinants and Effects', DESA Discussion Paper No. 16 (New York).

Yamori, N. (1998) 'A Note on the Location Choice of Multinational Banks: The Case of Japanese Financial Institutions', *Journal of Banking and Finance*, 22, pp. 109–20.

12

Spanish Foreign Direct Investment in Latin America, 1989–2004: A Constructivist Framework for Analysis

Pablo Toral

Since the Spanish government gradually eliminated the restrictions on foreign direct investment (FDI) by Spanish enterprises, between 1977 and 1992, Spanish FDI has reached significant proportions, making Spain the twelfth home country for FDI in the world in 2000 by stock. The 'position' or 'stock' of Spanish FDI abroad grew from US$1,931 million in 1980 to US$15,652 million in 1990, and to US$160,202 million in 2000 (see Table 12.1). This meant an increase of 8,294 per cent in this twenty-year period, the fifth largest percentage growth among the top home economies in the world (see Table 12.2).

Although the growth in the amount of Spanish FDI abroad during this short period was very large, what made these investments even more interesting was the fact that they were very highly concentrated in two geographic areas (the European Union and, in particular, Latin America (see Figure 12.1)), where Spanish FDI flows surpassed those coming from the USA in 1999 and 2000. The USA has been the main provider of inward FDI in Latin America since the mid-twentieth century (see Figure 12.2).

By the turn of the century, the seven Spanish firms included in this chapter (BBVA, SCH, Telefónica, Endesa, Iberdrola, Unión Fenosa and Repsol–YPF) had assets worth US$283,000 million and 128 million customers in Latin America, and they had become prominent actors in the economies of the region (BBVA, 1999, p. 22; 2001, p. 120; 2002, p. 17; SCH, 2002, pp. 5, 22; Endesa, 2002, pp. 9, 110; Iberdrola, 2002, pp. 101–4; Unión Fenosa, 2002, pp. 63–4). In this chapter, I will provide an explanation for these foreign direct investments. I conclude that the managers of the Spanish firms that invested in Latin America, especially in the 1990s, believed they had an advantage. They believed that this advantage manifested itself in a series of

Table 12.1 Foreign direct investment in outward stock, by home country, in 2000, US$ millions

Country	1980	1990	2000
USA	220,178	430,521	1,244,654
UK	80,434	229,294	901,769
France	23,599	120,179	496,741
Germany	43,127	148,457	442,811
Hong Kong/China	148	11,920	384,732
Belgium and Luxembourg	6,037	40,636	339,644
Netherlands	42,135	102,608	325,881
Japan	19,610	201,440	281,664
Switzerland	21,491	66,087	232,045
Canada	23,777	84,829	200,878
Italy	7,319	57,261	176,225
Spain	1,931	15,652	160,202
Sweden	3,721	49,491	115,574
Australia	2,260	30,507	83,220
Singapore	3,718	7,808	53,216
Finland	737	11,227	53,046
Taiwan Province of China	97	12,888	49,187
Denmark	2,065	7,342	46,111
Norway	561	10,888	44,133
South Africa	5,722	15,027	33,557
China, People's Republic of	39	2,489	27,212
Korea, Republic of	127	2,301	25,842
Argentina	6,128	6,105	20,189

Source: United Nations (2001), pp. 307–11.

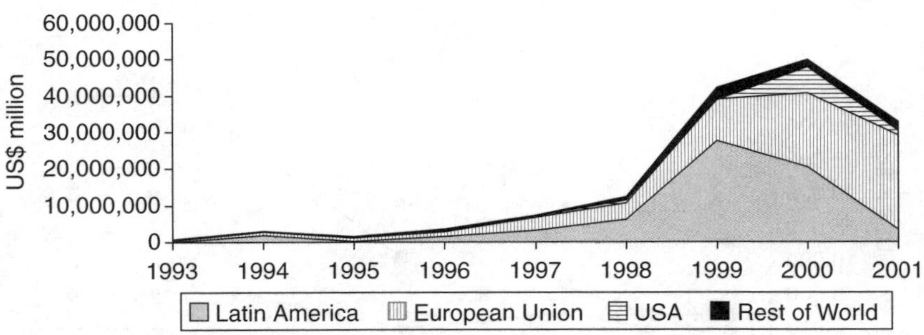

Figure 12.1 Flows of Spanish foreign direct investment by destination, 1993–2001, US$ millions

Source: Dirección General de Comercio e Inversiones, Secretaría de Estado de Comercio y Turismo (Spanish Ministry of the Economy) (2003).

Table 12.2 Position or stock of foreign direct investment by country of origin, first twenty-two home economies, percentage variation, 1980–2000

Country	Percentage variation
Hong Kong/China	259,954
China, People's Republic of	69,774
Taiwan Province of China	50,708
Korea, Republic of	20,348
Spain	8,296
Norway	7,866
Finland	7,197
Belgium and Luxembourg	5,626
Australia	3,682
Sweden	3,105
Italy	2,407
Denmark	2,232
France	2,104
Netherlands	1,738
Japan	1,436
Singapore	1,431
UK	1,121
Switzerland	1,079
Germany	1,026
Canada	844
South Africa	586
USA	565
Argentina	329

Source: United Nations (2001), pp. 307–11.

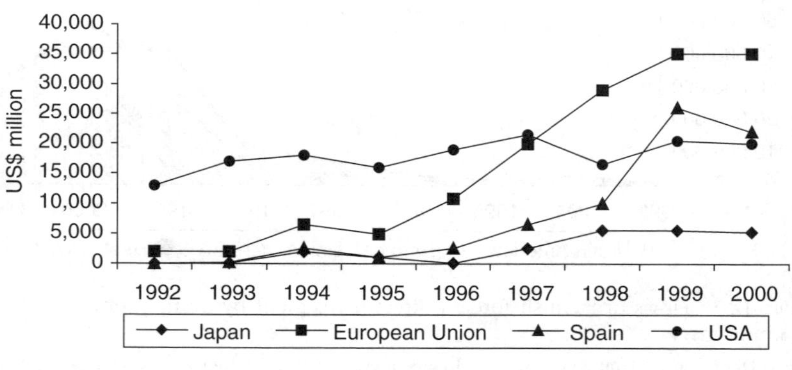

Figure 12.2 Inward foreign direct investment flows in Latin America and the Caribbean, 1992–2000, US$ millions

Sources: EUROSTAT (2002) and US Department of Commerce (2002).

Table 12.3 Sectoral allocation of Spanish foreign direct investment in Latin America, 1980–2000, percentage of total

Sector	1980–4	1985–9	1990–4	1995–2000
Energy	0.12	0.23	9.20	22.70
Communication	0.73	2.26	25.14	5.84
Banking and finance	48.86	57.48	57.38	40.50
Three sectors	49.71	59.97	91.72	69.04

Source: Dirección General de Comercio e Inversiones, Secretaría de Estado de Comercio y Turismo (Spanish Ministry of the Economy) (2003).

institutional factors. Subsequently, I will explain how the Spanish firms developed this advantage, and how they applied it in the markets where they invested. I will focus on seven firms that operate in the sectors that generated the largest amounts of FDI in Latin American banking, telecommunications, public utilities, and oil and natural gas. These sectors produced more than half of the Spanish FDI in Latin America. The companies were selected because they invested the largest share of FDI in their sectors. It is impossible to determine, based on the official statistics, how much money each of them invested, because the Spanish authorities do not provide this information in order to protect the privacy of the investors. Nevertheless, these firms were the largest in Spain in terms of market capitalization during the period of analysis (Dirección General de Comercio e Inversiones, 2003). While in the early 1980s these sectors absorbed barely half of the Spanish FDI in Latin America, mostly in banking, in the 1990s they attracted almost 70 per cent (including 'holding societies'), and the total amount was more evenly distributed among energy (which includes the public utilities and the oil and natural gas sectors), telecommunications, and banking (see Table 12.3).

Theoretical framework

Subsequently, I shall propose a model to explain the creation and the application of an advantage, using the empirical case of the Spanish firms mentioned above. The advantage of Spanish firms in Latin America was their 'knowledge of the market'. Their managers believed that they knew the needs of the Latin American markets very well, and thought that their firms had what was needed to provide the services and products that the markets required. Therefore, they decided to invest there.

This knowledge of the market was the result of two factors (see Figure 12.3). On the one hand, a shared culture between Spain and Latin America, the strong historical contact that has existed for centuries between Spain and Latin America, has left its mark in the Latin American culture, making it very similar to that of Spain. The managers of Spanish firms thought that the

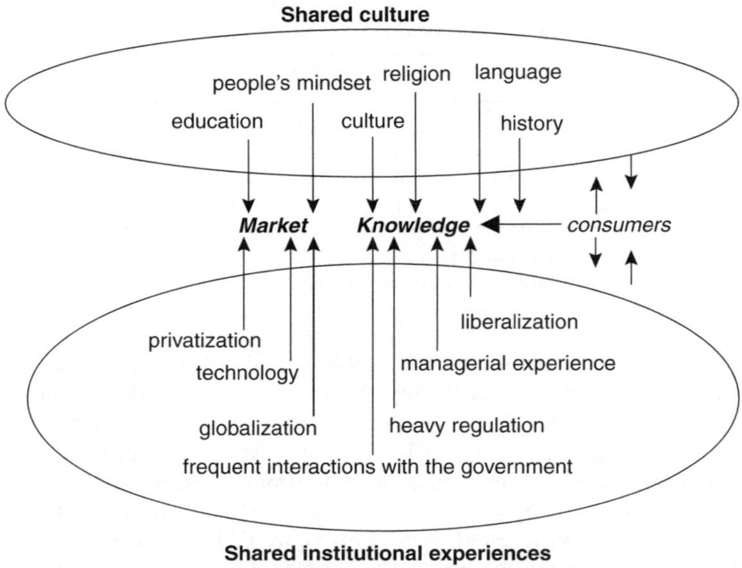

Figure 12.3 Development of the advantage

common language, and the predominantly Catholic religion, in both Spain and Latin America, and the similar educational systems, based on the same principles and similar values, had generated similar mindsets among people on both sides of the Atlantic. Therefore, they concluded that it would be easier for them to operate in this cultural environment.

Moreover, the linguistic and cultural similarity would also facilitate interactions with the employees of their potential Latin American subsidiaries, and would make it easier to move employees between the parent and subsidiaries. For all these reasons, they concluded that transactions would be easier and less onerous, and that the environment in which they would have to operate would be appropriate (*El Exportador*, 2003, p. 61). This is an important thesis, because it emphasizes a human aspect that is sometimes ignored by many disciplines. In other words, businesses are conducted by people. The impact of cultural differences in business has generated a great number of studies from an anthropological perspective.

On the other hand, knowledge of the Latin American market, in the more technical aspects, came out of the shared institutional experiences that were similar to Spain and Latin America, in each sector. That is to say, the institutional context in which Spanish firms operated was very similar to the one the managers believed they had found in Latin America. The markets had several characteristics: many state-owned firms were privatized, monopolies were eliminated by introducing competition (liberalization), the firms involved in these sectors had to devise technology very fast to meet the growing demands of the market, managers had to adjust the internal organization of their firms to be able to operate under these new conditions, the Spanish managers thought that globalization (which they defined as 'market liberalization') would increase competition and as a result only a few large multinational firms would survive in each sector, these Spanish firms operated in heavily regulated sectors; and this required their managers to establish frequent interactions with the government.

These conditions created a particular institutional and cultural context in which the Spanish firms found themselves in the 1990s. When they adjusted to these conditions, their managers decided to adopt the internal organizational processes that were more suited to the pursuit of their businesses. These organizational processes constituted the internal organization of the firm. They also developed a web of external relations with the regulators and with the government in order to lobby.

Both internally and externally, the firms adopted a 'ruled' behaviour – that is, behaviour based on a series of organizational rules or rules of internal behaviour (internal organization) and external behaviour (their relations with regulators and consumers) – which institutionalized their advantage and coerced their employees into adapting their behaviour on the basis of the products and services their managers wanted (or had) to produce. This institutionalized behaviour, both externally and internally, constituted the normative framework or organizational culture of the firms.

Here, I use the rule-orientated constructivist approach developed by Nicholas Onuf. In proposing a mode of analysis for the social sciences, he tackled the agency–structure debate and explained that agents and institutions (he prefers to use this term rather than structures) co-constitute each other. That is, the agents construct the social institutions in which they operate and these institutions, in turn, constrain agency. To understand this process of co-constitution, Onuf looked at social rules, which mediate between agents and institutions. The institutions are sets of rules that tell agents how to behave in a given setting. In our case, we regard the firm as an institution, governed by a series of rules created by its own employees (the agents). Outside the firm, the market is the institution and the firm becomes the agent. The rules of the market are determined by the regulating agents and by the firms that operate in them (Onuf, 1989).

When the executives of the Spanish firms included in this study considered the possibility of making FDIs, they saw that many regions of the world were going through the same processes of privatization and liberalization, including Latin America, Central and Eastern Europe, and Africa. They came to the conclusion that, although the institutional framework in which they had to operate was similar in all of these regions, the Latin American cultural framework was similar to Spain's, which led them to make FDIs in Latin America (see Figure 12.4).

Figure 12.4 Application of the advantage

In the following sections I provide an analysis of the historical context in which the Spanish firms developed their advantage and adopted the decision to make FDIs in Latin America. Their investments were facilitated by three variables. First, the development of Spain's economy (many Spanish companies benefited from a period of sustained growth and accumulated enough financial and managerial resources to expand overseas). Second, the European Union (EU) authorities set a schedule for the liberalization of several industries that until the 1990s had operated under monopoly (a group of Spanish companies decided to expand outside Spain, as a defensive strategy to withstand competition in Spain). Third, the new economic framework adopted by the Latin American governments stressed macroeconomic stability and gave foreign companies the same legal status as domestic companies.

Economic development in Spain

I follow the model developed by Dunning and Narula (1994) to explain the relationship between economic development and FDI. These scholars divide countries up into five categories based on the roles their economies play with regard to FDI. In stage one, a country's location advantages are not important enough to attract FDI, except in mining and exploitation of natural resources. Income per capita and domestic demand are low. Less industrialized countries that have unqualified labour and poor transport and telecommunications infrastructure are at this stage. FDI is small and concentrated in commercial activities related to export. Spain went through this stage in the nineteenth century and the first half of the twentieth century.

In stage two, the domestic market and the stock of capital in activities that generate value added are higher. There are some capital intensive industries, such as those related to steel, shipyards and a basic chemical industry. FDI is concentrated in the manufacturing sector and in the exploitation of natural resources. It works as an economic stimulus because it contributes towards increasing the productive capacity of those industries. FDI may spread to emerging industries that require intermediate technology, such as consumer goods, textiles, food and basic electric goods. Public expenditure emphasizes investment in education (mainly secondary education), transport, communications, and the provision of some public goods and services. The government also develops basic infrastructure to facilitate productive activities and pursues economic policies that promote macroeconomic stability. Spain went through this stage in the 1960s and 1970s.

In stage three, the standard of living is high, the tertiary sector is large, and consumers and firms start to give priority to high quality goods. Product differentiation plays an important part, along with investment in research and development (R&D). Firms demand workers with university degrees. Wages are higher and no longer play a part in the comparative advantages of firms. Salaries are not an incentive for investment to reduce production costs. Outward FDI is fairly high, especially motivated by the search for lower production costs (mainly cheaper labour). Spain went through this stage in the 1980s and early 1990s.

In stage four, the amount of inward FDI is equal to the amount of outward FDI. The comparative advantages of the country are created factors, rather than natural endowments. Domestic firms compete with foreign MNEs in the domestic market, as well as in international markets. There is a high degree of intraindustry trade and investment. Spain reached this stage in the mid-1990s. The fifth stage or 'information economy', is characterized by information-related activities such as telecommunications, computer technologies and software. Only a few post-industrial societies such as the USA, Japan, Germany, France and Sweden have reached this stage. Many of the economic transactions among these countries have been internalized by MNEs. These economies are very integrated. There are many acquisitions and strategic alliances among firms in these countries, seeking higher rates of efficiency.

Liberalization in Spain

The Spanish government played an important part in the process of internationalization of Spanish firms, by setting a deregulatory legal framework between 1977 and 1992, and pushing several publicly-owned Spanish companies to make investments outside Spain. The first step was the reduction of the legal requirements that outward capital flows had to go through. Until the mid-1970s, Spain had strong control mechanisms over capital movements to prevent capital flight, and investments outside the country had to be approved by the Spanish Council of Ministers. Reforms were introduced in 1977, 1979, 1986 and 1992 to make Spanish legislation comply with the stipulations of the European Union, which made the notification of the FDI for statistical purposes the only requirement (with no need of approval) (ICE, 1979, 1981, 1994; UNCTAD, 1996, pp. 239–43).

The incorporation of Spain into the European Union on 1 January 1986 was a powerful stimulus for Spanish exports to the EU and for FDI in Spain (by companies from the EU as well as from outside it). Inward FDI in Spain increased by 1,433 per cent between 1985 and 1995, from $8,939 million to $128,859 million, turning Spain into the sixth home of FDI in the world. The gradual liberalization of economic activities across the EU, especially in the public utilities (liberalization of telecommunications was set to be enforced in 1997 and in public utilities in 2007), contributed to push many Spanish firms towards Latin America. The Spanish government devised a defensive strategy to protect Spain's public utilities from European competition. Its goals were to push Spanish firms to new markets outside Spain, and to increase their competitiveness by forcing them to compete in open markets, where competition would compel them to raise efficiency. Latin America became the target.

In addition to the liberalization of financial flows, the strategy of the Spanish government comprised a reform of the tax system, a number of public funds to subsidize or finance Spanish FDIs, a system of public insurance to protect investments from the risks of the host country, and bilateral and multilateral treaties for protection of investments. A tax reform to prevent double taxation was implemented in 1990, in compliance with EU Directive 435. The Spanish legislature exempted Spanish firms from the payment of taxes on distributed dividends, and deducted from the tax payable in Spain the amount that their subsidiaries already paid in the host country, when this amount was lower than that stipulated by Spanish law (Morán, 1994, p. 13; Palacios, 1994, pp. 53–62; PriceWaterhouse, 1996, p. 572).

The Spanish government made a total of US$754 million worth of credit for FDI available through the Instituto de Crédito Oficial (ICO), the Ministry of Trade and Tourism, the Instituto de Comercio Exterior (ICEX), and the Spanish Company of Finance for Development (COFIDES) (Aceña, 1994; Dirección General de Comercio e Inversiones, 2003). The state-owned Compañía Española de Seguro de Crédito a la Exportación (CESCE), began insuring the FDI of Spanish companies in 1974. The 'Bilateral Agreements for Reciprocal Promotion and Protection of Investments' (BARPIs) sought to create a positive investment climate between Spain and the host countries. Between 1990 and 1995, Spain subscribed a BARPI with most Spanish speaking countries of the Western Hemisphere (García de Quevedo and Hontecillas, 1994, p. 79; Jiménez, 1994, pp. 86–7; IRELA, 1996, p. 30; UNCTAD, 1996, pp. 312–13).

Structural reforms in Latin America

This section explores the developments in the 1990s within Latin American countries that made their economies appealing to foreign investors, especially to Spanish MNEs. The magnitude of the crisis in the 1980s led to the search for new alternatives. According to the 'orthodox model', embraced by most economic agencies based in Washington, such as the World Bank, the International Monetary Fund (IMF), and the economic agencies of the US government, the economic crisis was caused by excessive state intervention (manifested in protectionist policies, excessive regulation of economic activities, and a large public sector) and the relaxation of fiscal policies.

The solution proposed was a package of ten policies to increase the role of the market forces including fiscal discipline, the use of public expenditure mainly for education and health care; to improve the efficiency of the tax system by increasing the tax base and moderating marginal taxes, to adjust taxes to the needs of the market; to liberalize external trade, to lift restrictions on FDI, to privatize public enterprises; to deregulate economic activities, and to protect property rights. In short, the orthodox approach recommended a reduction of the role of the state in production and a focus on macroeconomic stability (Bresser, 1993, pp. 18–20).

The liberalization of trade put an end to four decades of ISI. Governments eliminated non-tariff barriers (including quotas and prohibitions) and export taxes, and simplified tariffs, to promote exports and increase factor productivity. The creation of MERCOSUR, and the revitalization of other existing regional economic blocs (Andean Community, Central American Common Market – CACM, and the Caribbean Common Market – CARICOM) followed these principles. Between 1985 and 1992, over 2,000 state-owned firms were privatized in Latin America to generate public revenue, to reduce the degree of state involvement in the economy, and to increase the overall efficiency of domestic firms (Edwards, 1995, p. 170).

Several policies were adopted to deregulate capital markets and generate higher rates of domestic savings and private investment, including the deregulation of capital markets, deregulation of interest rates, elimination of the rules to establish direct credit, reduction and harmonization of deposit requirements for commercial banking, reduction of entry barriers, the development of capital markets, and the implementation of legislation based on the needs of the market. Previous administrations had set ceilings on interest rates, and channelled investment to certain sectors, based on social and political interests, rather than on the estimates of returns on investment. The role of the state was now reduced to legislation and supervision tasks (Edwards, 1995, pp. 200–24).

FDI was very important in the post-crisis strategies. Foreign firms would bring to Latin America new techniques and managerial styles, new technologies and innovations, and force domestic firms to increase productivity.

Chile and Argentina adopted these policies in the 1970s; Mexico in the mid-1980s; Peru, Colombia and Venezuela in the early 1990s; and Brazil in the mid-1990s. Every country gave foreign firms treatment equal to that of domestic companies (but did not allow FDI in some 'strategic' sectors), flat incentive policies (except in export sectors and investment in research and development), and allowed unlimited repatriation of capital and profits. The investments of Spanish firms in Latin America in the 1990s were concentrated in telecommunications, banking and energy (Edwards, 1995, pp. 246–51).

Telecommunications sector

Telefónica became one of the most prominent Spanish MNEs in Latin America, not only for its presence in most countries in the region, but also for the large amounts of money it paid in the privatization of some of the national telephone companies (US$2,000 million for the purchase of the Peruvian telephone company in 1992). Telefónica's investments were motivated by a series of economic, political, sectoral and firm-specific factors, including the liberalization of the telecommunications sector in Spain on 1 December, 1997, the culmination of Telefónica's process of privatization, which started in the 1970s and ended in 1997 with the sale by the state of the last stocks it held in Telefónica's subsidiary Telefónica Internacional Sociedad Anónima (TISA), and the evolution of the telecommunications sector in the world, which experienced the creation of large international telecommunications groups, integrated by some of the largest firms.

The process of economic globalization and the growth of economic interdependence raised doubts in the 1980s about the desirability for governments to maintain the condition of natural monopoly in telecommunications. This approach was based on the belief that telecommunications constituted a 'strategic public service', which the market did not price correctly. Many Latin American governments nationalized their telephone companies: Argentina in 1945, Brazil in 1962, Peru in 1970, Chile in 1971, and Venezuela in 1976 (Akinsanya, 1980, pp. 115–16; Sigmund, 1980, pp. 36–9). The Spanish government also nationalized Telefónica (created in 1926 by ITT) in 1944, under national security concerns (Carreras *et al.*, 1997, p. 32).

Economic integration in the 1980s increased the need of firms to have access to good and efficient telecommunications services. Technological innovations such as digitalization, optical fibres, mobile telecommunications and satellite communication increased the variety, quality and reach of telecommunications services that operators could provide. These advancements increased the technological demands of customers, but the national operators of traditional telephone services were unable to meet them. They used outdated technology inefficient systems, and, in general, could not upgrade their technology and infrastructure to satisfy the growing demands from the population and the business sector, thus hampering the internationalization and efficiency of firms.

The Latin American governments realized this in the 1980s and eliminated the consideration of 'natural monopoly'. This decision was based on their assessment of the performance of the domestic operators – long waiting lists for the installation of new lines, outdated technology, poor service, artificially maintained low prices, and the power of the workers' unions to influence the decisions of the companies (Ramamurti, 1996, pp. 1–45). They believed that privatization would be the best solution to upgrade the quality of the telecommunications services. It would also help to end the state's fiscal balance of payments crises, and send a signal to private investors that the change in approach was real. This aspect was very important, because in the new economic paradigm based on the Washington consensus, FDI played a prominent role. The importance of the telecommunications sector was high, given the zeal with which governments had protected it from private (possibly foreign) capital.

Telecommunications companies were privatized first, to let investors know that the reforms started by the new administrations were serious. The strategic importance of the telephone company would make governments appear to be truly committed to their structural reform programmes. By privatizing a 'plum' rather than a 'lemon', governments hoped to regain the interest of foreign investors (Ramamurti, 1996, p. 11). Telecommunications companies were the 'jewel in the crown', because they provided universal coverage and their growth potential was high. Thus, the governments' reforms were more credible and attractive. Telecommunications MNEs from the industrialized countries were ready to take part in the privatization of these Latin American state-owned enterprises. They had the technology needed to upgrade the system and were compelled to grow beyond their national borders, because they had made very large investments to upgrade their technology in the 1980s and needed to increase their sales to make those investments profitable.

Telefónica had no foreign ventures when it submitted its bid in the process of privatization of the telephone companies of Chile in 1987, Argentina in 1988 and Mexico in 1989. The liberalization prospects of the EU (1997 being the deadline set by the EU for governments to end national monopolies in the telephone sector) led Telefónica's executives to seek investment opportunities abroad. At that point the state was the largest stockholder. The goal was to expand Telefónica's businesses overseas to compensate for the potential loss of a share of its domestic market after the end of its national monopoly. Latin America offered Telefónica a very appealing market. To attract foreign investors, each Latin American government offered a period of monopoly to the highest bidder in the privatization of the state-owned telephone companies.

Telefónica had several advantages, *vis-à-vis* its North American, European and Asian competitors. A common language was one. Latin America provided Telefónica with the opportunity to offer its services and to conduct business in Spanish. A crucial advantage, however, was the similarity of political conditions in Latin America with regard to Spain. All the Latin American countries that Telefónica was interested in were nascent democracies. The communion of political interests between Spain and Latin America created a sense of political complicity between the government of Spain on the one hand, and some of the governments of Latin America on the other. This aspect facilitated political understanding among them, favoring all kinds of cultural, political, educational, commercial and economic exchanges. This complicity materialized in several investment treaties, as well as accords of political and cultural exchange signed between Spain and Latin American states, many of which were channelled through the Iberian–American summits that brought together the heads of state and government of Spain and Portugal and Portuguese- and Spanish-speaking Latin America.

Telefónica's strategy in Latin America followed some basic guidelines:

- Increasing the number of lines in each country
- Improving digitalization of lines, so that transmissions became better, cheaper and faster (this included the installation of a broadband network, with an emphasis on ADSL, from 1999)
- Focusing on the largest and fastest growing markets of Mexico and Brazil, since 2000, to achieve synergies in order to reduce operating costs (this included the coordination of the operations of its Latin-American subsidiaries to create a Panamerican Network that allowed Telefónica to provide comprehensive telecommunications service to the corporate sector, as well as to subcontract its services to other operators, thus becoming an operator of operators)
- Increasing labour productivity
- Diversifying into new products, with an emphasis on the convergence of telecommunications, internet and audiovisual services after 1999.

This strategy was based on Telefónica's previous experience in the Spanish market. Its managers believed that it would also be appropriate in Latin America (Telefónica, 1993, p. 36; 1996, p. 46; 2001, pp. 9, 35). Ignacio Santillana, CEO of Telefónica Internacional, SA, between 1990 and 1996 explained the firm's strategy in Latin America:

> The internationalization of Telefónica was established on the basis of the competitive advantages that Telefónica had *vis-à-vis* the American and European operators. It was based on the ability to undertake important investment programs in short periods of time. In the decade of the 1980s, and especially in its last years, Telefónica faced a crisis of demand for telephones and telephone services in Spain. In this period, Telefónica had close to one million demands to install a telephone. This crisis forced Telefónica to develop efficiently large investment programs quickly. This know-how, which some characterized as trench technology, was

very useful and extraordinarily attractive to satisfy the demands of the countries that needed an urgent expansion of their telephone systems, given the high demand of the people for telephones waiting to be installed. There was a coincidence, that the countries with these problems were involved in a process of privatization of the state-owned firms. These firms had a monopoly for the provision of telecommunication services. (Santillana, 1997, p. 94)

Telefónica had more than 48 million customers in Latin America in 2002 (and a total of 89 million customers across the world). It was the seventh largest telephone operator by market capitalization in the world, the sixth largest European firm, the largest in Spain, and the fourth-best performer on the Spanish stock exchange between 1996 and 2000, with an average profitability of 43 per cent, thanks to a large degree to its strategy of international growth after 1990. In 1999, it was the thirtieth-largest multinational enterprise in the world, and the most internationalized telephone operator (with the largest assets outside its domestic market), 38 per cent of its income in 2001 came from Latin America and there were 157,000 employees (see Table 12.4 for its Latin American subsidiaries). Before Telefónica began its international expansion in 1989, it was only a domestic telephone operator in Spain, with 11.797 million telephone lines, and 75,350 employees (Telefónica, 1990, p. 3; 2001, pp. 8, 11, 13, 30–4; 2002, pp. 12–14, 23; UNCTAD, 2001, p. 90).

Table 12.4 Telefónica's subsidiaries in Latin America and the Caribbean in 2003

Country	**Name**	**Area**	**Ownership percentage**
Argentina	Telefónica de Argentina	Land lines	98.03
	TCP Argentina	Cellular	97.93
	Telefónica Data Argentina	Business	97.92
	Terra Networks	Internet	99.99
	Atento Argentina	Customer relations	100.00
	Telefé	TV channel	100.00
	Torneos y Competencias	TV programming	20.00
Brazil	Telesp	Land lines	87.49
	Brasilcel	Cellular	50.00
	Telefónica Empresas Brasil	Business	100.00
	Terra Networks Brasil	Internet	100.00
	TPI Brasil	Directories	100.00
	Atento Brasil	Customer relations	100.00
Chile	CTC Chile	Land lines	43.64
	T.M. Aplic. Y Soluciones	Cellular	100.00
	Terra Networks Chile	Internet	100.00
	Publiguías	Directories	51.00
	Atento Chile	Customer relations	82.77

Continued

Table 12.4 Continued

Country	Name	Area	Ownership percentage
Colombia	Telefónica Data Colombia	Business	65.00
	Terra Networks Colombia	Internet	68.00
El Salvador	TEM El Salvador	Cellular	90.30
	Atento El Salvador	Customer relations	100.00
Guatemala	TEM Guatemala	Cellular	100.00
	Terra Networks Guatemala	Internet	100.00
	Atento de Guatemala	Customer relations	100.00
Mexico	Telefónica Móviles México	Cellular	92.00
	Telefónica Data México Holding	Business	100.00
	Terra Networks México	Internet	99.99
	Atento Mexicana	Customer relations	100.00
Peru	Telefónica del Perú	Land lines	97.21
	TEM Perú	Cellular	97.97
	Telefónica Empresas Perú	Business	97.07
	Terra Networks Perú	Internet	99.99
	Atento Perú	Customer relations	99.16
Puerto Rico	TLD Puerto Rico	Land lines	98.00
Venezuela	CAN Teléfonos de Venezuela (CANTV)	Land lines	6.92

Source: Telefónica, *Informe anual 2003*, pp. 122–3.

Banking sector

Banks were the leading Spanish investors in Latin America in the 1990s. Their decision to invest there was based on the general aspects already discussed in earlier sections, as well as on the strong competition in the Spanish banking system, and margin compression (the relationship between loans and deposits). When banks issued a high number of loans, their income may be increased greatly if their borrowers repay those loans in periodic installments, with interest. When the ratio of loans falls, relative to the ratio of deposits, the income of banks may fall, if banks cannot find profitable activities for the investment of deposits. The difference between loans and deposits in Spain fell from 7.39 per cent in 1991 to 4.38 per cent in 1995 (*Financial Times*, 1996). In the first half of the 1990s, Spanish banks faced a contradictory situation, with growing liquidity and falling profits. They had to devise new ways of investing their money profitably. Their solution was to seek new markets to invest part of those profits (Latin America), and to invest in new areas of economic activity with greater prospects of economic growth (mainly the energy sector and telecommunications).

In the 1980s, Spanish banks developed new products and services, such as investment funds, pension funds, public bonds, equities markets and corporate bonds, to adapt to the new needs of their market. The introduction of these products and services into Spain expanded the previous narrow role of the banks as deposit havens. New financial institutions (other than banks) soon appeared, taking advantage of the new banking market. Banks now had to develop these products and services, in order not to lose customers, reinvesting their funds with higher rates of return.

The expansion of Spanish banks in Latin America was facilitated by the process of financial and banking liberalization implemented by the Latin American governments in the 1990s, similar to that undertaken in the Spanish market in the previous decade, forcing domestic banks to adopt the new financial services. Spanish banks had already developed these products in the 1980s for the Spanish market and found a competitive advantage *vis à vis* domestic Latin American banks. They believed their financial products would be adapted easily to Latin America. Latin American banks, on the other hand, were compelled to develop these new services overnight. Moreover, the deep financial crisis of the 1980s had caused a severe reduction in the number of banks in healthy economic conditions, and governments tried to attract new foreign banking and financial institutions to strengthen that sector, to help rebuild the banking system, and to improve the quality of services and banking loans.

Public policies were in part responsible for the weakness of the Latin American financial systems when the crisis erupted. Most governments restricted the creation of new financial institutions, set ceilings on interest rates, even below inflation rates (thus generating negative interest rates and stimulating capital flight), and established concrete conditions to give credit based on non-economic or non-productive criteria. Banks had a high degree of liquidity (the relationship of liquid assets over deposits was high, and the relationship of credit to assets was low). High liquidity eliminated their incentive to set strict criteria for the concession of loans, thereby giving loans to many unproductive projects (Edwards, 1995, pp. 207–8). In Argentina, Mexico and Peru, the total of non-performing loans exceeded 20 per cent (Edwards, 1995, p. 14). and this decreased banking revenue, triggering a serious banking crisis. Governments tried to solve the crisis by extending credit to the state financial institutions. These institutions translated the funds to the troubled banks, which in turn, extended them to their clients. Finally, their clients invested the new credits in the same old unprofitable projects. The result was a drainage of state and banking funds, and the deepening of the banking crisis, when the resources of the state financial institutions dried up.

Things were a little better in Chile and Colombia, because the strict requirements of their central banks lowered the liquidity rate of the commercial banks. In 1982, Colombian and Chilean banks had relatively low ratios of cash assets to deposits and high ratios of loans to assets (Rojas-Suárez and Weisbrod, 1995, p. 14). At the outbreak of the crisis, foreign loans ceased, and the central banks became the major providers of credit to commercial banks. Thus, the central banks used this conjecture to promote 'credit discipline', by restricting lending to those commercial banks that gave credit only for profitable investments.

Elsewhere in Latin America, the consequences of the banking crisis were very serious. In Argentina, the largest private commercial bank and forty-two small- and medium-sized financial institutions went into liquidated between 1980 and 1982. In Chile, between 1981 and 1982, eleven financial institutions (whose portfolios represented almost 15 per cent of total loans) were liquidated, and in 1983 seven banks were taken over by the government (two of them were finally liquidated and five were rehabilitated) (Edwards, 1995, pp. 207–8). Moreover, excessive credit increased inflation and devalued national currencies. The crisis could not be overcome until governments tightened up credit. The governments gave conditional credit to banks that conducted a realistic appraisal of the possibility of their borrowers returning to solvency (lowering the ratio of cash assets to deposits and increasing the ratio of loans to assets) and liberalized the banking sector (Rojas-Suárez and Weisbrod, 1995, p. 15).

This change of approach facilitated the investment of Spanish banks in Latin America. Their universal character gave Spanish banks an advantage, derived from their experience in the provision of a large array of banking and financial services, ranging from traditional bank accounts to pensions and investment funds, corporate lending, mortgages and insurance. As in Germany, banks in Spain provided all kinds of financial services, in contrast to the British model, where banks were originally barred from some of those services.

In 2002, BBVA had US$88,850 million (€84,000 million) worth of assets in Latin America, mainly in Argentina, Chile, Mexico and Puerto Rico. It had over 23 million customers in 2001 in Latin America. SCH was Latin America's largest banking group in 2002, with 30 million customers and assets worth $114,805 million (€108,537 million), mainly in Argentina, Brazil, Chile, Mexico and Puerto Rico (BBVA, 1999, p. 19; 2001, p. 120; 2002, p. 17; SCH, 2002, pp. 5, 22) (see Tables 12.5 and 12.6). The expansion strategy of each of these banks was different. BBV sought a strong local partner, from which it bought between 30 per cent and 40 per cent of its stock. Eventually it increased its share of ownership in its subsidiaries to achieve full control over management. BS sought majority ownership of its Latin American subsidiaries from the beginning. Before the BS–BCH merger, BCH expanded in Latin America through its Chilean subsidiary, O'Higgins Central Hispano, and always sought a powerful local partner in each country. After the merger, SCH adopted BS's model and began a process of disinvestments in the smaller countries in which it had taken over local banks (Paraguay and Peru and, to a lesser extent, Uruguay), to focus on the main markets.

The expansion strategy of banks in Latin America also played an important part in the expansion of the Spanish energy companies, because the acquisition of energy producers and distributors became the second element

Table 12.5 SCH's main subsidiaries in Latin America and the Caribbean, 2003

Country	Firm	Ownership percentage
Argentina	Banco Río de la Plata, S.A.	99.09
Bahamas	Banco Santander Bahamas International Ltd.	100.00
Bolivia	Banco Santa Cruz, S.A.	96.34
Brazil	Banespa	98.01
Chile	Banco Santander Chile, S.A.	83.94
Colombia	Banco Santander Colombia, S.A.	97.64
Mexico	Banca Serfin	73.98
Panama	Banco Santander, S.A.	100.00
Puerto Rico	Banco Santander Puerto Rico, S.A.	88.63
Uruguay	Riobank Internacional SAIFE	100.00
Venezuela	Banco de Venezuela S.A., Banco Universal	98.25

Source: SCH, *Informe anual 2003*, pp. 196–8.

Table 12.6 BBVA's subsidiaries in Latin America and the Caribbean, 2004

Country	Firm	Area	Ownership percentage
Argentina	BBVA Banco Francés	Banking	76.14
	Consolidar AFJP	Pension funds	100.00
Bolivia	AFP Previsión	Pension funds	80.00
Brazil	Banco Bradesco S.A.	Banking	5.00
Cayman Islands	BBVA Global Finance Ltd.	Financial services	100.00
Chile	BBVA Chile	Banking	66.27
	AFP Provida	Pension funds	64.32
	BBVA Pensiones	Pension funds	100.00
Colombia	BBVA Colombia	Banking	95.37
	BBVA Horizonte	Pension funds	80.28
Dominican Rep.	BBVA Crecer AFP	Financial services	70.00
Ecuador	AFP Génesis	Pension funds	100.00
Mexico	Bancomer	Banking	99.70
Panama	BBVA Panamá	Banking	98.77
	BBVA Horizonte	Pension funds	90.00
Paraguay	BBVA Paraguay	Banking	99.99
Peru	Banco Continental	Banking	92.05
	AFP Horizonte	Pension funds	100.00
Puerto Rico	BBVA Puerto Rico	Banking	100.00
Uruguay	BBVA Uruguay	Banking	100.00
Venezuela	Banco Provincial	Banking	55.60

Source: BBVA, *Informe anual 2004*, pp. 234–7.

of the diversification strategies of Spanish banks. The result was the creation of two main industrial groups of companies, involving one or two of the main banks and several energy firms. In 1998, BBV, along with Barcelona's La Caixa, had important stocks in Telefónica, Repsol, Iberdrola and Gas Natural. BCH was a major stockholder of Endesa, Unión Fenosa (BS was also one of its main stockholders), Fomento de Construcciones y Contratas (FCC), and Dragados y Construcciones. BS, however, did not own significant amounts of stocks in any of these companies and it did not intend to develop a similar policy of diversification of its investments.

The fear of competition in Spain was not one of the factors that pushed Spanish banks to invest in Latin America, as in the case of Telefónica. In fact, the Spanish banking market opened to foreign competition in the 1980s. Spanish banks invested in Latin America because they were drawn by the great business opportunities they saw. The banking crisis hit many of the local banks severely, and some of the foreign banks that had investments in the region when the crisis began. The fear of instability in the Latin American banking sector kept many foreign companies out after the crisis, thus paving the way for the Spanish banks, which then faced very little competition from other large international banking groups. Given the seriousness of the Latin American banking crisis, the investments of Spanish banks were especially important for the regeneration of the banking infrastructure in many countries. They provided new credit for these cash-starved economies, developed new financial products, and helped to propagate a new banking and financial culture.

A vital aspect for both banks was the unification of management models across the Americas, adopting similar management techniques and strategies as those they had applied in Spain. They transferred their core products and services, risk policies and credit policies, as well as other core activities, such as advertising products and techniques and human resource models for evaluation of the potential of their employees. The adoption of the same type of management was based on the assumption that the organization, processes, products and services that their banks had developed in the Spanish context up to the 1990s were suitable for the Latin American markets in which they began to operate. Therefore, along with the transfer of managers from Spain and the adoption of the models applied by BBVA and SCH in Spain, came a transfer of know-how, which was embodied in the products and services that both banks introduced.

In the following statements, Emilio Ybarra, Chairman of BBVA in the late 1990s, and Francisco Luzón, SCH's CEO after the merger of BS and BCH, explained their strategy:

> In Latin America, our group's strategy is based on a long-term commitment to consolidate a regional franchise, which already has great value, in which the entrepreneurial model, the automation, and the systems platforms that our business units have in Spain, are in an advanced stage of implementation (Emilio Ybarra: BBVA, 1999, pp. 5–6).

> In the last twenty or twenty-five years in Spain, we developed risk management tools, we had to internationalize our enterprises in Latin America, we faced privatization, market concentration and liberalization. Banco Santander has a lot of experience operating in that kind of environment. Latin America offered us the opportunity to put our experience to work there (Francisco Luzón: Luzón, 2002).

Public utilities

The liberalization of the energy sector occurred simultaneously in Spain and Latin America. In Latin America, it was the response to expectations of economic growth and to the growing demand for energy that economic growth was expected to trigger. The World Bank estimated in 1995 that, between 1994 and 2000, an additional generating capacity of 70,000 MW would be needed in Latin America and the Caribbean alone. Meeting this demand would require additional investments of US$20,000–25,000 million (Siddique, 1995, pp. 18–21). In the midst of adjustment and debt-reduction schemes, many governments realized that the energy produced by state-owned companies would be insufficient to meet investment and production requirements and decided to privatize many of them, thereby relying on private companies, either domestic or foreign.

Based on the growth potential of the energy sector, foreign companies became anxious to operate in Latin America. Whereas demand for electricity was expected to grow by 1.9 per cent annually in the USA between 1995 and 2000, with returns on investment of 8–10 per cent, the growth of demand in Latin America was expected to be 5.5 per cent, with investment returns of 20 to 25 per cent (Siddique, 1995, pp. 18–21). Besides the greater growth expectation in Latin America, Spanish companies were concerned about the liberalization schedule set by the EU for the energy sector (in 2007 European governments will allow free competition). Once liberalization had been implemented, companies from other European countries would be free to expand into Spain. With liberalization in mind, the Spanish energy sector experienced major transformations in the 1990s. Inside Spain, competition led to major takeovers and mergers, reducing the number of operators to four: Endesa, Hidroeléctrica del Cantábrico (HC), Iberdrola and Unión Fenosa. Spanish operators also moved outside of Spain to grow, many of them into Latin America, where liberalization was under way.

Spanish energy companies completed a process of improvement of their infrastructure and technology to increase their productive capacity in the early 1990s. The fast rates of economic growth in Spain in the 1980s forced Spanish firms to increase their generation capacity, to keep up with market demands. Significant investments in technology increased their capacity beyond the energy needs of the Spanish market. The fast growth of the energy sector in the 1980s increased their revenue and profits. Since the expansion of productive capacity in the 1980s guaranteed their ability to satisfy energy demand in Spain, they decided to invest those profits in Latin America, where the growth potential was great.

Endesa was Spain's largest energy company in the mid- and late 1990s, and the one with the largest investments in Latin America. When Endesa moved into Latin America, the Spanish state still owned 41.1 per cent of its stocks, until its final privatization in June 1998 (Carcar, 1998). Endesa's first investments in Latin America occurred in 1995, with the acquisition of two power generation plants from Electroperú (Endesa, 1995).

Endesa's main purchase in Latin America was Enersis in Chile, in August 1997 (Endesa and Enersis had been allies in Peru prior to this operation). A month later, Endesa included Enersis in a consortium that submitted the winning bid in the privatization of Colombia's energy producer Emgesa and distributor Codensa (El País Digital, 1997b). In March 1998, both Endesa and Enersis reached an agreement to participate together in the privatization of several state-owned energy companies in Latin America, between 1998 and 2003 (Endesa, 1999). Since then, Endesa has conducted its Latin American ventures through Enersis and Endesa Chile.

Endesa engaged in a particular competition for the acquisition of a large number of electricity enterprises in Latin America with another Spanish energy firm, Iberdrola. Endesa bought Coelce in Brazil, beating Iberdrola, which submitted the second highest bid. In the mid- and late 1990s, Iberdrola was the second largest electricity company in Spain. It was headquartered in the Basque Country and the large Basque bank, BBV, was one of its main stockholders and investment partners. It began its operations in Latin America in 1992. In its particular race against Endesa, Iberdrola acquired 65.64 per cent of Coelba in North-western Brazil, in July 1997, and in December of that year it paid $500 million for Companhia Energética do Rio Grande do Norte (Cosern), also in North-western Brazil. Since then, Iberdrola decided to concentrate on the Brazilian and Mexican markets (El País Digital, 1997a; Endesa, 1997).

Another Spanish company with investments in Latin America was Unión Fenosa, which concentrated on the Caribbean, Central America and the Caribbean coast of Colombia. The investments of the Spanish electricity companies in Latin America were in part motivated by the fear of competition in their domestic market in Spain. The elimination of geographic restrictions on the operations of electricity providers within Spain originated a process of concentration in the Spanish market. This was the first phase of a strategy designed by the Spanish government to implement full liberalization in the energy sector by 2007. The second phase comprised the complete elimination of national limits to EU firms. This liberalization deadline led the Spanish firms to expand abroad, to grow in size and thus be better qualified to withstand European competition after 2007. The growth potential of the Latin American economies in the 1990s made them prime targets for the Spanish electricity firms, wanting to profit from business opportunities there.

As a result of their acquisitions in Latin America, the three Spanish firms became involved in three core activities, mainly in the generation and distribution of electricity and, to a lesser extent, its transmission. The first two activities were the ones liberalized by the governments of Latin America. Apart from these three traditional activities, Endesa, Iberdrola and Unión Fenosa also invested in non-traditional activities, such as water management, natural gas distribution or telecommunications (see Tables 12.7, 12.8 and 12.9).

Table 12.7 Endesa's main subsidiaries in Latin America, 2003

Country	Firm	Business area	Ownership percentage
Argentina	Central Dock Sud, S.A.	Generation, transportation and distribution	39.86
	Cía. Americana de Multiserv. De Argentina, S.A.	Energy infrastructure	60.62
	Comercializadora de Energía del MERCOSUR, S.A.	Commercialization	71.36
	Compañía de Transmisión del MERCOSUR, S.A.	Generation, transportation and distribution	71.35
	Edesur	Commercialization	45.68
	Transportadora de Energía, S.A.	Generation, transportation and distribution	71.35
	Yacylec, S.A.	Transportation	22.22
Brazil	Centrais Electricas Cachoeira Dourada, S.A.	Generation and commercialization	99.61
	Cerj	Generation, distribution and sales	59.20
	CIEN	Generation, transportation and distribution	71.35
	Coelce	Full energy cycle	44.59
Chile	Aguas Santiago Poniente, S.A.	Production and distribution of potable water	33.34
	Chilectra	Distribution and sale of energy	98.25
	Central Geradora Termelectrica Fortaleza, S.A.	Construction of a combined-cycle plant	80.78
	Endesa	Full energy cycle	36.36
	Enersis	Generation and distribution	60.62
	Gasoducto Atacama	Transportation of natural gas	36.36
Colombia	Central Hidroeléctrica de Betania, S.A.	Generation	31.13
	Codelsa	Distribution and commercialization	43.95
Dominican Rep.	CEPM	Generation, transportation and distribution	40.00
Panama	Empresa Propietaria de la Red, S.A.	Construction of the Central American Interconnection Network	14.29
Peru	Edegel	Generation and commercialization	13.78
	Edelnor	Generation, transportation and distribution	38.26
	Empresa Eléctrica del Piura	Generation	48.00
	ETEVENSA	Generation	43.50

Source: Endesa, *Informe anual 2003*, pp. 53–6.

Table 12.8 Iberdrola's main subsidiaries in Latin America, 2004

Country	Firm	Area of activity	Ownership percentage
Bolivia	Iberdrola de Inversiones, S.A.	Holding	99.99
Brazil	Iberdrola Energia do Brasil, Ltda.	Holding	100.00
Chile	Iberoamericana de Energía Ibener, S.A.	Energy	94.74
Guatemala	Gestión Empresas Eléctricas, S.A.	Services	99.99
Mexico	Enertek S.A. de C.V.	Energy	99.99
	Iberdrola Energía Altamira, S.A. de C.V.	Energy	99.99
	Iberdrola Energía de Monterrey, S.A. de C.V.	Energy	99.99
	Iberdrola Energía del Golfo, S.A. de C.V. (formerly Iberdrola Energía Altamira, S.A. de C.V.)	Energy	99.99
	Iberdrola Energía Tamazunchale, S.A. de C.V.	Energy	99.99
	Electricidad de Veracruz, S.A. de C.V.	Energy	99.99
	Electricidad de Veracruz II, S.A. de C.V.	Energy	99.99
	Iberdrola Energía La Laguna, S.A. de C.V.	Energy	99.99
	Iberdrola México, S.A. de C.V.	Holding	99.99

Source: Iberdrola, *Informe anual 2004*, p. 88.

Table 12.9 Unión Fenosa's subsidiaries in Latin America and the Caribbean, 2003

Country	Firm	Area of activity	Ownership percentage
Costa Rica	Central Hidráulica de La Joya	Generation	65.00
Colombia	Electricaribe	Distribution and	69.30
	Electricosta	commercialization	70.40
	EPSA	Generation	64.23
Dominican Rep.	Edenorte Edesur	Generation, distribution and commercialization	50.00
Guatemala	Deocsa Deorsa	Distribution	85.10
Mexico	Aeropuerto del Pacífico Noroeste, S.A. de C.V. Aeropuertos Mexicanos del Pacífico, S.A. de C.V. Combined cycle power station Hermosillo Naco Nogales Tuxpan	Holding Airport management Generation Generation Generation	48.99
Nicaragua	Disnorte	Distribution	79.50
	Dissur	Distribution	79.50
Panama	Edechi Edemet	Generation and distribution	51.00
Uruguay	Conecta	Transportation and commercialization of gas and construction of gas infrastructure	55.00

Source: Unión Fenosa, *Informe anual 2003*, pp. 94–9, 238.

In the following quotes, high ranking managers of the three firms summarize their philosophy in Latin America and the Caribbean:

> [The presence of Endesa abroad is] a purely entrepreneurial decision to search for new business opportunities, in which Endesa and its group of firms could capture the benefits of all of the knowledge that we had accumulated since our creation in 1944, the availability of experienced human resources that could apply adequately and efficiently their skills, as well as financial resources that could be invested profitably in countries that were going through deep processes of opening and sociopolitical change. (Rafael Miranda, CEO, Endesa: Miranda, 1998/99, p. 117)

> The expansion in new markets, in other business areas, and in other countries is vital if Iberdrola is to grow profitably in the future. This is a strategy designed to take the maximum advantage of our competitive advantages and to transfer the experience, management, and technological capacity of our Group to markets that have a great growth potential, with the goal of getting the return that we are looking for. (Íñigo de Oriol Ybarra, Chairman of Iberdrola: Iberdrola, 1997, p. 4)

> To be able to improve management it is essential to undertake a transfer of knowledge and experiences. It is necessary to enrich the capacity of the people and, with the experience accumulated in other projects, to take them to the belief that they have to break routines and that they have to be open to change ... This is the orientation that Unión Fenosa wanted to give initially to its international activity: a consulting job to modernize management and to share knowledge with professionals from other countries. The solutions that we proposed were the same that already existed in our own firm, and they could be appropriately tested and experimented by the professionals of the firms for which we worked. (Victoriano Reinoso, Vice-Chairman of Unión Fenosa: Reinoso, 1998, p. 65)

In 2002, Endesa and Iberdrola had assets worth US$26,259 million in Latin America. Endesa, Iberdrola and Unión Fenosa had around 22 million customers in distribution. Endesa had become the largest private public utility in Latin America. They had an installed capacity of generation of energy in Latin America of 22,493 MW (the energy consumption of Argentina in 2001 was 22,000 MW). In the six-year period between 1996 and 2002, the three firms increased the installed capacity of generation of energy of their subsidiaries by 9,073 MW (the consumption of Venezuela in 2001 was 11,938 MW), or 67.6 per cent, through the construction of new power plants. (The total installed capacity could increase by an additional 3,500 MW in the coming years if Endesa's plans to install windmills in Argentina materialize. In that case, the combined installed capacity of Spanish firms in the region would grow to 12,573 MW; that is, an increase of 93.6 per cent over the original installed capacity of their subsidiaries in less than a decade.)

These investments in generation were particularly important for Latin America, considering that the annual growth of demand for energy in that region in 2001 was 10,000 MW. Thus, the three Spanish firms developed the infrastructure to supply a large part of the additional demand needs.

Oil and natural gas

The other large Spanish company with investments in the energy sector was Repsol–YPF, an oil producer and distributor. Repsol was created in 1987 by the Spanish state as part of a reorganization of an older state-owned company, Instituto Nacional de Hidrocarburos. Repsol went through a slow privatization process that started in 1989 and was completed in April 1997. In its origins, Repsol was basically an oil distributor, and in 1996, refining and marketing still generated 78 per cent of the company's revenue, while exploration and production generated only 14.3 per cent. Profit margins in refining and marketing were very small in the 1990s. In 1997, Repsol only produced 25 per cent of the oil it processed. This reliance on external purchases of oil decreased its profit margins (Aparicio, 1997).

Repsol's managers adopted a new strategy in 1996, based on four guiding principles: strengthening its position at the head of the home market (Spain); growth in exploration and production by developing new discoveries and acquisitions, giving priority to natural gas reserves for the Spanish market (these activities had to be undertaken outside of Spain, because of the lack of oil and natural gas there), furthering international expansion (centring on Latin America), and generating power with its own natural gas (Repsol, 1996, p. 2; 1998, p. 5). They believed that Latin America was the more appropriate region in which to further the firm's strategy, because of the availability of resources, the opening of their markets, and the similarity of language and culture. However, Repsol's managers did not intend to use Latin America only as the source of oil and natural gas for its operations in Spain. They intended to operate as an integrated energy group in Latin America, in the oil, gas and electricity sectors, in wholesale and retail markets – as they did in Spain – (Repsol, 1996, p. 3).

They believed that they would gain an advantage if they managed to integrate production (upstream diversification) with market access (downstream). They wanted to be able to increase oil and gas production, and to be able to sell them through Repsol (without selling to domestic distributors), to achieve the efficient integration of all of the business areas. To achieve this goal, their objective was to gain the rights to oil and gas fields, in order to increase the supply of its own raw materials, and to gain market access through distribution networks in Latin America, to enable the company to sell finished products there. In all cases, the main objective of the firm's managers was 'to be leaders in those areas or businesses in which we concentrate. This way, the creation of value for our stockholders will have more solid bases and Repsol–YPF will set itself apart from the rest of the firms' (Repsol, 1999, p. 5; 2001, p. 4).

Repsol's major acquisitions in Latin America were carefully chosen to gain an advantageous position in both upstream (exploration and production) activities and in downstream (distribution) activities, especially in the two markets where the firm's managers wanted to expand, Argentina and Brazil. In 1996, the acquisition of a controlling stake of 37.7 per cent in Astra, and the purchase of 14.99 per cent a year later, were important steps in becoming a company integrated in the oil, gas and electricity sectors in Argentina (Repsol, 1997, p. 54; 1998, p. 6). The acquisition of 14.99 per cent of YPF from the Argentinean government in January 1999, and another 82.47 per cent in April to achieve control of 97 per cent of the stock made Repsol–YPF the local leader in Argentina's refining and marketing (the largest acquisition in the history of Latin America at the time: US$15,000 million). This acquisition was especially important to increase the group's reserves in oil and gas, given YPF's large reserves (Repsol–YPF, 1999, pp. 2, 6, 8). In Brazil, Repsol signed an agreement with Petrobras in 1999, whereby Petrobras agreed to exchange upstream (oil and gas production) and downstream (distribution networks) in Brazil for Repsol's assets in Eg3, one of its subsidiaries in the distribution industry in Argentina. Both parties also agreed to cooperate in the development of natural gas markets in Latin America, in gas supplies and in the production of gas-based electricity (Repsol–YPF, 1999, p. 6).

Natural gas became a major area of interest in the late 1990s. In Spain, Repsol's gas sales increased 28.3 per cent between 1994 and 1996, but in 1997 the gas division only generated 22.3 per cent of Repsol's total revenue. In 1997, Repsol controlled over 95 per cent of Spain's market of bottled gas and 90 per cent of the natural gas market. The inauguration of the African–European gas pipeline between Algeria and Spain in 1996, through the Straits of Gibraltar, indicated Repsol's commitment to natural gas for the future (Aparicio, 1997). Repsol also developed its natural gas business in Latin America, but not alone. It created a joint venture with Iberdrola and Gas Natural, called Gas Natural Latinoamericana (GNL). The main step in its expansion was the acquisition of YPF (Expansión, 1998; Repsol–YPF, 1999).

The strategic alliances among Spanish companies were particularly important in the energy sector. Repsol received financial support from BBVA. All the companies in which BBV had a stake (Gas Natural, Iberdrola, Repsol and even Telefónica) cooperated in their Latin American ventures. BCH also contributed resources to the Latin American expansion of the companies in which it owned stock (Endesa, Unión Fenosa and Cepsa), before the BS–BCH merger. This shows the importance of cross-sectoral alliances in the expansion strategies of Spanish companies, to raise funds, to develop synergies, and to share know-how and risk. The following quote by Repsol–YPF's CEO, Alfonso Cortina de Alcocer, expresses the firm's expansion philosophy in Latin America and the Caribbean: 'South America is an emerging area in the world economic stage, with an energy market in fast expansion, where we believe we have clear competitive advantages' (Repsol–YPF, 1996, p. 3).

Repsol–YPF became the sixth largest multinational oil enterprise in the world in 1999, and the sixteenth largest multinational enterprise by overseas assets, thanks mainly to the investments it has made in Latin America since the 1990s. In 2000, Repsol–YPF had 50 per cent of the proven reserves of oil and gas in Argentina, 60 per cent of refining capacity and 60 per cent of sales of gasoline and 71 per cent of the sales of natural gas. In Bolivia, Repsol–YPF had 68 per cent of the national production of oil and 54 per cent of natural gas. In distribution and marketing of gas, Repsol–YPF, through its subsidiary Gas Natural, has supplied gas to 71 per cent of the Argentinian market, 41 per cent in Chile, 49 per cent in Ecuador, 45 per cent in Mexico, 48 per cent in Peru, and 40 per cent in Bolivia since 2001. Repsol–YPF distributed gas to 5,565,331 customers in these markets. In 2002, 86.1 per cent of its production of hydrocarbons came from Latin America (76.4 per cent from Argentina alone), and 44.3 per cent of its employees (13,339) were in Latin America (see Table 12.10).

Table 12.10 Repsol–YPF's main subsidiaries in Latin America and the Caribbean, 2002

Country	Company	Activity	Ownership percentage
Argentina	Central Dock Sud, S.A.	Generation and commercialization of electricity	39.53
	Metrogás, S.A.	Gas distribution	
	Operadora de Estaciones de Servicio, S.A. (OPESSA)	Commercialization of hydrocarbons	98.90
	Pluspetrol Energy, S.A.	Exploration and production of hydrocarbons	44.57
	Poligás Luján, S.A.	Bottling, transportation and commercialization of LPG	50.01
	Refinerías del Norte, S.A. (REFINOR)	Refining and commercialization of oil products	49.52
	Repsol–YPF Gas, S.A.	Gas commercialization	85.00
	YPF, S.A.	Exploration and production of hydrocarbons	99.04
Bolivia	Repsol YPF Bolivia, S.A.	Holding	100.00
	Empresa Petrolera Andina, S.A.	Exploration and production of hydrocarbons	50.00
	Repsol YPF E&P de Bolivia, S.A.	Exploration and production of hydrocarbons	100.00

Continued

Table 12.10 Continued

Country	Company	Activity	Ownership percentage
	Repsol YPF Gas de Bolivia, S.A.	Commercialization of LPG	51.00
	Repsol YPF GLP de Bolivia, S.A.	Commercialization of LPG	100.00
Brazil	AESA Construcciones y Servicios	Engineering and construction	99.04
	CEG Río, S.A.	Gas commercialization	9.20
	Companhia Distribuidora do Gas do Río do Janeiro	Gas commercialization	6.92
	Gas Natural do Brasil, S.A.	Gas commercialization	24.04
	Gas Natural São Paulo Sul, S.A.	Gas distribution	24.04
	Operadora de Postos de Servicio, Ltd.	Service station management	100.00
	REFAP	Refining and commercialization of oil products	30.00
	Refinería de Petróleos Manguinhos	Refining and commercialization of oil products	30.71
	Repsol YPF Brasil, S.A.	Exploration and commercialization of hydrocarbons	100.00
Cayman Islands	A&C Pipeline Holding	Financial	17.83
	Repsol International Capital	Financial	100.00
Chile	Empresa Lipigás, S.A.	Commercialization of LPG	45.00
	Oleoducto Transandino Chile	Construction and management of pipeline	17.83
	Operaciones y Servicios YPF	Service station management	100.00
	Petróleos Transandinos YPF, S.A.	Commercialization and distribution of combustibles and lubricants	100.00
	Repsol YPF Chile, Limitada	Administ. of investments of YPF in Chile	100.00
Colombia	Gas Natural Cundiboyacense, S.A. ESP	Gas distribution	11.00
	Gas Natural, S.A. ESP	Gas distribution	14.20
	Gases de Barrancabermeja, S.A. ESP	Gas distribution	7.74
	Gasoriente, S.A. ESP	Gas distribution	7.74
Ecuador	Autogás, S.A.	Distribution and commercialization of LPG	60.36

Continued

Table 12.10 Continued

Country	Company	Activity	Ownership percentage
	Combustibles Industriales Oil Traders, S.A.	Commercialization of hydrocarbons	100.00
	Duragás	Distribution and commercialization of LPG	100.00
	Repsol YPF Comercial del Ecuador, S.A.	Commercialization of hydrocarbons	100.00
Mexico	Admón. Servicios Energía México, S.A. de C.V.	Services	20.85
	Comercializadora Metrogás, S.A.	Gas distribution	20.85
	Dynasol Elastómeros, S.A. de C.V.	Production and commercialization of chemicals	50.00
	Gas Natural México, S.A. de C.V.	Gas distribution	20.85
Netherlands Antilles	YPF Energy Holdings, N.V.	Holding	99.04
Peru	Grupo Repsol YPF del Perú, S.A.C.	Holding	100.00
	Limagás, S.A.	Distribution of LPG	29.85
	Refinería La Pampilla, S.A.	Refining	47.29
	Repsol Comercial S.A.C.	Combustibles trading	100.00
	Repsol YPF Comercial de la Amazonía, S.A.	Distribution of LPG	100.00
	Repsol YPF Comercial del Perú, S.A.	Commercialization of LPG	99.61
Trinidad & Tobago	Atlantic LNG	Gas logistics and procurement	20.00
	Atlantic 2/3 Company of Trinidad and Tobago	Gas logistics	25.00
	BP Amoco Trinidad and Tobago	Exploration and production of hydrocarbons	50.00
Uruguay	Adicor, S.A.		99.04
	Flawin SAFI	Exploration and production of hydrocarbons	100.00
Venezuela	Repsol YPF Venezuela, S.A.	Exploration and production of hydrocarbons	100.00

Source: Repsol–YPF, *Informe anual 2002*, pp. 124–35.

Conclusions

I have taken a constructivist approach to explain the conditions under which a number of Spanish firms made considerable direct investments in Latin America and the Caribbean since 1989. I have argued that managers perceived that their firms had an advantage in those regions and decided to invest there to put this advantage to work. Their advantage was the knowledge of the market conditions, which they perceived were similar to those they had been operating under in Spain in the 1980s. Their advantage was their ability to undertake deep processes of modernization and development of new products and services in a short period of time. The development of these products was based on a deep knowledge of the market, which resulted in a series of processes within the firm and outside of it (involving other market actors such as consumers and regulators), or organizational culture, to produce these products and services. When the Spanish firms made investments in Latin America and the Caribbean, they reorganized their subsidiaries there in order to introduce the same organizational culture, so they could develop the same types of products and services as in Spain, for the new markets.

Relations with the Spanish government and with regulators were an important part of the organizational advantage of Spanish firms. Their investments in Latin America were not based solely on microeconomic calculations, they were the result of the coordination of management decisions at the firm level with government policies at the macro level. One of the key aspects that facilitated cooperation between the Spanish government and Spanish firms was the Spanish government's fear of a takeover by foreign firms, especially in the sectors included in this chapter. The eventual liberalization of markets in the EU, especially in telecommunications and energy sectors, made the Spanish government fear the loss of 'national control' over the Spanish economy, if European firms took over key Spanish companies.

To prevent his loss of economic sovereignty, the Spanish authorities believed it was necessary to make domestic firms grow in size and increase their productivity rates, to make them more competitive. This would make a takeover by foreign firms more difficult. Given the small size of the Spanish market, the government tried to create a series of push–pull incentives to force Spanish firms to invest outside Spain. The 'push' factors were the stick provided by the liberalization deadlines set by the EU, which the Spanish government threatened to accelerate, and a series of economic incentives, such as subsidies, credits and insurance for FDI.

The main 'pull' factors were the reforms implemented by Latin American governments, and relations between the Spanish government and the governments of Latin America to overcome the anti-colonialist sentiment that existed among the people of some countries, mainly Peru and Mexico. Latin America was an 'appropriate' region for the expansion of Spanish firms, not only because of cultural and political similarities with Spain, but also because the Latin American governments decided to open up the banking and public utilities sectors to foreign investment. Liberalization was the main response of Latin American governments to the crisis of the 1980s. FDI played a fundamental role in their strategy, because, on the one hand, it brought capital into the cash-starved economies and, on the other, it brought in foreign firms with new technologies, products and services, with great potential to increase the overall productivity rates of the economies.

The sectors included in this study were the backbone of the economy, and their rejuvenation was fundamental to the resumption of economic growth. Spanish banks contributed to strengthening of the Latin American banking system. They introduced new credit (liquidity), and developed new financial and banking products, increasing domestic savings and channeling domestic investment into productive enterprises. The investments of Telefónica helped to improve the quality of the telecommunications systems. Good telecommunications were crucial for the efficient conduct of business on a daily basis. Finally, Spanish energy firms contributed to satisfaction of the growing demand for energy triggered by the acceleration of economic activities that followed the liberal reforms of the early 1990s.

Moreover, the competition that existed among Spanish firms to expand in Latin America, especially in the energy (Endesa versus Iberdrola) and banking (BBV versus BCH versus BS) sectors, helped introduce a new business culture into Latin America. Economic profit was now to be based on productivity gains and in the improvement of products and services, rather than on the concession of protectionist privileges, such as limits to competition and the subsidizing of losses. In this regard, some Spanish companies were forced to compete openly in some Latin American economies, while they were still being shielded from foreign competition in their domestic market in Spain. This was the case of the energy firms, such as Endesa, Iberdrola and Unión Fenosa, and Telefónica before 1997.

The expansion of Spanish firms in Latin America was also facilitated by the conditions of operation. The needs of the Latin American economies were basic, comprising the development of infrastructure in all sectors, such as banking, telecommunications and energy. These were the needs of the fast-growing Spanish economy in the 1970s and 1980s. In other words, Spanish firms brought to Latin America the same expertise, technology, products and services they had developed in previous years for the Spanish economy, to satisfy similar needs. This similarity made their managers believe that they had an advantage *vis-à-vis* the companies from third countries. They believed they knew what was needed in the market, and had the means to satisfy those needs. Their appreciation of the potential profits to be gained in these markets led them to offer more money than other European and North American competitors in the privatization of many of the Latin American banks and utilities.

Finally, to strengthen their position in Latin America and to increase their capital resources for expansion, some Spanish firms developed cross-sector alliances, in part thanks to their cross-investments. Two main groups of Spanish firms were created around each of the major Spanish banks. On the one hand, BBV, with its large investments in Telefónica, Repsol, Iberdrola and Gas Natural, facilitated the development of joint ventures among these companies, wherever they needed to pool resources and share expertise. The other group evolved around BCH, thanks to its investments in Endesa, Unión Fenosa, FCC and Dragados y Construcciones.

Notes

1 Figures for Repsol–YPF and Telefónica, foreign assets in 1999. Figures for BBVA are 2001, rest 2002.

2 I converted the amount into US dollars, but provided the original in parentheses. The conversion rates were those provided by the Federal Reserve for each year.

3 Endesa extended its participation in Enersis from 32 per cent to over 65 per cent on 14 April 1999. This provoked serious debates in the Chilean Congress. On 29 April Chile's Monopoly Commission blocked Endesa's move, but on 11 May 1999 it finally authorized the takeover.

4 He was referring here to the initial period in which Unión Fenosa began to operate in Latin America as a consulting firm.

5 Endesa had assets worth US$22,662 million (€21,425 million) and Iberdrola, US$3,597 million (€3,401 million) in Latin America. Unión Fenosa did not provide these figures in its annual reports. Endesa had a generation capacity of 13,265 MW, and 10.3 million customers in distribution. Endesa could add 3,500 MW to its generation capacity if its plans to install windpower generators in Argentina materialized after 2002. This project was under research by Endesa's experts in 2002. Iberdrola distributed electricity to over 7.5 million customers. It had a generation capacity of 6,374 MW (including the power plants under construction in 2002). Unión Fenosa had an installed capacity of 2,854 MW, and 4,264,393 customers. *Source*: Endesa, 2002, pp. 9, 110; Iberdrola, 2002; pp. 101–4; Unión Fenosa, 2002, pp. 63–4. Data on energy consumption in Argentina and Venezuela, World Energy Council, 2001, pp. 2, 70. Data on the increase in demand for electricity in Latin America in Rudnick and Zolezzi, 2000, p. 180.

6 The largest multinational oil enterprises were Exxon-Mobil Corporation, Royal Dutch-Shell Group, TotalFina S.A., British Petroleum and Nippon Mitsubishi Oil Corporation. See UNCTAD, 2001, p. 90; Gabilondo, 2000, p. 183; Repsol–YPF, 2000, p. 19; Repsol–YPF, 2001, p. 22; Repsol–YPF, pp. 2002, 29–30, 116.

References

Aceña, F. (1994) 'Instrumentos de financiación de inversiones', *ICE*, 735, November, pp. 63–74.

Akinsanya, A. A. (1980) *The Expropriation of Multinational Property in the Third World* (New York: Praeger).

Aparicio, L. (1997) 'Repsol, en Manos Privadas', *El País Digital*, 346, 14 April 1997, *Economía* section (accessed 14 April 1997).

Ariño, G. (ed.) (1999) *Privatizacion y liberalización de servicios* (Madrid: Universidad Autónoma de Madrid and Boletín Oficial del Estado).

BBV (1996–8) *Informe anual*, Madrid.

BBVA (1999–2003) *Informe anual*, Madrid.

BCH (1995–8) *Informe anual*, Madrid.

Bresser, L. C. (1993) 'Economic Reforms and Economic Growth: Efficiency and Politics in Latin America', in L. C. Bresser, J. M. Maravall and A. Przeworski (eds), *Economic Reforms in New Democracies. A Social-Democratic Approach* (Cambridge University Press).

Bresser, L. C., Maravall, J. M. and Przeworski, A. (eds) (1993) *Economic Reforms in New Democracies. A Social-Democratic Approach* (Cambridge University Press).

BS (1994–8) *Informe annual*, Madrid.

Carcar, S. (1998) 'La Euforia Bursátil Anima al Gobierno a Vender su 41% de Endesa para Ingresar 1,6 Billones', *El País Digital*, 700, 5 April, *Economía* section (accessed 5 April 1998).

Carreras, A., Tafunell, X. and Torres, E. (1997) 'Against Integration. The Rise and Decline of Spanish State-owned Firms and the Decline and Rise of Multinationals, 1939–1990', in Ü. Olson (ed.), *Business and European Integration Since 1800. Regional, National and International Perspectives* (University of Göteborg Press), pp. 31–49.

Dirección General de Comercio e Inversiones, Secretaría de Estado de Comercio y Turismo, Ministerio de Economía español, www.mcx.es/polco/InversionesExteriores/estadisticas (accessed 5 May 2003).

Dunning, J. H. and Narula, R. (1994) *Transpacific FDI and the Investment Development Path: The Record Assessed*, University of South Carolina Essays in International Business No. 10, May.

Edwards, S. (1995) *Crisis and Reform in Latin America. From Despair to Hope* (Oxford: Oxford University Press for the World Bank).

El Exportardor (2003) 'El español como recurso económico', p. 61, February., www.el-exportador.com (accessed 14 May 2003).

El País Digital (1997a), no. 320, 19 March, *Economía* section, http://www.elpais.es (accessed 19 June 1997).

El País Digital (1997b), 'Iberdrola Compra la Eléctrica Brasileña Cosern por 73.800 Millones', 589, 13 December *Economía* section (accessed 13 December 1997).

Endesa (1996–2003), *Informe anual* (Madrid).

Eurostat (2002) Themes. Economy and Finance, http://epp.eurostat.cec.eu.int/portal/page?_pageid=0,1136173,0_45570698&_dad=portal&_schema=PORTAL (accessed 16 May 2005).

Expansión (1998), 'Repsol Abandona el Capital de Gas Natural Latinoamericana', February 7, http://expansion.es (accessed 7 February 1998).

Financial Times (1996), 'Infrastructure in Latin America', 15 October Sp. III, p. 3.

Gabilondo, L. A. (2000) 'La inversión extranjera directa española en América Latina. El caso de Repsol-YPF', *Problemas del Desarrollo*, 21(123), p. 183.

García de Quevedo, J.C. and Hontecilla, R. (1994) 'Los acuerdos bilaterales de promoción y protección recíproca de inversiones', *ICE*, 735, pp. 75–80.

Hall, E. (1960) *The Silent Language* (New York: Anchor Books).
Hofstede, G. (1980) *Culture's Consequences* (Beverly Hills, Calif.: Sage).
Iberdrola (1995–2004), *Informe anual* (Bilbao).
ICE (1979) 1661, 1 February, pp. 349–50.
ICE (1981) 1765, 29 January, pp. 382–3.
ICE (1994) 2415, 6–12 June, p. 1403.
IRELA (1996) *The European Union and Mercosur: Towards a New Economic Relationship? Base Document*, Madrid.
Jiménez, C. (1994) 'La protección de las inversiones en el exterior. Instrumentos existentes', *ICE*, 735, pp. 81–8.
Luzón, F. (2002) 'La experiencia de Santander Central Hispano', presentation at 'Seminario Iberoamérica y las empresas españolas', Universidad Internacional Menéndez Pelayo, Santander, Spain, 19–20 August (F. Luzón was CEO of SCH in 2002).
Miranda, R. (1998) 'La experiencia de Endesa en Mercosur', *Economía Exterior*, 7, 1998/99, pp. 117–22.
Morán, P. (1994) 'La inversión directa española en el exterior en 1992', *BICE*, 2366, 26 April–2 May, p. 1115.
Onuf, N. (1989) *World of Our Making. Rules and Rule in Social Theory and International Relations* (Columbia, SC: University of South Carolina Press).
Palacios, J. (1994) 'Análisis comparativo del tratamiento fiscal de las inversiones en el exterior', *ICE*, 735, November, pp. 53–62.
PriceWaterhouse (1996) *Corporate Taxes. A Worldwide Summary* (London).
Ramamurti, R. (1996a) 'The New Frontier of Privatization', in R. Ramamurti (ed.), *Privatizing Monopolies. Lessons from the Telecommunications and Transport Sectors in Latin America* (Baltimore, Md.: Johns Hopkins University Press), pp. 1–45.
Ramamurti, R. (ed.) (1996b) *Privatizing Monopolies. Lessons from the Telecommunications and Transport Sectors in Latin America* (Baltimore, Md.: Johns Hopkins University Press).
Reinoso, V. (1998) 'Oportunidades del nuevo entorno energético internacional. La experiencia de Unión Fenosa en los mercados emergentes', *Economistas*, 76, February, pp. 62–8.
Repsol (1995–8), *Informe anual*, Madrid.
Repsol–YPF (1999–2002), *Informe anual*, Madrid.
Rojas-Suárez, L. and Weisbrod, S. R. (1995) *Financial Fragilities in Latin America. The 1980s and 1990s* (Washington, DC: IMF).
Rudnick, H. and Zolezzi, J. (2000) 'Electric Utility Deregulation and Restructuring. Electric Sector Deregulation and Restructuring in Latin America: Lessons to be Learnt and Possible Ways Forward', *IEE Proceedings* online, no. 20010230, DOI: 10.1049/ip-gtd: 20010230, accessed 15 November 2000.
Santillana, Ignacio (1997) 'La creación de una multinacional española. El caso de Telefónica', *Economistas*, 73, pp. 90–9.
SCH (1999–2003) *Informe anual*, Madrid.
Siddique, S. (1995) 'Financing Private Power in Latin America and the Caribbean', *Finance and Development*, 32(1), pp. 18–21.
Sigmund, P. E. (1980) *Multinationals in Latin America. The Politics of Nationalization* (Madison, Wisc.: University of Wisconsin Press).
Telefónica (1990–2003) *Informe anual*, Madrid.
UNCTAD (1996) *World Investment Report 1996* (New York: UNCTAD).

UNCTAD (2001) *World Investment Report 2001: Promoting Linkages* (New York: UNCTAD).

Unión Fenosa (1996–2003), *Informe anual*, Madrid.

Val, Maura de (2001) *La privatización en América Latina. ¿Reconquista financiera y económica de España?* (Madrid: Editorial Popular).

US Department of Commerce, Bureau of Economic Analysis (2002) *Survey of Current Business*, Washington, DC: US Department of Commerce.

13

Role of the International Monetary Fund in the Economic Policy-making and Growth of the Baltic Countries

Ulvi Vaarja

Developments in the world's economic situation have been extremely rapid since the 1980s. The enormous amounts of money handled in international trade and financial transactions make countries more dependent on international capital flows and investor sentiment. There have been unprecedented transitions from socialist planned economies to modern market economies; and numerous economic and financial crises have hit the countries.

Under these harsh conditions the Baltic countries (Estonia, Latvia and Lithuania) regained their independence in August 1991 and began to pursue an active policy of transition from central planning to market economy. As such an effort would have been almost impossible to accomplish by the countries on their own, they sought assistance from the International Monetary Fund (IMF) almost from the very beginning.

In this chapter, the author has tried to give a brief overview of the co-operation between individual countries and the IMF. The second section gives a short description of the creation and purposes of the international institution; and the third section concentrates on the theoretical basis for the macroeconomic programmes to be carried out with the help of the IMF. The fourth section gives a few comments on the specific issues of IMF programmes in the transition countries, and the fifth section offers a more detailed overview of the impact of the IMF programmes in the Baltic countries.

As the materials and this particular chapter were worked through, the author came to realize that the co-operation between the Baltics and the IMF has been quite close. It has evolved over different periods and economic conditions (initial recovery phase, economic growth, recession and preparations for EU accession) and in the author's opinion has been of enormous help to the countries in attracting foreign investment, re-entering the international community and thus initiating and favouring economic growth.

Creation and purposes of the International Monetary Fund (IMF)

The necessity for an international financial institution occurred during the crisis in the world economy in the 1930s, when individual countries tried to protect their producers by introducing trade barriers and a devaluation of their currencies. The economic crisis led to problems in the international monetary system, leading to numerous countries abolishing the gold standard and the fixed exchange rates that had been in use between currencies. It also caused disruptions to trade and many countries stopped exchanging their currency for foreign currencies.

A system to restore normal relations between countries and create a united financial system managed by a special co-operation organization was worked out almost simultaneously by H.D. White and J.M. Keynes. After long discussions, the final agreement on creating the IMF and the World Bank was signed by forty-four countries at Bretton Woods in 1944. The initial aim of the IMF was to ensure the liberalization of trade payments and fix the exchange rates of the members' currencies according to a par value system based[1] on the US dollar.

According to the Articles of Agreement of the IMF its purposes are:

(i) To promote international monetary cooperation through a permanent institution which provides the machinery for consultation and collaboration on international monetary problems.

(ii) To facilitate the expansion and balanced growth of international trade, and to contribute thereby to the promotion and maintenance of high levels of employment and real income and to the development of the productive resources of all members as primary objectives of economic policy.

(iii) To promote exchange stability, to maintain orderly exchange arrangements among members, and to avoid competitive exchange depreciation.

(iv) To assist in the establishment of a multilateral system of payments in respect of current transactions between members and in the elimination of foreign exchange restrictions which hamper the growth of world trade.

(v) To give confidence to members by making the general resources of the Fund temporarily available to them under adequate safeguards, thus providing them with opportunity to correct maladjustments in their balance of payments without resorting to measures destructive of national or international prosperity.

(vi) In accordance with the above, to shorten the duration and lessen the degree of disequilibrium in the international balances of payments of members (IMF, accessed 2003).

Nowadays the complex international economic system has caused changes in the issues overhauled by the IMF: the function of support to the members having balance of payments (BoP) problems has become that one field with which the organization is dealing. In addition, much time, money and energy are being spent on the issues of capital account liberalization, crisis prediction and avoidance, surveillance, and so on.

All the purposes of the IMF are fulfilled at various levels of co-operation with its members, and using its financial resources in case of need. The levels that are most commonly used, and which I shall concentrate on in the rest of this chapter are the loans from the IMF (stand-by or precautionary arrangements, or extended fund facilities) accompanied by the Memoranda of Economic Policies[2] (MEP) and surveillance under the Article IV consultations.[3]

Theoretical basis of the IMF supported economic programmes

Countries usually come to the conclusion of the memoranda on economic policies MEP programmes that the government and the IMF together work-out to solve the economic problems underlying the loans to be taken from the Fund. When they are facing serious economic problems (hyperinflation, decreases in GDP, debt crises and so on). The stabilization programmes are intended to improve the existing situation and should (but do not always) include:

(i) solving the problem and preventing its recurrence; and
(ii) achieving or reinstating domestic and external equilibrium (one sign of achieving it could be rapid economic growth).

The MEPs are prepared on the basis of a country's payment ability, which means that the main aim is to lower its current account deficit (achieving a balance in its BoP). Since they are made on the unified basis of the IMF's economic doctrine, they include many common elements regardless of the specific country in question. The IMF programmes are designed with an income/absorption and/or monetary policy approach on the BoP:

(i) *income/absorption approach* – trade balance is the difference between domestic output and absorption (where $A = C + I + G$)[4] and its size depends on the readiness to make various expenditure, and ratios to GDP; and
(ii) *monetary policy approach* – BoP is a monetary policy phenomenon because the main factors affecting it are money supply and demand.

The basis formula in composing MEPs and in financial programming carried out by the IMF can be stated as:

$$\Delta M = \Delta R + \Delta D$$

where ΔM – change in money; ΔR – change in the net foreign reserves of the banking system (shown in domestic currency); and ΔD – change in net domestic assets of the banking system.

An important role is played by:

(i) achieving the equilibrium in the money market $M^d = \Delta M$;
(ii) the formula giving the money demand $\Delta M = f(\Delta y, \Delta P, \ldots)$; and
(iii) the alternative cost of holding money (interest on deposits and other assets).

Combining the above, we shall obtain the formulas stating net foreign reserves:

$$\Delta R = \Delta M - \Delta D$$

$$\Delta R = f(\Delta y, \Delta P, \ldots) - \Delta D$$

where M^d – money demand; Δy – change in per capita real income; and ΔP – change in domestic price level.

The IMF also takes into account the influence of the change in domestic credit on income, domestic price level, interest, costs and exchange rate. So in order to forecast the effects of the change of domestic credit on the BoP we have (in addition to the money demand and the factors influencing it) to know its effect on money demand.

Both theory and empirical data suggest that an increase in the nominal money supply initially causes an increase in real money and a decrease in velocity. Accordingly, there might be no connection between the change in domestic credit and net foreign reserves in the short run. An assumption of the long-run equilibrium of money demand and supply in enforcing the IMF programmes might lead to errors in limits on domestic credit.

In addition to monetary policy, exchange rate (specifically devaluation) policy has an important part to play: it should decrease domestic demand and help to achieve a sufficient level of the trade balance. From the absorption point of view, the current account of the BoP, $CA = Y - A$, using

$$CA = \Delta R - \Delta FI \text{ and } CA + \Delta FI = \Delta M - \Delta D,$$

where CA – current account; ΔFI – change in net foreign debt of the non-bank sector; and Y – total income, we obtain:

$$Y - A + \Delta FI = \Delta M - \Delta D$$

Since the MEP are composed according to the central bank balance sheet, BoP and the limits on the government budget, the same relationships can also be shown according to the budget constraint:[5]

$BP = \Delta NFA$ and $BP = \Delta H - \Delta NDA$,

where BP – balance of payments; ΔNFA – change in the net foreign assets of the central bank; ΔH – change in base money; and ΔNDA – change in the net domestic assets of the central bank.

The first aim when designing the financial programme is to set the ceiling on the change of net foreign reserves in the specific time period. The next step is to forecast money demand (forecasting real income and prices). Finally, net domestic assets are specified.

In order to analyse the structure of the BoP, demand for imports needs to be assessed, assuming for simplicity that it is positively correlated to real income only:

$$IMV = \alpha y \qquad (1)$$

where IMV – import volume; α – constant; and y – per capita real income.

The balance of the BoP is:

$$\Delta R = X - IM + \Delta FI$$

where X – value of export of goods and services in local currency; and IM – value of import of goods and services in local currency.

So the financial programme will now be formulated as follows:

(i) setting the ceiling for net foreign reserves;
(ii) forecasting exports of goods and services and net capital flows of the non-bank sector;
(iii) derivation of the desirable level of imports:

$$IM^{*} = \Delta R^{*} - ({}^{-}X + {}^{-}\Delta FI) \qquad (2)$$

Where IM^* – desired level of imports; ${}^{-}X$ and ${}^{-}\Delta FI$ – forecasted levels of exports and capital flows; and ΔR^* – aim of change in net foreign reserves:

(iv) forecasting real income and setting the domestic price level target;
(v) deriving money demand;
(vi) calculating domestic credit growth; and
(vii) comparing the levels of import got from Equations (1) and (2).

Fiscal policy is added to the programme according to formulas:

$$\Delta FI = \Delta FI_p + \Delta FI_g \; \Delta D = \Delta D_p + \Delta D_g \text{ and } \mathrm{G} - \mathrm{T} = \Delta \mathrm{D_g} + \Delta \mathrm{FI_g}$$

where ΔFI_g – change in the net foreign debt of the public sector; ΔFI_p – change in the net foreign debt of the private sector; ΔD_g – change in loans given to the government; ΔD_p – change in loans given to the private sector; G – total government expenditure; and T – total government revenue.

As part of the programme, a ceiling is also set on the level of government borrowing in order to ensure a sufficient level of investment to and loan resources the private sector for the current economic activity and to avoid crowding out.

The programmes use a mix of different economic policies according to the country-specific situation. The list of policies used comprises expenditure switching (exchange rate policy), demand management (monetary, fiscal and income policies) and structural policies (increasing output by enhancing the efficiency of the distribution of existent resources or by increasing productivity). All the economic programmes have one or multiple nominal anchors, which can be money supply or the exchange rate or a combination of these with some supportive policies (for example, exchange rate as the stabilizer of prices is supported by an income policy of indexation of nominal wages).

Post-socialist economy and the IMF stabilization policy

As the transition from a socialist planned economy to a market economy is unique in the world history, there is no previous experience on the use of the IMF programmes in such a case. As a consequence, there are reasons that make the IMF principles discussed earlier somewhat inadequate. In my opinion, the main reasons for caution are:

(i) Insufficient consideration of the differences in the structure of the economy and the factors arising from it while formulating the financial programmes. Both open (when the overall prices rise) and shattered (deficit of certain goods) inflation occurred in the countries with a planned economy. The common feature (multiplicity) of the inflation process in the transition countries is caused by the structure of their economy generated by the central planning system, where financial policy adapts to the real processes and is not used to influence them. Price levels and ratios have to undergo significant adaptation in order to change their structure. As a result, correcting inflation occurs. Another factor to cause inflation pressure is servicing foreign debt, which decreases domestic expenditure.

(ii) Excess attention is paid to the measures decreasing demand and insufficient attention to the ones enhancing economic growth. Since the base level of growth is low in the transition countries, the initial growth achieved after stabilization is faster than in the industrial countries. However, the achieved effect in international competitiveness is eliminated quite rapidly by the remarkable increase in the price of labour, and if the country is not able to raise the level of productivity, initial growth may eventually be unsustainable.

(iii) Insufficient attention is paid to country-specific factors. The group of countries is often referred to as unified notwithstanding their historical, cultural and economic differences.

The MEPs were originally designed (and the assumptions therein made) on the historical experience of the industrial countries, and up to the transition period were usually orientated to developing countries.[6] The adequacy of the monetary approach in developing and transition countries is questionable, because the specific structural barriers that are typical to them decrease the efficiency of the use of the instruments of monetary policy in lowering inflation and redirecting resources into the external sector. Economic growth gets insufficient information because the main aim of the programmes is to improve the BoP (and decrease demand) of the country in question.

The IMF's opinion[7] on the MEPs in transition countries differing from traditional programmes seems to be that:

(i) excluding the exchange rate regime, there are no principal differences in the structure of the programme, either from the macroeconomic criteria or the structural reform points of view; and
(ii) fulfilling the macroeconomic criteria specified in the MEPs is related quite closely to sustainable stabilization and economic growth in the countries in question.

The influence of the IMF has been strongest in the transition economies that:

(i) were ready to enforce macrostabilization and structural reform policies;
(ii) were willing to take advice from the international organizations and use their experiences (especially small countries, with the aim of rapidly restoring connections with the international community and willing to give up relations with the former members of the Council for Mutual Economic Assistance and the former Soviet republics); and
(iii) had not yet reached a more developed stage of transition, where they might have been less eager to follow the IMF's advice.

Putting it another way: the IMF has been able to help those countries the most that were ready to help themselves.

IMF programmes, economic policy-making and growth in the Baltic states

The economic situation in the Baltic countries began to worsen in the 1980s. The causes were the problems arising from the beginning of the breakdown of the Soviet Union: the administratively regulated prices caused excess demand/supply of certain goods, price differences between goods in private and state shops were 100%-500% and GDP fell, depending on the country, roughly 5 per cent to 10 per cent. The problems deepened with the collapse of the Soviet planning system, which caused large disruptions in both trade and financial channels and brought with it a systemic shock.

As Russia moved into world market prices for energy and raw material exports to the Baltics, the countries faced a severe terms of trade (TOT) shock in 1992 (TOT deteriorated by more than 20 per cent of GDP). As a result, industrial production, employment and output fell rapidly, annual inflation reached triple and even quadruple digit levels (for example, year-on-year inflation in Estonia in June 1992 was 1080 per cent) and real income deteriorated (for example, in the first quarter of 1992 real wages in Estonia fell by 52 per cent).

To stabilize the economies in crisis, lower the hyperinflation and restore GDP growth, the countries turned to the IMF for assistance. This initial period in the relationship between the Baltic countries and the IMF may have been the most important. As discussions went on, the local authorities and the IMF staff came to an agreement that under the circumstances there was no choice but to use 'shock therapy' – that is, to adjust rapidly.

The main aim was to achieve economic stabilization with the help of tight monetary and fiscal policies accompanied by strong packages of structural measures for institution building and creation of favourable conditions for business development. As the new (endogenous) growth theories suggest that one important reason for differences in economic growth across countries[8] is inflation. At the same time empirical analysis[9] shows that the growth rate increases the most when stabilization includes bringing its level down to about 20 per cent a year. Taking this into consideration, the countries concentrated on tight anti-inflationary monetary policies.

The first country to leave the rouble area – and by doing so to try to insulate its economy from the inflationary impulses of the former Soviet Union – was Estonia, in June 1992. Despite opposition from the IMF,[10] the decision to use the most radical method of fixing the exchange rate of the local currency versus some other, the currency board system was adopted, since the theoretical knowledge is that fixed exchange rates help to lower inflation and interest rates. The local currency (the kroon) was fixed to the German Mark at the rate of 1 DEM (Mark) to 8 EEK (Kroon).

Latvia left the rouble area a month later and introduced the Latvian rouble (with an initial rate of 1 : 1 with the Russian one) that was eventually replaced with the lat. This was initially allowed to float, and in February 1994 was informally pegged to the IMF's accounting unit SDR.

Lithuania was the last of the three to exit the rouble zone, in October 1992, when the talonas (their interim currency) came into use. Because of weak monetary discipline, the limited independence of the central bank and political pressure to extend credit being high, the talonas depreciated greatly. The monetary policy was tightened in May 1993, with preparations for adopting the currency board system and the introduction of the litas.

Structural reforms, price and trade liberalization and introduction of a two-tier banking system (central bank and commercial banks) supported the financial measures.

Did this generate the hoped-for stabilization and restore growth? By analysing the first MEPs one can conclude that it was not as fast as forecast (for example, in the case of Estonia, the IMF forecast growth within a year of stabilization – that is, in 1993, but it in fact first occurred only in 1995). Why the excess optimism? I believe that there are three reasons for the IMF being overoptimistic:

(i) the other international institutions, rating agencies and the private sector take the IMF's opinion into account when assessing the economy of a country, and by being optimistic the IMF is hoping to help it to gain access not only to the financial resources of the IMF, but also to international financial markets;
(ii) it is hoping to create self-fulfilling positive expectations; and
(iii) the Executive Board of the IMF only approves programmes showing the ability of members to repay the funds borrowed (that is, if the MEP is not approved, the country having economic problems will not have any access to financial resources, because turning to the IMF is one of its last choices).

The first phase in the co-operation between the Baltic countries and the IMF involved a banking crisis in Estonia (in 1992–3) and in the next phase crises also emerged in Latvia (1995) and Lithuania (1995–6). The early stages of these crises involved government intervention in support of problem banks, a central bank moratorium on some of them, and the subsequent closure or liquidation of a number of large ones. About a third of the broad money stock was destroyed during these banking crises, but even the failure of the larger banks had only limited systemic effects. The short-term reaction to the problems with the banking sector was strengthening supervision and legislation governing the banking industry.

Thus growth was restored and initial stabilization achieved from 1995. The main elements were the continuation of financial stabilization through tight financial policies and a speeding up of further structural reform to lay the foundation for economic growth. Lithuania chose to use a special line of credit provided by the IMF to assist countries with structural reforms (the Extended Fund Facility (EFF) – a type of loan commitment by the IMF) whereas Estonia and Latvia used precautionary stand-by agreements.[11] The key achievements of this period were a remarkable decrease in inflation (it came down to single digits) and rapid economic growth (double digits in

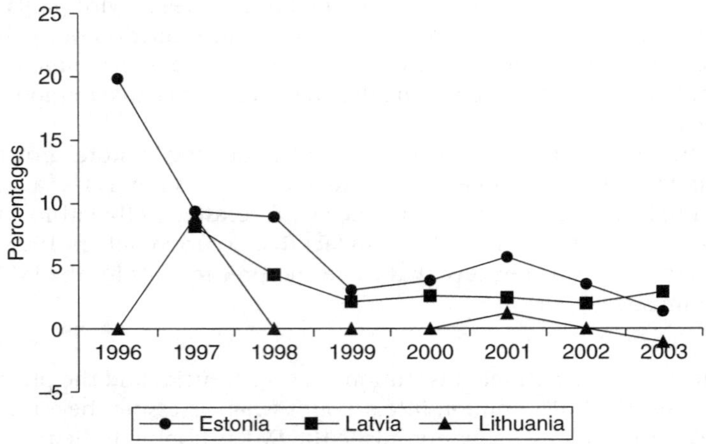

Figure 13.1 Inflation in the Baltic countries

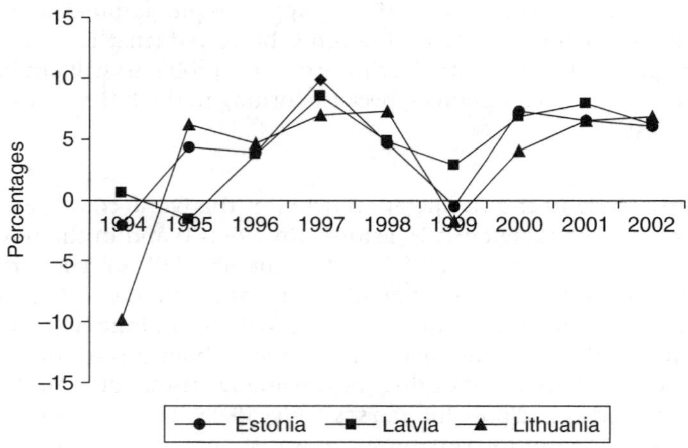

Figure 13.2 GDP real growth in the Baltic countries

Estonia in 1997). The drawback of the fast recovery was, however, the large current account deficits in all the three countries.

In 1997, the Estonian economy showed signs of overheating, caused by large foreign capital inflows and resulting in large domestic credit expansion and sky-high stock prices. As a result, the central bank of Estonia, in close co-operation with the IMF, worked out a long list of measures curbing credit expansion and making control over the banking system more efficient. Among others measures, this included raising the levels of capital adequacy and minimum capital of the banks, increasing required reserves, and amending legislation on the banking industry. It resulted in the closure of some banks and a slowdown of the economy. The stock market crash in late 1997 further added to the slowdown.

Then in 1998, the Russian crisis hit. Even though a lot of effort had been made in reorientating the external trade of the Baltic countries towards the West, trade relations with Russia were still strong. Export shares of Russia and the CIS (Commonwealth of Independent States) were, respectively, 15 per cent and 20 per cent for Estonia; 20 per cent and 30 per cent for Latvia; and 25 per cent and 45 per cent for Lithuania.[12] As exports fell, output declined and the economies went into recession. The problems in Estonia deepened and Latvia faced a similar crisis, where heavy strains emerged in the banking sector and some banks went down. In Lithuania, the response was a loosening of fiscal policy and the budget deficit rose from 3.5 per cent in 1991 to 8.5 per cent in 1999. Monetary policy remained tight in all three countries, with no changes to the currency boards in Estonia and Lithuania or the exchange-rate peg in Latvia.

As a result of these serious efforts, the Baltic countries recovered from the effects of the Russian crisis quite rapidly. Exports to the West (mainly to European Union (EU) countries) rose quickly after 1999, and the attention of the countries was turned to preparations for EU accession. In fact, negotiations with the EU became the most important policy issue, and the possible upcoming membership enhanced further structural reforms (especially in Latvia and Lithuania).

Since the economies were growing stronger by the day, a new era in relations with the IMF also began. The IMF now became an adviser on how to be more efficient in the reform process that had yet to be completed. There was no longer any need for official credit or commitment in the form of economic programmes, so Estonia was the first of the three Baltic countries to move into surveillance mode (Article IV consultations) in relations with the IMF. The focus in the consultations shifted toward the analysis of specific topics, such as an assessment by the IMF on competitiveness[13] or the financial markets[14] in the Baltic countries.

By the end of March 2003 all the Baltic countries had moved to surveillance mode with the IMF, and one of the important policy issues had become the accommodation of the public expenditure necessary for EU accession in the tight fiscal requirements for an early entry into the euro area. So date policy advice from the IMF on budget issues remains an area of close co-operation. To date the countries have fared well: there is a budget surplus in Estonia and the deficits in Latvia and Lithuania are fairly small (the 2003 deficit for Lithuania was 0.3 per cent of GDP, and for Latvia 1.8 per cent of GDP).

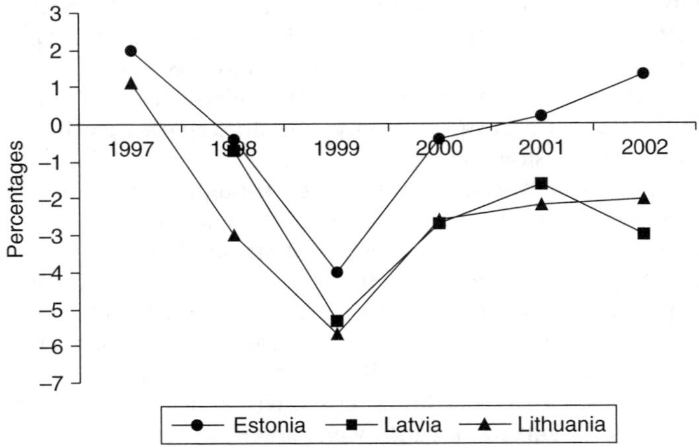

Figure 13.3 Public balance in the Baltic countries

Summary and conclusion

The relationship with the IMF is important for industrial countries, but especially so for developing and emerging countries. The poorer countries, and the ones with economic difficulties, can apply for IMF loans. The prerequisite for getting one of these advantageous loans is the memorandum of economic policies (MEP) agreed between the government of the particular country and the IMF. The MEP is a document where the main economic problems and steps to be taken to solve the problems are formulated.

The IMF's financial assistance has been extremely important in helping the transition countries in their efforts to reform their economies and integrate them with the rest of the world. It even created a special facility for the group of countries, under which they could obtain loans for the systemic transformation of their economy (the EFF), of which Lithuania from the Baltic countries took an advantage.

The role of the IMF in the Baltic countries has also been quite substantial. Estonia, Latvia and Lithuania have completed arrangements with the IMF in different forms since becoming members. Since the economic development of these countries has been very rapid, the advice given by the IMF has had to keep pace. The targets of the first MEPs included halting the decline in GDP, and the liberalization of prices, trade and the exchange rate of the local currencies. The next targets were formulated within the framework of economic growth and dealt with related problems (a slowing down of growth of domestic credit and a reduction in the current account deficit). Then there was a period of recession to be dealt with, and then the Baltics became EU members in May 2004.

The advice on economic policy given by the IMF to the local authorities has, in the author's opinion, been quite adequate. The international experience and the financial assistance from the IMF have helped to reform the economies, integrate them with the rest of the world and avoid a long-term recession. I think that the economic objectives set in the MEPs and the steps to achieve these objectives have increased the confidence of international investors, who otherwise would not have had as much information available about the Baltic countries. The IMF's positive attitude towards the countries' economic situation also contributed to their comparatively high sovereign credit ratings from the leading rating agencies of the world within a few years of the initial recovery. So, I believe that the impact of the IMF on the economic policy-making and growth in the Baltic countries has been quite substantial.

Notes

1 Article VIII of the Articles of Agreement of the IMF prevents the members from imposing barriers on trade payments.
2 Programmes of economic policy (including aims set for the period and policy mixes to be used) intended to be carried out within the specified program period backed by the IMF loan.
3 Article IV of the Articles of Agreement specifies the co-operation with the members who do not need financial support from the IMF as to be carried out on a yearly policy discussions basis.
4 *A* is absorption; *C* is consumption; *I* is investment; *G* is government expenditure.
5 Fischer (1997).
6 Kolodko (1992).
7 From various articles and statements by the IMF on the internet.
8 Olson (1997).
9 Bruno (1995).
10 To enhance flexibility, the IMF usually suggests floating exchange rate regimes.
11 Loan agreements where the commitment is made and MEP formulated, but no real borrowing takes place.
12 Knöbl and Haas (2003).
13 IMF (2003a).
14 IMF (2003b).

References

IMF (2003) *Articles of Agreement: Article I – Purposes* www.imf.org, accessed.
Bruno, M. (1995) 'Does Inflation Really Lower Growth?', *Finance and Development*.
Fischer, S. (1997) 'Applied Economics in Action: IMF Programs', *AEA Papers and Proceedings*, 87(2).
IMF (2003a) 'Competitiveness in the Baltics in the Run-Up to EU Accession', IMF Country Report No 03/114.
IMF (2003b) 'Capital Markets and Financial Intermediation in the Baltic States', IMF Country Report No 03/115.

Knöbl, A. and Haas, R. (2003) 'IMF and the Baltics: A Decade of Cooperation', IMF WP/03/241.

Kolodko, G. Gotz-Kozierkiewicz, D. and Skrzeszewska-Pacsek, E. (1992) *Hyperinflation and Stabilisation in Postsocialist Economies* (Kluwer Academic Publishers).

Olson, M., Sarna, N. and Swamy, A. (1997) 'Governance and Growth: A Simple Hypothesis Explaining Cross-Country Differences in Productivity Growth'.

Index